Injustice, Inc.

The publisher and the University of California Press Foundation gratefully acknowledge the generous support of the Anne G. Lipow Endowment Fund in Social Justice and Human Rights.

Injustice, Inc.

How America's Justice System
Commodifies Children and the Poor

Daniel L. Hatcher

UNIVERSITY OF CALIFORNIA PRESS

University of California Press
Oakland, California

© 2023 by Daniel L. Hatcher

Library of Congress Cataloging-in-Publication Data

Names: Hatcher, Daniel L., author.
Title: Injustice, Inc. : how America's justice system commodifies
    children and the poor / Daniel L. Hatcher.
Description: Oakland, California : University of California Press,
    [2023] | Includes bibliographical references and index.
Identifiers: LCCN 2022030859 (print) | LCCN 2022030860 (ebook) |
    ISBN 9780520386679 (cloth) | ISBN 9780520396050 (paperback) |
    ISBN 9780520386693 (epub)
Subjects: LCSH: Criminal justice, Administration of—Economic
    aspects. | Criminal justice, Administration of—Corrupt practices.
Classification: LCC HV9950 .H394 2023 (print) | LCC HV9950 (ebook)
    | DDC 364.973—dc23/eng/20220902
LC record available at https://lccn.loc.gov/2022030859
LC ebook record available at https://lccn.loc.gov/2022030860

Manufactured in the United States of America

32 31 30 29 28 27 26 25 24 23
10 9 8 7 6 5 4 3 2 1

For my parents, James and Barbara,
for my children, Landon, Raina, and Ava,
and for Banafsheh—my partner in love and life

Contents

Contents

Acknowledgments

First, I would like to thank my clients, who continue to teach and inspire me through their perseverance. Although I frequently use the term "vulnerable" to describe populations impacted by the practices uncovered in this book, I do not intend to imply weakness. Rather, vulnerability requires great strength. Ultimately, we are all vulnerable, and we are all interdependent—with each other and with the government agencies and justice systems intended to serve us.

I am grateful and honored to publish this book with the University of California Press. Since I first met with Maura Roessner when this book was only an idea, her support, encouragement, and professionalism have been invaluable.

I remain thankful for the opportunity to teach at the University of Baltimore School of Law and for the encouragement and support from Dean Ronald Weich and all the excellent faculty and staff. And I could not be more grateful for being part of the University of Baltimore's outstanding clinical program, where I have the privilege of learning with wonderful students, staff, and faculty as we engage in a struggle for justice for those who are struggling.

Many of my colleagues and friends at UB and elsewhere provided helpful feedback and encouragement in the writing process, including Michele Gilman, Jane Murphy, Robert Rubinson, Barbara Babb, Shanta Trivedi, Garrett Epps, Colin Starger, Jana Singer, Jack Frech, and Ezra Rosser. I am also thankful for the assistance and support of Rosalind

Williams, who recently retired from UB—and her excellent service to the law school, students, and our clients will be greatly missed. Patrick Brooks also provided helpful research and insightful support as a research assistant. Further, I would like to thank my former colleagues from the Maryland Legal Aid Bureau and Children's Defense Fund—all tireless advocates for justice.

Portions of my earlier article, which appeared in the New York University *Annual Survey of American Law*'s tribute volume to the amazing life work of Marian Wright Edelman, provided foundational research and material for parts of this book. I thank the excellent student editors at the journal.

I am also incredibly grateful to family and friends for their endless support and helpful suggestions during the writing process, including David Hatcher, Behzad Ghassemi, Pam Wallis, Kella Hatcher, R. J. Wallis, Valerie Crabill, and my wonderful parents-in-law, Mehdi and Pooran Ghassemi. To my children, Landon, Raina, and Ava, thank you for being the magically beautiful souls that you are, thank you for providing excellent insights to improve my writing, and thank you for inspiring me daily with your brilliantly creative and unique approach to life's journey. I love you all.

For Banafsheh, you have my heart. I am in eternal gratitude for your love, your trust, and your truth. In the translated words of Hafez, "to fall in love is what the bold souls dare." And you opened my heart to be daring. I cannot thank you enough for reviewing multiple drafts and for your support, understanding, and advice as my research and writing process takes me into a seemingly unending matrix to piece together the stories of harm that I seek to expose.

Finally, I thank my parents, James L. and Barbara J. Hatcher, who taught me the meaning of life. After a long struggle with dementia, my father passed away during the first year of the pandemic. In our last talk before he took a fast turn for the worse after a fall, we sat on his back porch, discussing my work on this book. He was able to express how important he thought the book was and how proud he was that I was writing it. I submitted the full draft on his birthday. There is nothing he couldn't do, and everything he did—he did for love. His excellent book is titled *Going to Camp: A Memoir of Twin Boys' Quest for Education in the Rural South*. And my mother has a smile that can welcome and heal the world. I have learned and continue to learn so much from her, from her lifelong devotion to helping others through her volunteer efforts and work as a nurse—and from her tireless empathy and compassion for family, friends, and everyone she encounters. She's never met a stranger. From our small home where I grew up in the Midwest, my mother was able to expose me to the wonders of the world, and she instilled in me a devotion to equal justice. I love you, Mom and Dad.

Introduction

The juvenile courts in Ohio run like a business. Processing tens of thousands of children's cases with an inconsistent patchwork of state and county funding, the courts have evolved—or, more accurately, devolved—in the pursuit of revenue and efficiency.[1]

Mostly unknown to the public, the juvenile courts began a strategy in 1996 to make money when removing children from their homes.[2] Although the federal government provides funding intended for foster care agencies, the courts entered contracts to take over the agency role to claim the money for themselves. Through the "subgrant agreements," if the courts rule that children are delinquent or "unruly" and take them into court custody, the courts can then use their contractual role as foster care agencies to leverage the children into court revenue. Federal law requires judicial review of the agency actions, so the courts literally review themselves through the dual roles and increase their payments when reviewing themselves favorably. At least twenty-seven Ohio juvenile court systems have now entered these deals, using children to obtain millions in revenue.[3]

The juvenile courts process children through factory-like operations. In just one year, the Summit County court processed 5,402 cases with only one judge, the Montgomery County court processed 18,455 cases with only two judges, and the Hamilton County court churned through 23,923 new case filings—with 109,265 hearings—with only two judges.[4] The judges hire attorneys to act as magistrates for much of the caseload and combine services that are supposed to be independent into business structures with hundreds of employees. The courts operate their own juvenile detention centers, jailing children as young as age ten.[5] The courts oversee work programs in which children as young as twelve work to repay court-ordered costs.[6] Although children are supposed to have independent advocates, the courts run the child advocacy programs. The courts operate their own probation departments, with probation officers using the children to claim more foster care revenue.[7] Some of the courts run their own residential treatment centers, allowing the courts to claim yet more foster care funds when placing children in their facilities.[8] Several courts even started their own schools, and more. All the court employees, even the teachers, serve at "the pleasure of the judge."[9] And similar to factories that have turned to automation for greater efficiencies, one of the courts, which provides only "five to seven minutes" per child in its treatment docket, has partnered with IBM Watson to use artificial intelligence in helping to decide children's cases.[10]

In such operations, revenue and efficiency can reign over justice, and children can become commodities. After one of the smaller juvenile court systems in Jefferson County entered such a foster care contract, the court reported that its revenue from children equaled over half of the court's total budget for the year.[11] As another county juvenile court judge explains, "[T]he more kids that are placed out of their homes, the more money the court gets, which might lead some people to question the court's motivation: helping the youngsters or getting the money?"[12]

Ohio's juvenile courts are emblematic of the several examples detailed in this book, exposing how America's foundational justice systems have struck a Faustian bargain to monetize children and the poor.[13] Courts, prosecutors, probation departments, police, sheriffs, and detention facilities are all operating like divisions of a factory business, trading impartiality, independence—and justice—to use vulnerable populations in an efficiency-seeking and revenue-generating enterprise.

The methods are many, and the harm is high. The injustice enterprise inflicts a starkly disproportionate racial impact while using hundreds of thousands of children and impoverished adults as fuel for a money-making fire that burns the ideals of justice. Courts are contracting to make millions from children in juvenile proceedings and are contracting to make millions more from struggling children and families in child support proceedings. Prosecutors, probation departments, sheriffs, and police have all joined the money-driven contractual processing. Our foundational justice systems are also simultaneously using impoverished litigants to pursue billions in fines and fees, incentivizing arrests, pirating property from the poor and dividing the loot, collaborating with private debt collectors and a massive debt-buying industry, privatizing justice functions, and even using artificial intelligence. And after these factory-like systems process children and the poor for revenue, countless forms of detention facilities are profiting from warehousing the humans treated as remnants.

It's not easy for me to provide the analysis and conclusions for this book—because I still believe in the pursuit of justice. For over twenty-five years, I've been an advocate for vulnerable children and adults, trying to help overcome the unending and intertwined legal challenges of poverty.

I almost quit law school in 1994, with my idealistic hopes to learn about striving for equal justice facing a barrage of disillusionment from first-year classes. But then I started volunteering at a legal aid office in a small nearby Virginia town. I was supposed to help with new client intakes by telephone, but one man did not have a phone, so he came into the office. He was probably twice my size, still dressed from work as a construction laborer. I wore my only suit, trying to look like a lawyer. I nervously reached out to shake his large, callused hand, and I began to stumble through the process of gathering information about his request for legal assistance. He started crying as he spoke. After finishing the intake, I remember rolling down the windows in my car as I drove away in the late sun, freeing the wind and a wave of emotions—realizing the calling to help.

In my first legal aid job after law school, I represented children pulled into the chaotically dysfunctional Baltimore foster care system, hundreds of children each facing heartbreaking circumstances. I still see their faces. I still carry guilt, wondering how they are now, wondering if there is more that I could have done. I have also represented almost countless adults, first as a legal aid lawyer and continuing as a clinical law professor, teaching students while helping clients with all their poverty-related legal challenges. Each case is a human story of struggle that I carry with me.

Despite all the injustices I have encountered through my clients' eyes, I still believe in striving for justice. I still believe that when hardship and unfairness appear, advocacy can spur our agencies to provide needed services and our courts to fulfill their solemn duty to balance the scales so that wrongs can be righted. Thus, I am the most alarmed when encountering circumstances in which the ideals of our institutions have been structurally compromised.[14] In my first book, *The Poverty Industry*, I set out to expose how state human service agencies have subverted their service missions, partnering with private companies to turn vulnerable populations into revenue tools.[15] In this book, I seek to reveal an even greater concern: our foundational justice systems—intended to review agency actions and protect the rights of the vulnerable—have become active participants in the same poverty industry.

This book does not aim to demonize individual judges, justice officials, or staff, especially those who tirelessly pursue the ideals of equal justice despite insufficient resources. But this book does hold all individuals in our justice systems accountable, including those pure in their purpose and those who are not. And as attorneys are considered officers of the court, I also hold myself accountable. Institutions of justice are not built of marble or brick but of people within, and the words "Equal Justice under Law" carved over the towering pillars of the Supreme Court only have meaning if we give them meaning. Thus, when we encounter systemic threats to the ideals of justice, we cannot feel content or absolved by simply knowing our individual actions are pure when the system around us is not.

The struggle for equal justice can never end, and the effort necessitates awareness. Otherwise, as James Baldwin forewarned, "ignorance, allied with power, is the most ferocious enemy justice can have."[16]

In *The Poverty Industry*, I introduced a hypothetical foster child: "Sarah—who like most foster children comes from a poor family—becomes '$arah' as she is mined for potential funds."[17] Here, we meet her brother $hawn, who first reminds us how human service agencies and private contractors use vulnerable children and adults as a source of revenue. Then, as we move through the chapters of this book, he helps us to understand how our justice systems have joined in the commodification. $hawn is simultaneously hypothetical and real. His story is a conglomeration of data and research surrounding vulnerable youth and my own experiences representing children and impoverished adults pulled into the juvenile and family court systems.

$hawn is twelve years old. The juvenile court initially ordered him removed from his home at age eight—the average age of a foster child—due to allegations of neglect resulting from poverty, the same as for most foster children. $hawn is Black, as are a disproportionate percentage of children in foster care.[18] After $hawn's father died, his mother struggled with unemployment and temporary homelessness, and she was seeking assistance when $hawn was removed. The child welfare agency shuffled $hawn between multiple foster care placements, including a for-profit group home with a history of abuse, before he was allowed to return home last year. Although only twelve, $hawn suffers from PTSD (post-traumatic stress disorder), which foster children experience at twice the level of soldiers of war.[19]

$hawn is scared that he may be taken from his home again. His mother is also scared as she continues to struggle for economic stability in an unstable world. She is also worried because $hawn has been experiencing behavioral difficulties in school due to his trauma, and likely a learning disability, at a school with a reputation for quickly referring children to juvenile court for "unruliness" and delinquency proceedings—especially Black children. The statistics are triply lined up against $hawn. Through the school-to-prison pipeline, school administrators and enforcement officers refer Black children into the juvenile justice system at about twice the percentage of their population, with a similar disproportionate rate imposed upon disabled children.[20] For boys, the numbers are higher still.

Also, $hawn faces a hidden gravitational pull back into the system: he is the source of multiple revenue streams and is the commodity that keeps the system running. If he is taken back into the foster care or juvenile delinquency systems, the revenue operations will immediately begin. $hawn may have a small trust fund containing $2,000 from his deceased aunt. If he lives in Iowa, an agency manual provides specific instructions for taking those funds.[21] If $hawn lives in Georgia, the agency will immediately process him through its "Revenue Maximization (RevMax) Unit" for a long list of revenue extraction operations against $hawn and his mother.[22] If he lives in Maryland, the agency has crafted a regulation to obtain "the child's own benefits, insurance, cash assets, trust accounts," and even his own earnings when $hawn is old enough to work.[23] If he lives in Nebraska, the agency regulation provides a detailed dissection of $hawn, with twenty-three categories of possible resources to obtain from him, even taking his burial space.[24]

Realizing $hawn may be entitled to funds resulting from his father's death, the agency refers $hawn to its revenue contractor. The company gains access to confidential information and determines he is eligible for Social Security survivor benefits that his father earned by working and paying taxes into the program. Then, without telling $hawn, the foster care agency takes his money. If his father died during military service, the agency would also take his Veterans' Assistance survivor benefits.[25]

If $hawn's father was alive, the agency would ask its revenue contractor to apply for $hawn's Supplemental Security Income (SSI) disability benefits. And again, the agency would take his money. Contract documents describe foster children as "units," using them in "data match algorithms" and "predictive analytics" "and prioritizing and 'dissecting' the population of foster children in terms of which children will bring in the most money."[26] A contractual report for the Maryland agency refers to foster children as a "revenue generating mechanism."[27]

Some states will also use $hawn in a strategy to take his Medicaid resources. If $hawn lives in New Jersey, the state has hired another revenue contractor to help run its "Special Education Medicaid Initiative" and requires schools to collaborate, using low-income children to maximize Medicaid funds.[28] Then, although the federal aid is supposed to help schools serve the children's health and special education needs, New Jersey redirects 82.5 percent of the money to its general coffers.[29] Tellingly, New Jersey oversees the initiative through its Department of Treasury rather than its Department of Education.[30]

While scouring $hawn for resources, the agency will also pursue child support against his impoverished mother. Then, rather than using the payments for $hawn's benefit, the agency will take the child support as yet another revenue source. As his mother struggles for economic stability to reunify with $hawn, the agency undercuts her efforts with punitive enforcement tools: suspending her driver's license, garnishing two-thirds of her meager wages, and seeking her incarceration for contempt when she falls behind. In some states, a parent's inability to keep up with the state-owed child support is even grounds for terminating parental rights. $hawn is collateral.[31]

The details of the practices vary from state to state, but the moneyed theme is the same. If $hawn is removed from his home, the agencies will mine $hawn for multiple sources of revenue while simultaneously using him as collateral to force more payments from his mother—when all they both want is to be together.

In the chapters that follow, $hawn helps to guide us beyond the human service agency practices. We uncover the disturbing reality of how America's foundational justice systems are also using $hawn in their moneyed pursuit.

Chapter 1 begins by describing the ideals of justice and how those ideals have been subverted since America's founding through a history of inequality that fuels current commodification practices. The ideals are necessary in every institution of justice, from our nation's highest court to our thousands of local justice systems, and the ideals are palpably crucial in the "lower" foundational systems that we often encounter in our circumstances of greatest vulnerability. However, the closer the justice systems are to the people, the more the systems are overwhelmed with inconsistent state and county funding, crowded dockets and caseloads, frustrated or jaded judges and justice officials, and inadequate legal representation. These justice systems devolved through a distorted mix of Darwin-like self-preservation and capitalism, entering contracts to run more like profit-seeking businesses than justice-seeking institutions. Through details of the deals, vulnerable litigants are harmed, constitutional principles are shredded, and the foundations of justice are broken. This chapter also places the contractual schemes in the broader context of other mechanisms that have allowed the injustice operations to grow, including billions in fines and fees collections coursing like destructive venom through justice's veins, a massive debt-buying industry taking over the courts, "rocket dockets" and "cattle calls" of impoverished litigants, and even judgeless courts. And our justice systems continuously seek increased factory efficiencies, including privatization and automation of judicial functions, focused on the moneyed bottom line.

Chapter 2 exposes the details of how Ohio juvenile courts enter contracts to obtain revenue when removing children from their homes in juvenile delinquency proceedings, also by labeling and processing children as "foster care candidates," and explains how other state juvenile court systems are following Ohio's lead. An increasing number of Ohio juvenile court systems have signed interagency contracts to claim foster care revenue through the children, and many of the courts have hired a revenue maximization consultant to help. Other states have shown signs of implementing similar practices, including Louisiana, Arizona, Iowa, Missouri, Illinois, and Texas. Seeing the millions to be made through this processing of children, more states will likely follow suit unless the strategy is stopped. Thus, this chapter also provides legal analysis of how the courts' revenue schemes are unconstitutional, violating required separation of powers and due process, and how the practices directly conflict with state codes of judicial ethics.

Chapter 3 sheds light on how juvenile and family courts are also making money from impoverished children and their parents in a vast child support business. The practices are even more widespread than the foster care revenue strategies but similarly unknown to the public. The revenue schemes range from courts selling off their judicial magistrates as child support mercenaries to the courts contracting to take over the entire executive branch child support agency function. Through these unconstitutional and unethical interagency contracts, courts are financially incentivized in maximizing their child support operations and in deploying a barrage of punitive enforcement tools, all while churning fragile families into revenue production.

Chapter 4 uncovers how prosecutors' offices have joined the factory. Like the courts, prosecutors have entered contracts to generate revenue from vulnerable litigants through foster care, juvenile justice, and child support proceedings. In some jurisdictions, prosecutors can increase contractual revenue when more poor children are removed from their homes, and the prosecutors can further increase funding by seeking to permanently terminate parental rights. Prosecutors are similarly incentivized in massive and harmful child support operations, with the goal of profiting from struggling families. Further, prosecutors often work with the courts, probation departments, and police to ruthlessly pursue the poor for court fines and fees. Through such money-driven business operations, prosecutors' offices are monetizing economic and racial inequality, harming impoverished children and adults, undermining justice, and abdicating their constitutional and ethical obligations.

Chapter 5 explains how probation departments also form a large component of the operations, contractually collaborating with the courts and prosecutors. As the juvenile court and prosecutor's office generate revenue from $hawn and his mother, the factory doors are further opened for the probation business to join the moneyed pursuit. Through additional foster care and child support contracts, probation departments are similarly making millions by harmfully processing the poor. Probation departments have also formed a mafia-like division of the fines and fees business, unconstitutionally extorting fees on top of fees, mandating punitive supervision with more fees, and using probationers as forced free labor while charging them yet more fees to work for free. Georgia even enacted a structure it calls "pay-only probation" for the sole purpose of extracting money from vulnerable populations.[32] Further, counties in multiple states have shed any veneer of restorative justice by hiring for-profit probation companies to generate the revenue, then dividing the takings.

Chapter 6 provides the story of how policing is part of the injustice business. Police and sheriff's departments have joined the courts, prosecutors, and probation departments in their contractual strategies to make money from foster care, juvenile justice, and child support, including financially incentivized arrests. Further, sheriffs, city marshals, and constables—relics from colonial times—act as modern-day bounty hunters to generate fees, commissions, and "poundage" by carrying out evictions, collections, arrest warrants, utility shut-offs, foreclosures, car repossessions, and more. Many sheriffs' offices sign additional contracts to profit by targeting and jailing undocumented individuals and by hiring revenue consultants to help. Law enforcement agencies also make money from seizing property in civil forfeitures, with sheriffs and police keeping a large percentage of the takings and often sharing a cut with the prosecutors. Also, this chapter provides the disturbing history of how sheriff's offices profited by selling enslaved persons to enforce court-imposed debts, originating the "sheriff's sales" still used today as a revenue-generating tool that targets the poor. And taking the business mindset to its fruition, several jurisdictions are now granting full police authority to for-profit private police companies.

Chapter 7 delves into stark details of how the business of jailing children and the poor provides warehousing for the commodified resources. The structures vary: some are public facilities, and some are private, including for-profit, nonprofit, and religious organizations. However, while varying in structure, all the jails, prisons, detention centers, correctional facilities, residential treatment centers, reform schools, "farms," "villages," and "camps" are detaining or jailing children and profiting from the same simple and harmful strategy of seeking increased occupancy rates—maximizing bodies in the beds—while minimizing the costs of care. Cities and towns use juvenile jails to spur economic development and to generate government revenue. Detained children are essentially bought and sold as for-profit juvenile facilities are purchased by larger private equity firms, "real estate investment trusts," and other companies traded on the stock market. Large private entities structure themselves as "nonprofits" while generating millions in revenue from vulnerable youth. Facilities claim religious status to avoid taxes, licensing, and regulation, while profiting from children's harm. In all these structures, vulnerable children and adults frequently suffer from poor care, abuse, or worse.

Chapter 8 reflects on the systemic racialized harm of the injustice enterprise. Our foundational justice systems are permeated by a racist history that enslaved and commodified Black children and their parents. And that history reverberates into current revenue operations.[33] For example, looking back to the Ohio juvenile courts, census data in Hamilton County, Ohio, shows that Black individuals account for about 26 percent of the county population.[34] However, a 2019 news report found that 81 percent of minors issued warrants through the juvenile court were Black youth, who can then be used to generate court revenue.[35] Similarly, Black individuals account for about 21 percent of the population in Montgomery County, Ohio, but the juvenile court's 2018 data shows that almost 50 percent of those charged as delinquent or unruly were Black youth, and 85 percent of those committed by the court to its own corrections facility were Black youth.[36] The several revenue schemes uncovered in this book used by courts, prosecutors, probation departments, police, sheriffs, and detention facilities all draw a concerning historical connection: the factory of injustice profited from racial and economic inequality at America's beginnings and still does today.

The book concludes by taking us back to the beginning, calling for us to open our eyes to our failings in order to walk a better path toward instilling truth into the words "Equal Justice under Law." The path inevitably begins with realigning our foundational justice systems with trued mission and ethics, to provide our vulnerable populations with justice rather than using them to make money.

History has witnessed the rise and fall of democracies—and the rise and fall of human rights for their inhabitants—in correlation to their adherence to the ideals of equal justice. Around the world, member states of the United Nations recognize that "the importance of a competent, independent and impartial judiciary to the protection of human rights is given emphasis by the fact that the implementation of all the other rights ultimately depends upon the proper administration of justice."[37] If justice falls, all else falls with it.

CHAPTER I

Crumbling Foundations of Justice

Justice is an ideal. And justice is built from subparts that are ideals in themselves, each inextricably necessary for justice to serve both the individual and collective good of civil society: independence, impartiality, ethics, and equality. Frustration surrounds the pursuit of justice, as progress encounters regress in a struggle as endlessly certain as time itself. Because of the inherent flaws in humanity, the ideals of justice and its subparts—like any ideal—will never be fully attainable. But we must persevere through the frustration and continuously strive to get as close as humanly possible. Otherwise, the ideals will inevitably be overcome by their opposites.

The functional operation of justice is carried out by America's justice systems, powered by adjudicatory and enforcement arms at the federal, state, and local levels. The federal system is immense in national power and often the recipient of the greatest attention and resources. However, the vast majority of us—we the people—are most likely to encounter one of the thousands of state and county "lower-level" justice systems, and this likelihood is heightened for the most vulnerable among us.

The "lower-level" systems are in fact the foundations of the structure on which justice in America either stands or falls. And those systems are faltering.

This book exposes how our foundational institutions of justice are using contractual tools to harness America's history of racial and economic inequality, converting the harm into revenue through factory operations. Rather than providing vulnerable populations with equal justice, the institutions are mining them, using commodification tools strengthened and modernized through time and technology.

The coming chapters uncover the operations. But first, this chapter sets the stage, pausing to look back at how we got here by examining the history of America's ideals of justice, then bringing us back to the present by flipping on the light switch to introduce the conveyor belt churning justice into a business.

FOUNDATIONAL IDEALS OF JUSTICE

Justice is a paradox, permanently imperfect, requiring the permanent pursuit of perfection. The intertwined ideals described here are each crucial to the foundation of justice. However, each of these subparts was also undermined from the outset, permeated by inequality at America's beginnings.

Independence

After seven years of revolutionary war against the British monarchy, the "founding fathers" and drafters of the US Constitution tried to create a structure of government to prevent tyranny, to promote the public welfare, and to pursue justice and individual liberty. Before the revolution, the colonies struggled and grew for over 160 years under the oppressive and self-serving control exercised by one entity—the British Crown. Thus, understanding all too well that tyranny is inevitable when governmental power is concentrated in a single entity, the founders created a structure built upon independence, a separation of powers between three independent branches of government so that no single branch or individual can take control. As James Madison wrote in the *Federalist Papers*, "The accumulation of all powers, legislative, executive and judiciary, in the hands of one, a few, or many, and whether hereditary, self-appointed, or elected, may justly be pronounced the very definition of tyranny."[1]

While drafting a structure for the pursuit of ideals, the founders recognized an inherent flaw: humanity. Thus, Madison focused his pen on human nature, seeking to form a government to protect ourselves from ourselves, which is ultimately our greatest struggle to preserve our constitutional democracy: "But what is government itself, but the greatest of all reflections on human nature? If men were angels, no government would be necessary. If angels were to govern men, neither external nor internal controls on government would be necessary. In framing a government which is to be administered by men over men, the great difficulty lies in this: you must first enable the government to control the governed; and in the next place oblige it to control itself."[2] To account for humanity, Madison explained that the separate branches must be simultaneously intertwined with a careful overlap of checks and balances to counteract the flawed human condition, such that "[a]mbition must be made to counteract ambition."[3] Therefore, attempting to prevent any one branch from usurping all power, each branch is provided with a back and forth of safety valve controls over the others. Congress can pass laws, the president can veto laws, Congress can override vetoes and can impeach the president and other governmental officials, the president appoints federal judges, Congress approves judicial appointments, the judiciary has power to review the constitutionality of all actions by the legislative and executive branch, and Congress can amend the Constitution.

Within this structure of separation of powers combined with checks and balances, the founders understood that an independent, impartial, and ethical judiciary must be at the core, reviewing the actions of the other branches. Alexander Hamilton, writing in support of the separation of powers in the *Federalist Papers*, explained that "[t]he complete independence of the courts of justice is peculiarly essential in a limited Constitution," and that the constitutional structure "can be preserved in practice no other way than through the medium of courts of justice, whose duty it must be to declare all acts contrary to the manifest tenor of the Constitution void."[4]

However, the deep human failings—which Madison described—undermined the founders' words of protecting liberty and justice. Madison enslaved people. Although historical debates continue regarding Hamilton, he may have personally held people in slavery, and he bought and sold enslaved persons for his in-laws.[5] The founders also did not recognize the equal rights of women—and treated Native Americans as "merciless Indian savages."[6] Yet through this disturbing irony, although the language of liberty was written into the Constitution in 1787 by flawed men who contributed to slavery, denied rights to women, and sought to destroy our Native American population, those words would provide the necessary structure for the future and ongoing struggle for equal justice.

Fast-forward almost two hundred years after the Constitution was ratified: Senator Sam J. Ervin Jr. was selected to chair the Senate committee that investigated the Watergate scandal and led to articles of impeachment against former president Richard Nixon. Two years before the constitutional crisis that shook the nation, Senator Ervin wrote of the importance of judicial independence: "[J]udicial independence is the strongest safeguard against the exercise of tyrannical power by men who want to live above the law, rather than under it. The separation of powers concept as understood by the founding fathers assumed the existence of a judicial system free from outside influence of whatever kind and from whatever source, and further assumed that each individual judge would be free from coercion even from his own brethren."[7] Again, disturbing hypocrisy adhered to the individual who wrote words about protecting liberty. Senator Ervin labeled himself a champion of civil liberties for southerners, while he fiercely opposed civil rights for Black Americans.[8] In 1956, Ervin had even helped to draft the "Southern Manifesto" that encouraged defiance of school desegregation. However, ideals have the potential to overcome human failings—and the synched ideal of judicial independence with the separation of powers, which Ervin supported, allowed for the unanimous Supreme Court school desegregation decision in *Brown v. Board of Education*, which Ervin fought against.

Impartiality

Impartiality almost sounds like not caring, but it is quite the opposite. The ideal requires an individual to care so deeply for the pure pursuit of justice that inherent human failings and temptations to succumb to bias, self-interest, and outside pressures are all overcome. To ensure that justice officials embrace the ideal, our Constitution requires it.

The due process clause in the Fifth Amendment, applied to the states through the Fourteenth Amendment, requires that no person shall be "deprived of life, liberty or property without due process of law." As part of the due process requirements, as interpreted by the courts, individuals have a fundamental right to a fair trial and impartial justice systems.

Impartiality is required of all officials in the adjudicatory and enforcement arms of justice, and the ideal is most paramount in the judiciary. If our courts systemically succumb to human failings, hope for justice is lost—and if justice falls, our constitutional democracy falls. As Paul Verkuil, former president of the College of William and Mary, explains: "Conflicts of interest destroy the independence that is the hallmark of the judiciary, and by extension of all public officers. Yet the judiciary must internalize that principle because judges are the arbiters of justice; if they fail, civil society in Locke's sense fails, and we revert to a state of nature."[9] Thus, US Supreme Court justice Robert Jackson explained in 1950 that the importance of impartial tribunals cannot be overstated: "The right to fair trial stands guardian over all other rights."[10] Also, US Supreme Court justice Hugo Black described this right in 1955 while overturning a lower court decision in which a judge acted both as the accuser in a "one-man grand jury" and as the trial court judge to rule on his own accusations: "A fair trial in a fair tribunal is a basic requirement of due process. Fairness, of course, requires an absence of actual bias in the trial of cases. But our system of law has always endeavored to prevent even the probability of unfairness. To this end, no man can be a judge in his own case, and no man is permitted to try cases where he has an interest in the outcome."[11] Justice Black recognized that "[s]uch a stringent rule may sometimes bar trial by judges who have no actual bias and who would do their very best to weigh the scales of justice equally between contending parties."[12] However, he also explained that the Constitution requires that judges must avoid both actual bias and systems in which bias is perceived: "[T]o perform its high function in the best way, 'justice must satisfy the appearance of justice.'"[13]

Justice Black was a Supreme Court justice for thirty-four years and became known "as a champion of civil rights and liberties."[14] But again, this champion of justice had previously supported racialized injustice. Before becoming a US senator and later being appointed to the Supreme Court by President Franklin D. Roosevelt in 1937, Justice Black had been a member of the Alabama Ku Klux Klan (KKK).[15]

Ethics

Ethics is the ideal that lifts humans toward ideals. Ethical codes of conduct seek to hold judges, attorneys, and other justice officials personally accountable to adhere to the professional and constitutional requirements of the positions they hold. Without ethics, the words of justice can become meaningless.

Like the constitutional ideals toward which ethics lifts us, the ethical requirements in our justice systems also grew from human failings and inequality. Alabama was the first state to adopt codes of attorney ethics in 1887, during the same time that Alabama justice systems were enforcing vagrancy laws designed to keep Black Americans in bondage of forced work after the end of the Civil War.[16]

Thomas Goode Jones, the drafter of Alabama's ethical codes for the legal profession, fought in the Confederate Army before becoming the state's governor in 1890. Jones carried his fight for White supremacy into his governorship: "During Jones' tenure as governor, Alabama passed laws segregating blacks and whites on common carriers" and "Jones helped draft the 1901 Alabama Constitution that established racial segregation as a fundamental principle of social organization in the state."[17] A subsequent Alabama governor delivered a eulogy for Jones, praising his racism with these words: "After the close of the Civil War [Jones] was one of the leaders of our people in their struggles to restore good government and maintain their civilization, and by his eloquence, his courage and his wise counsels, and statesmanship, he rendered material assistance in leading our State back from the slough of dishonor and corruption to the high secure ground of White Supremacy, security and safety."[18]

Thus, a man who fought for slavery and racial segregation drafted the first state codes of attorney ethics. Those ethical codes would become the model for other states and eventually were incorporated by the American Bar Association in its original Canons of Professional Ethics in 1908.[19]

Equality

Equality is a subpart of justice so crucial that the word is carved over the entrance to the US Supreme Court. But simultaneously, the ideal of equality has been more ignored, degraded, and compromised than any other component of justice throughout America's history. The American equality deficit is deep, as it was dug with more than four hundred years of an unequal past—from when the first enslaved persons were brought to Jamestown.

America's founders struck a deal in drafting the Constitution that treated enslaved persons as less than human while simultaneously leveraging the enslaved population to give the South greater electoral power. While every state would have two senators, the number of a state's seats in the House of Representatives would depend on its population. Thus, strategizing to increase power through humans they treated as property, representatives of the southern states demanded that enslaved people be counted.[20] The "three-fifths compromise" was disturbingly immortalized in Article I of the Constitution: "Representatives and direct Taxes shall be apportioned among the several States which may be included within this Union, according to their respective Numbers, which shall

be determined by adding to the whole Number of free Persons, including those bound to Service for a Term of Years, and excluding Indians
not taxed, three fifths of all other Persons." As a result of the three-fifths
compromise, the more people a state held in slavery, the more representatives the state obtained in Congress. The impact on the political power
of the South and corresponding growth of slavery was enormous. In the
1790 Census, three years after the Constitution was first signed, about
654,000 enslaved persons were held in the southern states—amounting
to over one-third of the South's total population. In Virginia, almost
40 percent of the population were enslaved persons.[21] By the 1860 census, on the eve of the Civil War, the southern states had expanded the
enslaved population to almost four million.[22]

James Madison, commonly hailed as the "Father of the Constitution,"
enslaved more than one hundred persons, and he advocated for the three-
fifths compromise: "Let the compromising expedient of the Constitution
be mutually adopted, which regards them as inhabitants, but as debased
by servitude below the equal level of free inhabitants, which regards the
slave as divested of two fifths of the *man*."[23] In rationalizing his support,
Madison argued that enslaved people were like property, and the Constitution should protect property, so the Constitution should therefore
give greater power to enslavers.[24]

Madison also helped design the electoral college to support states that
relied on slavery. A transcript of a public debate reported Madison's view
that the best method of electing the president would be by popular vote:
"The people at large was in his opinion the fittest in itself. It would be as
likely as any that could be devised to produce an Executive Magistrate
of distinguished Character."[25] However, Madison was concerned that
southern states would be at a disadvantage if the presidential election
occurred by popular vote because enslaved persons accounted for over
a third of the southern population—and were not allowed vote: "There
was one difficulty however of a serious nature attending an immediate
choice by the people. The right of suffrage was much more diffusive
in the Northern than the Southern States; and the latter could have no
influence in the election on the score of the Negroes. The substitution
of electors obviated this difficulty and seemed on the whole to be liable
to fewest objections."[26] Therefore, to ensure enslavers had more power
over presidential elections, Madison devised the electoral college system
that leveraged the three-fifths compromise.[27] Each state's citizens would
select a number of electors based on its number of representatives in
Congress, which increased as a state increased the population of people

it held in slavery, and the electors would pick the president. Thus, although the Constitution is founded on ideals of liberty and justice, the southern states harnessed their political power into the Constitution through slavery.

Hamilton also supported the electoral college and advocated for its acceptance in the northern states by appealing to elitism. In *Federalist* no. 68, written "To the People of New York," Hamilton argued for using electors rather than the popular vote: "It was equally desirable, that the immediate election should be made by men most capable of analyzing the qualities adapted to the station, and acting under circumstances favorable to deliberation, and to a judicious combination of all the reasons and inducements which were proper to govern their choice. A small number of persons, selected by their fellow-citizens from the general mass, will be most likely to possess the information and discernment requisite to such complicated investigations."[28] As part of his argument, Hamilton included ominously incorrect predictions that the electoral college "affords a moral certainty, that the office of President will never fall to the lot of any man who is not in an eminent degree endowed with the requisite qualifications," and that "there will be a constant probability of seeing the station filled by characters pre-eminent for ability and virtue."[29]

Hamilton's elitist argument against the popular vote is even more concerning when we understand that every state already included vastly unequal treatment and disenfranchisement based on race, gender, religion, and wealth. When the Constitution was ratified, voting rights were left to be determined by the states. Both southern and northern states restricted voting to White male landowners. Multiple states only allowed Christians to vote. When George Washington was elected as the first president in 1789, only 6 percent of America's population was eligible to vote.[30]

After the founders embraced wealthy White males, Andrew Jackson emerged as the first populist and champion of the "common man." But Jackson ratcheted up the harmful hypocrisy another level. Even as he spoke of liberty and the rights of the poor, he again only sought to protect the interests of White men. He ignored the rights of women, brutally enslaved hundreds of people, and savagely sought the elimination of the Native American population. When an enslaved person escaped from bondage on Jackson's plantation, Jackson took out an advertisement in the *Tennessee Gazette* offering a reward for his return "and ten dollars extra, for every hundred lashes any person will give to him."[31] In his annual message as president, Jackson argued for White supremacy—that Indigenous peoples should yield to the "superior race" and "ere long disappear": "They have neither the intelligence, the industry, the moral habits, nor the desire of improvement which are essential to any favorable change in their condition. Established in the midst of another and a superior race, and without appreciating the causes of their inferiority or seeking to control them, they must necessarily yield to the force of circumstances and ere long disappear."[32]

Jackson caused the slaughter and removal of tens of thousands of America's Indigenous peoples, including on the Trail of Tears, in which Cherokee men, women, and children were rounded up, removed from their homes, and forced to walk thousands of miles at gunpoint, with thousands dying along the way.[33] Disturbingly, after signing the Indian Removal Act in 1830, Jackson updated Congress with these words: "It gives me pleasure to announce to Congress that the benevolent policy of the Government, steadily pursued for nearly thirty years, in relation to the removal of the Indians beyond the white settlements is approaching to a happy consummation."[34]

Decades of tension between the northern and southern states over the South's continuation and growth of slavery culminated in civil war. As the war ended in 1865, President Abraham Lincoln was considering plans for Reconstruction to reintegrate the southern states and to begin rectifying the inequalities of slavery. However, the plans were weakened when Lincoln was assassinated and Andrew Johnson became president. Also considering himself a champion of the "common man" like Jackson, President Johnson implemented Reconstruction in a manner to appease White southerners—including taking back land that had been provided to formerly enslaved persons and redistributing the land to the pre–Civil War enslavers.[35] Southern states began enacting laws known as "Black codes," severely restricting the rights of Black Americans and continuing forced labor. Black adults were forced into contracts with plantation landowners. In an excerpt from the 1865 Black Codes of Mississippi, the section purposefully misnamed "An Act to confer civil rights on freedmen" explains how if a "free" Black adult tried to escape such a contract, the county justice system would force him or her back into contractual bondage:

Sec. 7. . . . Every civil officer shall, and every person may, arrest and carry back to his or her legal employer any freedman, free Negro, or mulatto who shall have quit the service of his or her employer before the expiration of his or her term of service without good cause; and said officer and person shall be entitled to receive for arresting and carrying back every deserting employee aforesaid the sum of five dollars, and ten cents per mile from the place of arrest to the place of delivery. . . .

Sec. 8. Be it further enacted, That upon affidavit made by the employer of any freedman, free Negro, or mulatto, or other credible person, before any justice of the peace or member of the board of police, that any freedman, free Negro, or mulatto, legally employed by said employer, has illegally deserted said employment, such justice of the peace or member of the board of police shall issue his warrant.[36]

While Black adults were forced into contracts, the county justice systems forced Black children into "apprenticeships," with preference given to the children's former enslavers:

Sec. 1. . . . It shall be the duty of all sheriffs, justices of the peace, and other civil officers . . . to report to the probate courts . . . all freedmen, free negroes, and mulattoes, under the age of eighteen . . . who are orphans, or whose parent or parents have not the means or who refuse to provide for and support said minors; and thereupon it shall be the duty of said probate court to order the clerk of said court to apprentice said minors to some competent and suitable person . . . Provided, that the former owner of said minors shall have the preference when, in the opinion of the court, he or she shall be a suitable person for that purpose.[37]

The "master or mistress" was given the statutory authority to beat the children for purposes of "management and control," and if the children tried to escape, the justice systems would send them back.[38]

Reaction to the Black codes in the northern states temporarily led to renewed congressional interest in reducing the severe inequalities. Black Americans obtained citizenship and the right to due process and equal protection through the Fourteenth Amendment in 1868, and Black men obtained the right to vote through the Fifteenth Amendment in 1870.[39] However, also during this time, a group of former Confederate soldiers in Tennessee formed a secret society, the KKK, which quickly grew into a paramilitary terrorist group that spread across the South, using severe violence and intimidation against the Black population, and sought to undermine Reconstruction.[40]

Then came the presidential election of 1876 between the northern candidate Rutherford Hayes and the southern candidate Samuel Tilden.[41] The results were disputed in some of the southern states because of widespread violent efforts to disenfranchise Black voters. After initially establishing an electoral commission to resolve the dispute, the North and South reached a compromise. In exchange for the southern states agreeing to accept Hayes as president, the northern states agreed to end Reconstruction, withdrawing federal troops who were protecting the civil rights of Black Americans, and White southerners were then free to rule their states as they wished.[42] As a result, violently unequal treatment and lynching spread, and the Black codes were replaced with Jim Crow segregation laws that reigned across the South—and parts of the North—for almost another one hundred years, until the Civil Rights Act of 1964.[43]

Meanwhile, White women were denied the right to vote until 1920. Black women and other women of color had to fight decades longer for the right to vote. Asian American residents were denied citizenship with the right to vote until the Immigration and Nationality Act of 1952. The Native American population did not receive citizenship with the right to vote until 1924, and many states continued to block voting rights to Native Americans, Black Americans, and other historically disenfranchised persons until protections in the 1965 Voting Rights Act—which have since been severely weakened—and disenfranchisement efforts have now been renewed.

Still today, reverberations of inequality from America's founding are deeply felt across the country. And the reverberations are deepest in America's justice systems.[44]

JUSTICE BECOMES AN INJUSTICE BUSINESS

Destabilized from the outset due to America's history of inequality, our foundational justice systems began with a desperate need for realignment toward their intended ideals. But instead, the components of these institutions of justice devolved into rattling parts of a factory business. Our lower-level justice systems have often openly embraced the poverty and inequality experienced by vulnerable litigants, developing mechanisms to abdicate the ideals of justice to generate revenue from the despair. Before exposing details of those revenue schemes in the coming chapters, this section first provides the context of the injustice business operations in which the contractual deals grew.

Inverted Reality: Neglected Importance of Lower-Level Justice Systems

In addition to the impact of historical inequality, the devolution of justice into an injustice business has also been spurred by the lack of attention, resources, and reform at the state and county levels that could provide better potential for the ideals of justice to heal and grow. Although the strength of any structure lies in its foundation, our lower-level justice systems—those that serve the masses in our circumstances of greatest vulnerability—are often the most overlooked and overwhelmed. Because the systems are "lower," they are perceived as lesser in terms of importance. But estimates have indicated that up to 95 percent of all US cases are in state courts, not federal.[45] Of those cases, over 99 percent are in the state trial courts, the courts of first resort.[46]

Further, judges, attorneys, and other justice officials often consider lower-level justice systems stepping-stones. Prosecutors' and public defenders' offices frequently send their newest attorneys to juvenile courts as a place to learn, as the attorneys hope to quickly "move up." Also, newer judges often start in our foundational courts to gain experience as they hope for assignments that they view as more prestigious.[47] Moreover, many law schools contribute to the problem by clambering to climb national rankings—scored by a for-profit media company—and often focusing more on perceived prestige than on the workings of our foundational systems.

Perception has impact. In 1966 Professor Monrad Paulsen—who would become the first dean of the Cardozo School of Law—described his observations and concerns with the New York Family Court, titled *Juvenile Courts, Family Courts, and the Poor Man*: "'It is a poor man's court.' . . . Each morning a hundred stories of poverty are suggested by the faces and the personal effects of those who wait to appear before the judges. The cold atmosphere of the room only intensifies the feelings of helplessness, fear, and frustration which accompany poverty. '[C]ourtrooms are bare, toilet walls are defaced. The court's waiting rooms resemble those at hospital clinics.' . . . Impersonal attendants perform their duties with clipped routine, underscoring alienation."[48] Paulsen further observed that while "[t]he poor may be the principal customers of juvenile court services," their needs are not the focus, but rather "the chief concern of those who administer the court is to meet the convenience of the judges and the staff."[49] Half a century later, the cold atmosphere of despair continues. In 2009 a New York State Senate committee noted that the Family Court "is perhaps the saddest place in New York," and a 2016 report explains that "[e]ven the wins in Family Court are sad."[50] And to the extent that change is occurring in foundational justice systems in New York or elsewhere, the focus is primarily on running like a business: increased efficiency and revenue rather than equal and impartial justice.

Revenue and Efficiency Replace Justice

Rather than issuing reports that focus solely on transparency and justice, county justice systems often publish annual reports and public relations communications similar to those of for-profit companies. Like presentations to prospective investors, the reports include emphasis on financial data and accomplishments in efficiency as if the justice systems are in capitalistic competition with neighboring county systems, fighting for revenue rather than collaborating for the common cause of justice.

Ohio's Lucas County Juvenile Court is one of the court systems that started contracting to generate revenue from foster care and child support, described in the following chapters. In its 2018 annual report, the court highlights its "Fiscal—Business Office" achievements as including $2 million in foster care and child support revenue and lists its fines and fees revenue at over $252,000.[51] The court celebrates how "2018 was a banner year for the Lucas County Juvenile Court" and then highlights the number of children it processes: "In 2018, our Court engaged a stunning 11,743 cases."[52] The court also highlights that its new mission statement includes a statement in support of equity.[53] But in that same year, almost 70 percent of the children that the court "engaged" into its detention center were Black youth, while the percentage of Black individuals in Lucas County is only 20 percent.[54]

The prosecutor's office in Cuyahoga County, Ohio, also contracts to generate millions in revenue from impoverished children and families in foster children and child support contracts.[55] The office explains: "Ours is a very large office with many important responsibilities . . . Last year, we handled more than 10,000 adult felony criminal cases and another 5,500 juvenile cases. That doesn't count more than 10,000 child support cases. . . . It's too big and too important to the public not to be run like a business."[56] The prosecutor's office further describes its business mindset as if it is in competition with other counties to show statistics of success: "We have asked our IT team to create and continually refine statistical measures of how we perform . . . Soon we will post statistics from comparable counties to provide benchmarks and to begin the hard process of setting goals. Successful businesses do that all the time."[57]

While county justice systems increasingly act like businesses competing for revenue, the county governments also use the justice systems—and the vulnerable children and adults pulled into the systems—to generate county general funds.[58] For example, a news report explains that Victoria County, Texas, has used its juvenile detention center to maximize county revenue by jailing children from multiple jurisdictions, and the County Judge "credited the juvenile detention center as a growing source of revenue for the county that helped to offset a decline in property values."[59] As the *Victoria Advocate* explains: "Victoria County is projected to almost double the revenue it brings in by housing youths from outside the county in its juvenile detention center. . . . The proposed 2019 budget for Victoria County projects that contracts at the juvenile center will bring in almost $2.3 million for the county in the next budget year."[60] The County Judge reportedly elaborated that "[w]e have a lot of improvements out at the juvenile detention center," and "[d]ue to our work out there in improving trends, increasing populations, better payment rates, we were able to budget upward $450,000 in revenue at juvenile detention."[61] Thus, the county justice system, which should be hoping fewer children need to be imprisoned in its detention facility, instead lauded its own efforts at "increasing populations" of detained children as a means of making money.

Building business structures to focus on efficiency and revenue rather than ensuring equal justice, county justice systems often bring multiple nonjudicial services in-house that are typically intended to be independent from the court. Similar to the Ohio juvenile courts described in the introduction, a juvenile court in Tennessee provides another example of such a structure. The court is introduced here and revisited in chapter 8.

The Juvenile Court of Memphis and Shelby County heard more than forty-six thousand cases in 2019, with only one actual judge and about eleven magistrates who serve at "the pleasure of the judge."[62] The court runs its own corrective and protective services departments, probation services, psychological services, collections department, a school, foster care services, foster care review board, the guardian ad litem office that is supposed to provide independent legal representation to children and parents, and multiple other programs intended to be independent but that report to the judge.[63] Further, the court is one of several juvenile court systems described in chapter 3 that entered interagency contracts to generate revenue when issuing and enforcing child support orders against impoverished parents.[64] The court describes a focus on efficiency and stated that one of the goals of its clerk's office is "to generate revenue through collection of court ordered fines and fees, grant contracts and state reimbursement to offset the cost of court operation."[65]

Focused on revenue and efficiency, the juvenile court lost sight of its intended mission of equal justice. The court asserted in its 2012 annual report that many of the court's initiatives "have been adopted as models for other programs in Tennessee and across the nation."[66] However, the US Department of Justice's (DOJ) Civil Rights Division also issued a report in 2012, finding that the court's "administration of justice discriminates against Black children," "fails to provide constitutionally required due process to children of all races," and that the court "violates the substantive due process rights of detained youth by not providing them with reasonably safe conditions of confinement."[67]

Judges Who Are Not Judges

As part of increasing efficiency in their business operations, county justice systems often do not use actual judges for high-volume court proceedings that impact vulnerable populations, but rather employ lower cost officials such as magistrates, masters, hearing officers, and referees, who in some states are not even required to be attorneys. Juvenile court "referees" in New Jersey are not required to be lawyers and only need a four-year college degree.[68] North Carolina magistrates who decide civil and criminal cases do not need a four-year college degree.[69] North Carolina also allows nonattorney juvenile court counselors to order juveniles into secure and nonsecure custody.[70] In Alaska, magistrates who can hear all sorts of criminal, civil, and juvenile matters do not even need a high school degree but are simply required to be twenty-one and a citizen of the state.[71]

The situation is often not much better in states with seemingly stricter requirements. Pennsylvania does require that its juvenile court hearing officers be licensed attorneys but only requires the attorneys to receive six hours of specific juvenile law instruction before they start deciding the fate of children.[72] As a comparison, Pennsylvania requires six hundred hours of direct training and instruction before someone can be a licensed massage therapist.[73]

Privatization and Automation

Continuously looking for mechanisms of efficiency, many justice systems have started privatizing and automating judicial functions. For example, as mentioned in the introduction, the juvenile court in Montgomery County, Ohio, partnered with IBM Watson. Focusing on efficiency while processing tens of thousands of children through its operations, a judge on the court's treatment docket may have "less than 10 minutes per child to review information from many parties and make potentially life-changing decisions."[74] So, the court collaborated with IBM Watson to use artificial intelligence (AI) in helping to decide children's cases.[75] According to a news report, the goal of the pilot project was to "put the lightning-fast, artificial intelligence system into the hands of judges across the country."[76] After the court's administrative judge was elected president of the National Council of Juvenile and Family Court Judges in 2017, IBM Watson became the presenting sponsor of the organization's national conference the following year.[77]

Multiple reports have now highlighted concerns with courts across the country relying on algorithms and AI, including concerns regarding racial and economic bias programmed into the assessment tools themselves, further bias in the interaction between the algorithms and humans using them, and significant problems with transparency as litigants and lawyers often cannot gain access to information about the assessment tools.[78] For example, a 2016 investigation by ProPublica into the algorithm used in Florida criminal courts revealed that an "analysis of Northpointe's tool, called COMPAS (which stands for Correctional Offender Management Profiling for Alternative Sanctions), found that black defendants were far more likely than white defendants to be incorrectly judged to be at a higher risk of recidivism, while white defendants were more likely than black defendants to be incorrectly flagged as low risk."[79]

The business opportunity is not small. In 2017 Northpointe, Inc., Courtview Justice Solutions Inc., and Constellation Justice Systems Inc. "were united as equivant under a single brand," which is "owned by Constellation Software, Inc., a publicly traded company on the Toronto Stock Exchange" with "$1.67 billion in gross revenue."[80]

Despite reported concerns, most states now use some form of risk assessment algorithms in their criminal court systems.[81] And state agencies serving vulnerable populations also use algorithms in life-changing decisions, such as child welfare agencies deciding whether to remove children from their homes and agencies deciding whether to deny needed public assistance or health services to the elderly and the poor.[82]

Also, many courts now use online dispute resolution (ODR) systems, under contract with private companies, which in turn again often rely on algorithms.[83] Some courts are now mandating that litigants participate in ODR before they can access actual court proceedings.[84] Illustrating the business interest, the individual who reportedly helped develop the ODR platforms for eBay and PayPal later cofounded one of the companies that now provides ODR to courts.[85] County courts that primarily pursue revenue from fines and fees are increasingly considering ODR as a means of enhancing their revenue-producing efficiency.[86]

The trend continues, as justice systems try to run like businesses and often contract out their operations directly to private companies. Our prisons and detention centers are often privatized, our probation departments are often privatized, prosecutors are often privatized, and even our police are often privatized.[87] And as our institutions of justice increasingly look to privatize their operations, America is one step away from companies operating our courts.

Court Fines and Fees Revenue

The efficient pursuit of revenue rather than justice is a theme that has continued to grow in our foundational justice systems. As an example of the moneyed mindset, courts, prosecutors, probation departments, and police are all collaboratively profiteering in the pursuit of court-ordered fines and fees against impoverished populations.

As the coming chapters uncover details of contractual revenue mechanisms, it is important to consider those practices as interconnected with revenue operations that are fueled by fines and fees. The harm from our justice systems profiting from these court-ordered debts has continued to receive increased attention in numerous policy reports, investigations, and scholarship, gradually leading to incremental improvements in some states—but most of the vast fines and fees business unfortunately continues.

Courts across the country are incentivized to order fines and additional fees in criminal, traffic, juvenile, and other minor offenses to generate court and county revenue.[88] The courts often collaborate with prosecutors, probation officers, and police in the collections, partnering in mafia-like pursuit against the impoverished litigants—including threatened or actual arrests—in shakedowns for whatever pennies they can pay, and then dividing up the loot. The initially ordered amounts of fines and fees are frequently unmanageable for impoverished litigants at the outset, and the debts quickly balloon through interest and seemingly endless additional fees on top of fees. As a result, fines and fees revenue has become a big business for our foundational justice systems, a business that diverts justice toward money and harm.

For example, the Judicial Council of California, which oversees the policies and practices of all the state's courts and is led by the chief justice, publishes an annual report that is not about justice but rather designed to encourage the collection of court fines and fees from poor litigants. Called the *Report on Statewide Collection of Court-Ordered*

Debt, the fiscal year 2019–20 report explains that California courts' "statewide collections programs collected $1.163 billion in total revenue," with an outstanding delinquent debt from the fines and fees of $8.6 billion that the courts were still pursuing.[89] To give context to those numbers, California receives $3.6 billion in federal Temporary Assistance for Needy Families (TANF) to provide welfare cash assistance to impoverished families across the state, but the state courts ordered and are pursuing delinquent court debt of well more than twice that amount, likely against many of the same families.

The Judicial Council acknowledges at the beginning of its report the "disproportionate impacts of fees, fines, and assessments on low-income and minority communities," but then continues with over two hundred pages all aimed at maximizing collections. As just one example, the Judicial Council report provides "best practices" to improve collections: "The best practices identify a variety of strategies designed to improve the collection of delinquent court-ordered debt. For example, best practices include permitting courts to finalize judgments when violators do not appear in court after repeated notices, utilizing Franchise Tax Board's collections programs, and contracting for the services of third-party collections vendors. Statewide collections programs are encouraged to follow as many best practices as possible to enhance collections efforts, resolve accounts in a timely manner, and increase revenue collections."[90] These "best practices" are thus not about how to best administer justice, but about how to obtain the most revenue from the poor. The suggestions include encouraging courts to hire private collections companies that are incentivized by a contingency fee from any court debt they collect. And because they are collecting court debts rather than private debts, the companies are not held back by the federal or California Fair Debt Practices Act and can thus use aggressive tactics.[91]

As another example, the "Justice Court" in Clackamas County, Oregon, partners with sheriffs and police to generate revenue by pursuing fines and fees from vulnerable populations. The court reported concerns in its 2020–21 budget report with losing fines and fees revenue during COVID-19 "due to a reduction in the number of violations filed," and the court was also concerned with "a further reduction in civil case revenue due to a moratorium on evictions."[92] But looking forward, the court anticipated increased fines and fees revenue to over $4 million for the year. And the court's budget shows that that amount of revenue is almost twice the court's total expenditures.[93] The "Justice Court" is instead a profit court.

Courts, Debt Buyers, and "Judgeless Courts"

As courts themselves hire private debt collectors to enforce such court-ordered fines and fees, the courts also collaborate with companies and debt collectors pursuing impoverished individuals for credit card, health-care, and other consumer debt. Moreover, the companies often sell the alleged debts to a massive debt-buying industry that now overwhelms the dockets of trial courts around the country. And the courts are often partnering with the industry by providing efficient mechanisms in the private collection effort rather than ensuring that impartial justice is provided for the low-income litigants.

The debt-buying industry operates by bidding on "portfolios" of old consumer debts that are packaged and sold and often resold, through a process in which the Federal Trade Commission found that "[o]n average, debt buyers paid 4.0 cents for each dollar of debt."[94] The older the debts, the lower the price debt buyers pay, including for debts likely past the statute of limitations.[95]

The business opportunity for debt buyers is significant, as 28 percent of Americans have at least one delinquent debt in collections.[96] One of the largest debt buyers, Midland Credit Management, is owned by another company, Encore Capital Group, publicly traded on the NASDAQ.[97] In a 2020 letter to shareholders, the company asserts that "[f]or years Encore has been helping consumers recover from financial difficulty and regain their personal economic freedom."[98] However, at the end of 2018, the company agreed to settle an investigation by the attorneys general of forty-one states and the District of Columbia "into Midland's debt collection and litigation practices and its pattern of signing and filing affidavits in state courts against consumers in large volumes without verifying the information printed in them—a practice commonly called robosigning."[99]

After purchasing millions upon millions of consumer debts, various debt buyers have flooded America's foundational trial courts. A 2020 report by the Pew Charitable Trusts provided stark examples: in Massachusetts, only nine debt buyers accounted for 43 percent of all the civil and small claims caseloads, and in Oregon, just "six debt buyers accounted for 25 percent of all civil cases."[100] Similarly, an investigation by the *News-Press* in Lee County, Florida, found that out of all the small claims cases filed over a five-month period, more than 45 percent of the cases were initiated by debt buyers.[101]

The courts in turn have developed methods to process as many cases as possible with as few resources as possible, while obtaining filing fees and often court costs from the proceedings. An investigation by Human Rights Watch describes "judgeless courts" in several jurisdictions, similar to practices I previously encountered in Baltimore courts, where impoverished litigants are ordered to court for forced and unsupervised settlement conferences with debt collection attorneys. The structure "allows plaintiffs to commandeer the coercive machinery of the courts in service of their own claims to the detriment of defendants' due process rights and the courts' own neutrality and integrity."[102]

Further, when alleged debtors are actually allowed their day in court, their cases are rushed through a crowded conveyor belt-like process in which the courts seem to align with the debt collectors and their attorneys rather than providing fair and impartial procedures. Although the impoverished litigants may often have multiple defenses to all or part of the claimed debts, they rarely have lawyers and are forced through a system focused on efficiency rather than fairness.[103] I have sat through countless busy collections dockets over the years as I wait for clients' cases to be called, and while contemplating the proceedings unfolding before me, justice is rarely a word that comes to mind. An excellent 2019 investigation by the *Atlanta Journal-Constitution* describes how "[s]wamped by the caseloads, the courts cycle through what attorneys refer to as 'rocket dockets,'" and "[t]he presiding magistrates handle case after case in a matter of minutes."[104] The attorneys use the term "cattle call" to describe the mechanics of shuffling poor litigants through the proceedings.[105] The investigation provides examples from a day in a Georgia collections court, including a confused and scared mother: "[A] mother of four walked out of the courtroom close to tears. The magistrate had told her that the debt collector would have the power to garnish her wages or pull money out of her bank account if she missed a single payment on her debt. 'They just let the attorneys go in and make a deal,' she told the AJC, speaking on condition she not be named. 'They're really not hearing our cases. The attorneys come talk to us and just scare us. We're all just scared.'"[106]

Such examples of the machinery of efficient injustice continue, day in, day out, across the country. And the next chapters uncover how our foundational justice systems have added numerous contractual mechanisms to these factory operations—to directly monetize children and the poor.

CHAPTER 2

Juvenile Courts Monetizing Child Removals

Moving through this book, we see that the revenue operations of each component of our justice systems are harmfully interlinked. We can envision $hawn and his family continuously processed through the operations of courts, prosecutors, probation, police, and detention facilities—through which justice is converted into a distorted form of capitalism that profits from economic and racial injustice.[1] This chapter starts with the courts.

The stark details provided here expose how juvenile courts in multiple states are entering into contracts to generate revenue when removing children from their homes or by pulling children into the juvenile justice system under constant threat of removal. Increasingly embracing a businesslike focus in their search for funds, some courts have carried out this practice for years, tucked away in little-known interagency contracts. Courts are trading away their impartiality and independence, and violating the Constitution and judicial ethics, to monetize harm to children.

The juvenile court revenue strategies target children from poor families and disproportionately impact Black children and other children of color. The children's parents face endless barriers to economic stability and do not receive adequate services to help their families stay intact. After enduring the pain and confusion of being removed from their homes, children face further difficulties in the "system" from overworked social workers and probation officers, poorly monitored foster placements, unsafe group homes and juvenile facilities, and overcrowded juvenile courts. The children have struggled with the trauma of poverty and now face even greater trauma after being removed from their homes. And as they leave the foster care and juvenile justice systems, the statistics are even more daunting.[2]

I should pause. As I write with concern for vulnerable youth and seek to shed light on funding mechanisms that threaten the foundations of equal and impartial justice, I should disclose more of my own background.

During my first day in court in my first legal aid job, I was assigned to represent several foster children in one afternoon. The processing of their cases started in the basement of a historic Baltimore courthouse, constructed in 1896. After walking with a fleeting feeling of grandeur through the imposing entrance of granite and marble, towering columns, and carved lions, I abruptly encountered a line of mostly Black children shackled in chains as they were shuffled to delinquency proceedings. And then I descended into a small, dank room with flickering florescent light encased in broken yellow plastic over stained flooring, crowded with worn metal tables and mismatched office chairs with torn vinyl—the "stip" room.

The court directed all the attorneys for the children, parents, and the foster care agency to this room, along with the social workers, to reach "stipulated agreements" that would be presented the same day to judicial masters to avoid the time needed for actual court hearings. If no agreement was reached, one of the attorneys had to request a "contest" before a judge, a step that was disfavored by the court system.

The room smelled of jaded apathy, packed with bodies sluggishly struggling over access to the chairs or a few inches of wall space on which to lean. A handful of outdated DOS-based computer terminals were surrounded by attorneys haggling over agreements while typing out sparse summaries of the lives of children with blinking cursors over green text. I learned that day that some of the foster care agency attorneys engaged in a sort of hazing practice of purposeful delay with new lawyers for the children. Then, one of the judicial masters sent a message demanding our immediate presence to quickly dispose of the cases because the Baltimore Orioles game was scheduled to start soon. Priorities.

The routine replayed itself, as I would also scramble to find times and locations to meet with my child clients, occasionally in my office when social workers would bring them, sometimes at their schools that felt more like prisons, or in their often dilapidated and constantly changing foster care or group homes, and sometimes left with no option but to meet with the children on benches in the chaotic courthouse halls. As I sat next to child-clients on oak benches worn by decades of the grasping fear of those who had sat there before us, I did not feel the presence of justice.

Much of that experience is now a blur of memories, mixed with specific moments and images seared into my mind. I was overwhelmed. I feel that I tried my best, but I simultaneously feel that I should have done more. I have even thought about trying to file an attorney-grievance complaint against myself, years later, for attempting to juggle more cases than ethically possible—to help draw attention to the failing system in which I worked.

So, as my research has uncovered structural concerns that further undermine the possibility of equal and impartial justice for vulnerable children and adults, I feel driven to provide accurate and detailed facts paired with legal analysis to expose the structural failings so that the systems can hopefully improve. The analysis for this chapter turns to Ohio.

OHIO JUVENILE COURTS CONTRACTING TO MAKE MONEY FROM CHILDREN

Normally, foster care agencies provide foster care services. The federal government provides Title IV-E foster care funds to help the state agencies. Juvenile courts conduct review hearings to ensure the agencies comply with legal requirements and act in the best interests of children. Independence between the courts and agencies is crucial. But in Ohio, the juvenile courts have created a plan to combine all this so the courts can make money from the children.[3] The devil is in the details.

In 1996 four Ohio juvenile courts developed a convoluted contractual process unlikely to be known or understood by the public.[4] Like all states, Ohio has three branches of government that are intended to be independent: the executive, judicial, and legislative branches. The Ohio Department of Job and Family Services is part of the executive branch and is responsible for statewide foster care services, including for children removed from their homes after delinquency proceedings. The agency is also responsible for the receipt of federal funds to help run the foster care agency services. The juvenile courts are supposed to carry out an independent judicial branch function, including judicial review of the agency actions.

EXHIBIT A

OHIO DEPARTMENT OF JOB AND FAMILY SERVICES
SUBGRANT AGREEMENT

G-1213-06-0242

11-303

RECITALS:

This Subgrant Agreement between the Ohio Department of Job and Family Services (hereinafter referred to as "ODJFS") and the Summit County Juvenile Court (hereinafter referred to as "SUBGRANTEE"), and the Summit County Board of Commissioners (hereinafter referred to as "COMMISSIONERS") is created pursuant to the Subgrant awarded by ODJFS to SUBGRANTEE and COMMISSIONERS. SUBGRANTEE hereby accepts the Subgrant and agrees to comply with all the terms and conditions set forth in this Agreement.

FIGURE 1. Ohio Department of Job and Family Services, 2011 Subgrant Agreement with Summit County Juvenile Court. *Source:* https://council.summitoh.net/files -legislation/20203/file/2011_303_exhibit_a.pdf.

However, the juvenile courts created interagency contracts, called "subgrant agreements," for the courts to take over the agency functions while simultaneously carrying out their judicial role.[5] The courts enter these contracts to claim federal foster care funds (IV-E funds) for themselves through juvenile delinquency proceedings. Through the contracts, each juvenile court agrees to a subservient role as "subgrantee," contractually agreeing to serve the state agency as its local foster care agency— and to simultaneously serve as the court to review its own actions as the foster care agency—in order to generate foster care revenue.[6]

Thus, when a juvenile court judge rules that a child is "unruly" or delinquent and orders removal from the family home, the court can claim the IV-E foster care funds intended for the foster care agency. The more children a juvenile court removes from their homes, the more money the court can claim. Also, in addition to generating revenue from child removals. the courts can claim additional funds by labeling other children "foster care candidates." Once the children have been labeled and pulled into the system, the courts can keep processing them—at a constant risk of removal—to claim IV-E revenue for the courts' operations.

In such a distorted system, $hawn is a commodity, and the payoff is significant. Strikingly, the Jefferson County juvenile court reports that such IV-E revenue provided over half of the court's total budget in 2016.[7] The Muskingum County juvenile court reported in 2015 that after ordering just two children "into Temporary Custody of the Court," it was able to leverage the two youth into $140,843.44 in foster care revenue.[8] The Cuyahoga County juvenile court showed a cash balance of

$4 million resulting from the strategy in 2017, and the court was adding about $1.5 million a year in IV-E revenue from the children as of 2019.[9] The Montgomery County juvenile court pulled in over $3.2 million in IV-E revenue in 2018 and over $2.3 million in 2019, which doesn't include millions in revenue obtained from the court's residential treatment center.[10] In the pursuit of money, at least twenty-seven Ohio juvenile courts have now signed these interagency contracts.[11]

Children Plugged into Revenue Equations

To begin the process, children removed from their homes must be poor, like $hawn. The courts can only obtain the funds if the child is IV-E eligible, meaning the child must come from an impoverished family. Therefore, the juvenile courts received training about maximizing IV-E funds, including how to focus on such "allowable youth."[12] $hawn is plugged into math that leads to the money through the "eligibility ratio," often called the "penetration rate," that measures the percentage of children removed from poor rather than nonpoor families. One of the training slides provides the equation:

> The Eligibility Ratio (ER) is computed by taking:
> The number of placement days experienced by Title IV-E program eligible children housed in allowable settings
> *Divided by*
> The total number of placement days experienced for all children in custody/care placements for the reporting period.[13]

The resulting ratio is then used as a multiplier by the courts in claiming IV-E revenue. Thus, the way the equation works, the greater the percentage of poor children removed by the courts into foster care, and the longer those children are held in foster care compared to nonpoor children, the more money the juvenile courts can obtain. To further illustrate the math, another of the training slides uses the names of cartoon characters from the *Flintstones* and *Jetsons* TV shows, apparently trying to be humorous about using children to generate revenue. Following the "Tally List" chart portrayed by the state agency, children labeled as "George Jetson" and "Fred Flintstone" are both IV-E eligible and thus from poor families, while a child labeled as "Betty Ruble" is not from a poor family.[14] Through the chart, court personnel learn that if the nonpoor child is held in custody for fewer days, and instead the poor children are held in custody for more days (or if more poor children are added), then the "Eligible Days in Allowable Setting" will be higher, and thus the eligibility ratio will be higher. Then, when the higher eligibility ratio is used as a multiplier by the courts in claiming various IV-E administrative costs revenue, the courts can obtain more money.

Bidding on Children

After the court rules that $hawn is delinquent or unruly and that he should be removed from his home and adds him to the eligibility ratio, the court then picks among qualifying placements, which can include foster care homes, group homes, treatment foster care, and residential treatment facilities. The Families First Act of 2018 added new requirements for facilities to be IV-E eligible as "Qualified Residential Treatment Programs," but the list of available facilities continues to be long. The state agency provides courts with a several-page spreadsheet of hundreds of organizations to choose from, with reimbursable costs listed as if the facilities are bidding on the children.[15] If $hawn lives in a jurisdiction like Montgomery County, the juvenile court operates its own residential treatment center, allowing the court to place children in its own facility and claim IV-E revenue.

Although the placements must be "nonsecure," they are certainly not voluntary. The children usually receive a probation officer along with the placement, and if rules are broken, a prison-like juvenile facility awaits. Further, as detailed in chapter 7, children like $hawn often face significant maltreatment—or worse—in facilities that seek to maximize their occupancy rate of children while minimizing operational costs.

To qualify for IV-E funds, government-run facilities are limited in size to twenty-five children. However, there is no restriction on the size of private facilities, so the children can be packed in to make more money.[16] The facilities can be public, nonprofit, religious, for-profit, and out-of-state.[17] One example company is Ohio Mentor, part of National Mentor Holdings, Inc., which a news investigation explained "turned the field of foster care into a cash cow."[18] The investigation described concerns with abuse and neglect at the facilities and "found that the problems at Mentor are not limited to a few tragic cases but are widespread" and led to a 2017 US Senate investigation.[19] Despite the reported concerns, Ohio governor Mike DeWine appointed the head of Ohio Mentor to his Children Services Transformation Advisory Council in 2019.[20] National Mentor is owned by Civitas Solutions, Inc., which in turn was purchased in 2019 "in cash by Celtic Intermediate Corp., an affiliate of Centerbridge Partners, L.P. and The Vistria Group, LP."—private investment firms—for approximately $1.4 billion.[21] The "troubled youth" business is big.

An annual report from the Hamilton County juvenile court provides an example of the revenue-focused view of child placements. The court partnered with a private organization that operates juvenile facilities called Rite of Passage to run the Hillcrest Training School, a 142-bed residential treatment center, which led to more court foster care revenue: "In 2013, the Court began realizing the benefits of this collaborative partnership through the receipt of increased Title IV-E funds for the reimbursement of placement cost."[22] The court explained how it used this collaboration to increase revenue to offset county funding cuts, "[i]n a continuing effort to manage the budget reductions": "For example, with the public-private partnership the Court formed with Rite of Passage to assume operational control of the Hillcrest residential treatment facility, the Court realized new revenues from federal IV-E funds totaling approximately $877,000. . . . The Court has also allocated three of its magistrates to preside over child support cases exclusively whereby increasing its entitlement to federal IV-D funds."[23] The court's $877,000 new IV-E revenue, acquired through child placements at this facility, was in addition to other IV-E revenue claimed by the court, for a total of over $1.8 million for the year.[24] In fact, the court lists that its IV-E revenue for the year was greater than its IV-E-related expenses by over $277,000.[25] Further, the report's description of using magistrates to generate IV-D funds foreshadows further widespread court revenue strategies exposed in the following chapter, in which courts use impoverished children and families to obtain revenue from child support proceedings.

Using Children to Fund Court Overhead

In addition to seeking funds from direct foster care placement services, the training materials explain how courts can obtain even more revenue from youth through a seemingly endless list of administrative costs. After ruling that $hawn is delinquent or unruly, the courts begin using him as a resource to fund overhead and operations, such as

- payroll and fringe benefit costs of court staff;
- equipment and supply costs;
- postage and telephone costs;

- the cost of liability insurance;
- travel and per diem costs;
- costs of rent, leases, and utilities;
- a listing of over a dozen categories of training costs;
- costs of contracted services; and
- other "shared administrative costs," which can include the costs of court staff such as administrative assistants and receptionists, as well as utilities and supplies.[26]

The training slides even explain how a court can use $hawn to recover depreciation costs of court buildings. And were that not enough, the court can use a pyramid-like strategy to obtain revenue by claiming the administrative costs of the process of claiming administrative costs.

The training materials also show the courts how to use an accounting gimmick to claim more administrative costs than actually occur. The materials provide an example showing that although "actual costs" of supplies for juvenile court IV-E staff may be $2,000, the court could instead use a "Percentage of Full Time Equivalent (FTE) Method" to charge $2,500, or 25 percent more than the actual costs.[27] Using such a method, the courts would be knowingly submitting inaccurate claims.

This pursuit of revenue from overhead costs leads to inverted operational goals. Nonprofit organizations face constant criticism regarding how much they spend on overhead compared to direct services, often targeting less than 15 percent on administrative costs. But for the juvenile courts' IV-E strategies, this goal is flipped. For example, the Lucas County Juvenile Court's 2016 annual report lists $457,381.01 to reimburse IV-E administrative costs, about 370 percent more than the amount in direct placement services of $123,124.12.[28]

Courts Hiring Contractors to Maximize Revenue from Children

Because the process of maximizing IV-E funds from children can be confusing, many Ohio juvenile courts hired a private revenue contractor, Justice Benefits, Inc. (JBI). The company explains that "JBI has been working with Ohio Juvenile Courts since 2003," and that "[c]urrently, JBI works with over 20 Ohio Juvenile Courts to successfully file IV-E quarterly claims."[29] Searching through county records, a Miami County commissioners' meeting explains how JBI is incentivized by a percentage of money claimed through the children: "JBI is paid 22% on monies recovered through claims submitted by the Court, and will be paid from the Juvenile Court Title IV-E Fund."[30] Thus, as courts issue more rulings that children are delinquent or unruly, JBI can help the courts obtain IV-E funds from the children, increasing the company's contingency fee.

Further, in addition to child removals, the courts can also generate revenue by labeling children as "candidates" for foster care. Through this part of the strategy, a court first rules that $hawn is delinquent or unruly and orders him into court supervision through probation. Then, as long as the court keeps processing $hawn through the system of intrusive probation monitoring, continual hearings, and numerous evaluations, with the constant fear of removal, he can be used to pay for court operating costs. With changes under the Families First Act, children considered candidates for foster care can trigger IV-E funds regardless of the income of the child's family, whereas for child removals into foster care the IV-E funds are still only available when the children are poor. Again, the courts contracted with JBI for help with this strategy, including "candidates for foster care" trainings.[31]

OTHER STATE JUVENILE COURTS FOLLOWING OHIO IN MAXIMIZING REVENUE FROM CHILDREN

As in Ohio, other state juvenile court systems are also using children to claim foster care funds. The stories of the strategies are often buried in budget documents. For example, public financial statements of Louisiana's Jefferson Parish Juvenile Court from 2005 reveal "the Judicial Expense Fund budget was favorably impacted by the accrual of $326,286.45 in Title IV-E money." Digging into the reports makes clear how the juvenile court strategy makes money from children: "As indicated by the financial statements and mentioned previously, the Court has identified Title IV-E funding as a significant new revenue source. Essentially this money represents Federal reimbursement, passed through the Louisiana Department of Social Services, of various indirect, administrative, and direct expenditures associated with the provision of services to children in the foster care system."[32] Reading further presents a picture of court personnel wearing pagers that are programmed to alert them to record information in a way that maximizes revenue from the children: "Eligibility determination is accomplished by a Random Moment Time Study, whereby eligible participants are given pager-like devices that are programmed to alarm at various points throughout the day. Participants are also given a legend of Title IV-E activities, and are required to indicate which activity they are performing when the alarm sounds. This information is compiled on a quarterly basis, and with various other cost and eligibility indicators, the claim is calculated."[33]

Included within its more recent 2017 financial statement, the juvenile court explains its continuation of the strategy, how the resulting revenue "has steadily increased over the last 3 quarters of 2017 due to additional training," and that "Title IV-E revenue is expected to continue on this pattern throughout 2018."[34] Then, in the Jefferson Parish's legally required public notices are resolutions showing that the parish followed Ohio's example of using a revenue contractor to help with "consulting services regarding the identification and obtaining of available federal grant funds, including Title IV-E reimbursement and other resources that may be available to the Department of Juvenile Services for a total cost not to exceed 12% of the total resulting revenues received by the Parish through Justice Benefits, Inc."[35]

In addition to Ohio and Louisiana, other state documents reveal that similar strategies to generate revenue from children have been implemented by juvenile court systems in Missouri, Iowa, Arizona, Illinois, and Texas—and possibly more states.[36] In Missouri, 2021 budget documents indicate that the state agency "contracts with certain juvenile courts or family courts to reimburse the court the federal [IV-E] match for the children who are placed in the court's custody and in an out-of-home placement."[37] In Iowa, responsibility for administering IV-E programs "extends to Juvenile Court Services through an interagency agreement that authorizes Juvenile Court Services to provide child welfare services."[38] The Pima County, Arizona, Juvenile Court reports IV-E revenue "derived via cost reimbursement from the federal government through the Administrative Office of the Courts."[39]

Multiple state court systems use their court-run juvenile probation departments to claim the funds from children.[40] In Illinois, the Juvenile Probation and Court Services Departments report directly to each county's chief judge.[41] Therefore, the Cook County Office of the Chief Judge Juvenile Probation and Court Services entered a contract with JBI to help claim IV-E funds under a contingency fee structure.[42] In Texas, the Juvenile Justice Department entered an "interagency cooperation contract," with a value up to $10,500,000, for the agency's juvenile probation departments to maximize IV-E revenue.[43] Although the Texas juvenile probation offices are part of the state Juvenile Justice Department, each of the county probation offices is run by a juvenile board comprised of judges.[44] And again, some of these Texas county juvenile boards entered contracts with JBI for help maximizing the funds.[45]

UNCONSTITUTIONAL AND UNETHICAL JUVENILE COURT SYSTEMS

Through their contractual deals, juvenile court systems have lowered their sights from the pursuit of justice for children to obtaining revenue from children. And the courts twist and tear constitutional norms in the process.

Separation of Powers Violations

As set out in chapter 1, our US Constitution establishes the separation of powers between the three branches of government. Each state also drafted its own constitution, with most including a separation of powers, and states still recognize the separation of powers doctrine when not explicitly stated in their constitutions.[46] Courts have differed over the years in how strictly to interpret the doctrine, ranging between what constitutional scholars describe as "formalism," which is a purist view requiring strict separation between the branches of government, and "functionalism," a more pragmatic approach that recognizes some shared functions may be necessary for efficient operations in our more complex modern government.[47] However, even under the functionalist approach, any shared branch functions must be necessary for a legitimate government need, must not disrupt the intended balance of power, and must be limited when conflicts of interest are present.[48] Moreover, some circumstances are an afront to the constitutionally required separation of powers regardless of what line of reasoning is applied. The Ohio juvenile court IV-E contracts provide such a story of constitutional destruction.[49]

As described earlier, foster care services are supposed to be provided by foster care agencies, which are part of the executive branch of state government. Juvenile courts are supposed to review the actions and decisions of the foster care agencies. However, the Ohio juvenile courts twist themselves into contracts to carry out both the judicial and foster care agency roles so they can generate revenue from children. First the courts act like courts and rule that children are unruly or delinquent. Next the courts act like foster care agencies and use the children to claim foster care IV-E revenue. Then the courts act like courts again to review themselves acting like foster care agencies so they can increase the IV-E money. Simultaneously, the courts let the actual statewide foster care agency have contractual control over the courts in their role as both courts and local foster care agencies.

This all seems confusing because it is. But what is clear is that the revenue strategy violates the principles of separation of powers and judicial independence. Deciphering the courts' unconstitutional contractual path requires digging into the details.

The story turns to 2006, ten years after the juvenile courts first created the IV-E contracts, when one Ohio county justice system paused to question their legality.[50] Butler County officials expressed concerns to the Ohio Supreme Court's Board of Commissioners on Grievances and Discipline, questioning if a juvenile court could ethically take on the additional role as a foster care agency and then review its own actions. The specific question is striking: "(W)hether or not it is permissible, within the canons, for a juvenile court to act as a child placing agency for the purpose of receiving reimbursement through Title IV-E of the Social Security Act when provisions of that act require the court to make judicial determinations concerning whether or not continued placement in the home is contrary to the welfare of the child, and whether or not the placing agency (in this case the court) has made reasonable efforts to prevent the need for the placement of the child in order to receive such reimbursement."[51] Rather than answering, the Ohio Supreme Court's Board sent the question back to a committee of juvenile court judges. The judges reviewed themselves in the actions of reviewing themselves and found themselves to be fine: "It is the position of the juvenile judges of Ohio, in light of the preceding arguments that optional juvenile court participation as a Title IV-E placing agency is supported by law and consistent with the ethical standards embodied in the Judicial Canons."[52]

Disturbingly, the judges only briefly addressed the separation of powers violations by attempting to minimize their conflicting roles: "Applying the law to the facts of this case, the constitutional function of courts as adjudicators is not impeded by incidental administrative activities such as providing for the placement of children."[53] This description by the judges of the care and placement of vulnerable children as merely "incidental administrative activities" is concerning and incorrect.[54]

To grasp the weight of this role, the US Department of Health and Human Services summarizes the foster care placing agency responsibility as being "legally accountable for the day-to-day care and protection of the child who has come into foster care." In addition to critically important placement decisions, the responsibility "also ensures that the State

provides the child with the mandated statutory and regulatory protections, including case plans, administrative reviews, permanency hearings,
and updated health and education records."[55] Because of its heightened
importance, the child placing agency role is subject to detailed federal
statutes and regulations, all with the overarching purpose of ensuring the
safety and well-being of children. Also, along with the extensive federal
law requirements, Ohio law sets out a long list of agency responsibilities.[56]

Thus, the foster care agency responsibilities are not merely "incidental
administrative activities." In fact, because of the importance of their role,
federal law requires continuous judicial review of the agencies, which
means the Ohio juvenile courts are reviewing themselves in multiple specific and crucial judicial determinations intended to protect children's
well-being, including (1) reviewing the agency's child removal decision to
determine whether "continuation in the home would be contrary to the
welfare" of the child; (2) reviewing whether the agency made "reasonable efforts" to provide assistance and services in order to prevent the
need for the child's removal; and (3) conducting a "permanency hearing"
within twelve months of the child's entering foster care, to determine if
"reasonable efforts have been made to finalize a permanent placement
for the child."[57] Also, the courts must conduct hearings every six months
to review the foster care agencies (which are the courts) in their case plan
and progress, including efforts toward family reunification or alternative permanency goals. Moreover, the courts have continuing jurisdiction
over the actions of the agencies (themselves) throughout the time when
the child is in foster care, and any party can bring a matter regarding the
agencies' actions or services to the courts' attention by motion at any
time.[58] The juvenile courts are even in a position where they can review
and issue orders controlling the conduct of the current custodians of the
children, who again are the courts themselves.[59]

In each of these crucial court decisions, the juvenile courts are reviewing themselves in their contractual foster care agency role, contra-
dicting a principle that has existed since the beginnings of American
jurisprudence, as stated by James Madison: "No man is allowed to be
a judge in his own cause; because his interest would certainly bias his
judgment, and, not improbably, corrupt his integrity."[60] Further adding
to the conflict, the courts are financially incentivized to rule in their own
favor because such determinations in turn trigger the courts' ability to
claim and maximize IV-E foster care revenue, as discussed earlier.

Digging deeper into the interagency contracts reveals even more
separation of powers concerns in language giving the executive branch

agency "final and binding" control over the courts. Through the contracts, each juvenile court becomes a "subgrantee" of the state executive branch agency, the Ohio Department of Job and Family Services (ODJFS). The court then "agrees to allow ODJFS to periodically assess and monitor SUBGRANTEE's [the juvenile court's] adherence to all the requirements" of the contract (which includes carrying out both the foster care and the judicial functions). If the court disagrees with ODJFS, the agency "will inform [the court], in writing, of its final determination related to the matters in the dispute." Then, the court "agrees to accept the decision of ODJFS as final and binding."[61] This contract language illustrates unconstitutional control by the state executive branch agency over the courts, and additional contractual provisions exert more control, even the agency's control over and contractual ownership of records and documents produced by the court.

Thus, the contracts result in a conflicted and convoluted arrangement whereby the juvenile courts are conducting judicial reviews regarding their own actions as the IV-E placing agencies, with financial incentives—which is a significant conflict in itself—and then the courts are simultaneously agreeing to submit to the final determinations of the state executive branch agency regarding the courts' performance of both their foster care agency and judiciary role. Such intertwined conflicts are precisely what the separation of powers doctrine exists to prevent, and why the doctrine is so clearly violated by the juvenile court interagency agreements. In fact, in 2015 the DOJ's Civil Rights Division found comparable separation of powers concerns when investigating the Family Court in St. Louis: "The organizational structure of the Family Court, wherein both prosecutor and probation officer are employees of the court, the prosecutor is counsel for the probation officer, and the probation officer acts as both an arm of the prosecution as well as a child advocate, causes inherent conflicts of interest. These conflicts of interest are contrary to separation of powers principles and deprive children of adequate due process."[62] The DOJ's opinion supports the conclusion that the juvenile courts' interagency agreement structure violates the separation of powers doctrine and leads here to further consideration of due process violations.

Due Process Violations

Combined with the separation of powers, our Constitution also enshrines the right to procedural due process, including the right to impartial justice systems. To meet the impartiality requirement, justice officials must meet two tests: (1) the reality of impartiality, so that the individuals are not actually biased; and (2) the appearance of impartiality, so that a reasonable person with full knowledge of the facts would not think the circumstances create the appearance of likely bias.

Impartiality is necessarily intertwined with the separation of powers. Otherwise, if the executive branch gains power and control over judicial functions, the opportunity for impartial tribunals to render justice is lost.

The juvenile court interagency contracts undermine these constitutional ideals.[63] Rather than judicial independence and impartiality, the courts now have a direct financial interest in the outcome of judicial hearings. When the Ohio judges reviewed the constitutionality of their own contractual agreements, their analysis ignored long-standing US Supreme Court precedent that originated in their own state. First, in a case from the Prohibition era, the Supreme Court in *Tumey v. Ohio* found the structure of the Ohio mayor's court violated due process when the mayor also sat as a judge and received a financial incentive to convict defendants, and his village received revenue upon each conviction:

> There, the mayor of a village had the authority to sit as a Judge (with no jury) to try those accused of violating a state law prohibiting the possession of alcoholic beverages. Inherent in this structure were two potential conflicts. First, the mayor received a salary supplement for performing judicial duties, and the funds for that compensation derived from the fines assessed in a case. No fines were assessed upon acquittal. The mayor-judge thus received a salary supplement only if he convicted the defendant. . . . Second, sums from the criminal fines were deposited to the village's general treasury fund for village improvements and repairs.[64]

Forty-five years later, the Supreme Court found similar due process violations, again with the Ohio mayor's courts, in *Ward v. Village of Monroeville*, in which the mayor/judge did not receive direct compensation, but his village received revenue for each conviction. In finding the structure violated the defendants' due process guarantee to an impartial tribunal, Justice William J. Brennan Jr. explained "that 'possible temptation' may also exist when the mayor's executive responsibilities for village finances may make him partisan to maintain the high level of contribution from the mayor's court."[65] The same unconstitutional temptation applies when juvenile court judges are incentivized in their decisions to seek IV-E revenue for their courts.

In more recent decisions following the Supreme Court's reasoning, the US Court of Appeals for the 5th Circuit issued opinions that are directly applicable to the juvenile court IV-E revenue schemes. The court in *Caliste v. Cantrell* held that the Louisiana trial courts violated defendants' due process rights when the court received fees every time a judge required a secured money bond as a condition of release.[66] And in *Cain v. White*, the court similarly held that the institutional financial interest of the courts from judges ordering court fines violated the due process clause.[67] The Ohio courts' due process violations are even more severe, with the abdication of impartiality further emboldened by the separation of powers violations. The courts are financially incentivized to issue orders that children are delinquent or unruly, and the courts are further incentivized in reviewing themselves in their foster care agency role to obtain more revenue.[68] Even if an individual judge can somehow ignore the clear financial conflict, the appearance of impartiality is knowingly destroyed.

Documents from the Cuyahoga County Council illustrate an example of the conflict, revealing that the juvenile court used IV-E funds resulting from its interagency contract for over $1.8 million in court salary increases.[69] The large amount of revenue illustrates that there is unfortunately no shortage of poor children the juvenile court can use to obtain IV-E payments, with almost half of Cleveland's children living in poverty. As noted in the introduction, an Ohio juvenile court judge from Franklin County bluntly expressed his concern with the conflict, explaining that "the more kids that are placed out of their homes, the more money the court gets, which might lead some people to question the court's motivation: helping the youngsters or getting the money?"[70]

Simply put, for our courts to be impartial and independent, they cannot be financially incentivized in their decisions. Vulnerable youth and adults should have access to needed services, but in a manner wherein justice systems are not incentivized to use them for revenue. However, even the Ohio RECLAIM program (Reasoned and Equitable Community and Local Alternatives to the Incarceration of Minors), which has a good stated goal of diverting the juvenile population from state-run juvenile prisons to local community alternatives, is structured to directly financially incentivize juvenile court decisions. According to the Ohio Department of Youth Services, "RECLAIM Ohio is a funding initiative which encourages juvenile courts to develop or purchase a range of community-based options to meet the needs of each juvenile offender or youth at risk of offending."[71] While encouraging fewer juvenile placements in state correctional facilities, the incentivized formula is structured in a concerning way that can actually provide increased funding to a juvenile court if the court's number of juvenile felony adjudications is greater than the state average.[72] Our justice systems are supposed to be ethically motivated by pursuing their justice missions, not by chasing money.

Violations of Judicial Ethics

In addition to being unconstitutional, the court revenue schemes are unethical. The ABA Model Code of Judicial Conduct begins with the core principles in Canon 1: "A judge shall uphold and promote the independence, integrity, and impartiality of the judiciary, and shall avoid impropriety and the appearance of impropriety." The juvenile court interagency agreements undermine those goals.

Even if an individual judge tries to avoid being influenced by the unconstitutional structure that surrounds her, she must confront an ethical truism: a judge cannot ethically carry out her judicial functions in a justice system where independence and impartiality are compromised. A case from Washington state provides an excellent example. In *Matter of Dependency of A.E.T.H.*, the judge recused herself because the juvenile court structure violated the due process right to an impartial tribunal. The case involved a structure in which the volunteer guardian ad litem program (VGAL) is an agency of the court, although the VGALs are supposed to independently advocate for children's interests. In her recusal decision, the judge entered a memorandum explaining the structural due process violations, including that "the acts of VGAL Program employees are the acts of the Superior Court, and judging or sanctioning the acts of VGAL Program employees is the Judge judging or sanctioning himself or herself."[73] The Court of Appeals agreed, recognizing that the "right to a fair trial before an impartial tribunal" is "especially critical" in child welfare proceedings, and further explained that "'even if there is no showing of actual bias in the tribunal, . . . due process is denied by circumstances that create the likelihood or the appearance of bias.'"[74] Thus, although the judge showed no personal bias, she could not ethically carry out her judicial functions when surrounded by an unconstitutional court structure.[75]

If this same reasoning is applied to the juvenile court IV-E contracts and other similar examples addressed in this book, not only is there concern with the structural conflicts, but the judges are also financially incentivized in their judicial actions.

Moreover, in addition to violating the principles of judicial ethics in Canon 1, the courts' contracts also violate more specific ethical rules.

For example, the Ohio Code of Judicial Conduct follows the ABA Model Code in prohibiting a judge from serving as a fiduciary in matters that come before the court. This prohibition includes serving as guardian for a foster child (who is considered a "ward"): "A judge shall not serve as a fiduciary if it is likely that the judge as a fiduciary will be engaged in proceedings that would ordinarily come before the judge or if the estate, trust, or ward becomes involved in adversary proceedings in the court on which the judge serves or one under its appellate jurisdiction."[76] This explicitly prohibited scenario is exactly what occurs when a juvenile court signs an interagency agreement to become a foster care child placing agency. Through the contract, the judge and her court become a fiduciary for children in the foster care agency role, while the judge is simultaneously carrying out her judicial role in proceedings involving the children (wards).

Thus, juvenile courts are violating ethical and constitutional requirements through their foster care contracts, and unfortunately, what has been revealed in this chapter is just the tip of the iceberg. The following chapters further expose how the court systems, prosecutor's offices, probation departments, police, and sheriff's departments—and even detention centers and group homes—are all using multiple interlinked schemes to generate revenue from the struggles of children and impoverished adults. The resulting ripples of harm cannot be overstated. As vulnerable populations are harmed, we are all harmed, and the foundational ideals of justice are crumbling.

CHAPTER 3

Judicial Child Support Factory

America's child support system is supposed to be about helping children. The overarching mission is unequivocally to serve the best interests of children. However, as with the child welfare system, the child support mission has been traded for revenue operations, with vulnerable children and their families often pulled into an industrialization of harm. And our courts, which are supposed to exist as guardians of rights and monitors of mission, have instead become part of the factory.

This chapter reveals how across the country, our foundational juvenile and family courts have developed contractual deals to generate revenue from child support, in strategies ranging from selling off court officials as child support mercenaries to the courts contracting to take over the entire executive branch child support agency function—again destroying ethical and constitutional norms. The practices are even more widespread than the foster care revenue strategies but similarly unknown to the public.

Before exposing details of the courts' contractual efforts, it is important to delve into a bit of history of the IV-D child support program, which sets the stage for the harm that comes from child support's unfortunate beginnings from poor laws and bastardy acts, from which our foundational justice systems are now profiting.

But first I need to pause to be transparent with more details of my own history that now drive me to write this part of the book. During my years as a legal aid lawyer, I was asked to create a new child support advocacy project with the goal of helping children and their impoverished families, but with a focus on representing noncustodial parents. I was hesitant. At the time of the request, I had already transitioned from the foster care child advocacy unit and represented countless clients who were struggling with all types of poverty-related issues, from threatened housing evictions to Medicaid and Social Security appeals. I achieved numerous successful outcomes for clients, which helped to motivate me, and the unsuccessful outcomes motivated me even more.

And then there are the losses that haunt me. Some of my clients died while I was trying to help them. A client hanged herself, overwhelmed by thousands in medical debt and denials of Medicaid eligibility that we were seeking to overturn. I hear her nervous voice as I write this, as we were sitting on her worn brown couch, just starting to dig though disheveled stacks of documents. A different client was barely able to talk after multiple strokes and seeking desperately needed Social Security disability benefits, but the administrative law judge explained he thought she was faking her symptoms despite medical reports. She died during the appeal. Another client faced a denial of disability benefits after the administrative law judge ruled he was not bad enough off to qualify. The client shook my hand and thanked me for trying—with a tired smile—as we discussed plans to appeal the decision, but I later received a call from his family member saying that he had died. These cases occurred over twenty years ago, but the memories refuse to depart my mind and continue to inspire my efforts to fight for struggling individuals against systemic failings and opposing forces that are causing them harm.

So, several years ago when I was asked to start the new child support project, I was hesitant. I had already done a significant amount of legal work for low-income parents in family law matters, including child support. But this project was different. My prior child support experience had involved helping impoverished custodial parents, usually the mothers. In this project, I was to provide legal representation for the noncustodial parents. I was uncertain, because I was to represent individuals whom I had previously viewed as the harmful opposing forces I was fighting against. Society labeled these individuals "deadbeat dads," many of whom were also labeled "ex-offenders" with criminal histories. In my heart, I would always be a child advocate first and foremost, so I was unsure to say the least about helping noncustodial parents. I was wrong.

Through the project, I met parent after parent, mostly fathers but also several mothers, who were struggling to overcome difficulties that would already have broken most people. I encountered countless circumstances in which the fathers, mothers, and children were all being harmed by the workings of a system that was supposed to help them. And as it turns out, I learned that there are starkly different and separate child support systems, one that serves the interests of parents with money and lawyers and a forced system that seeks to generate revenue from the poor.

WHEN CHILD SUPPORT IS CONVERTED TO HARM: TITLE IV-D CHILD SUPPORT PROGRAM

When parents in family law matters have money, the IV-D child support agencies are usually not involved. The parents hire lawyers, and their cases are served by experienced judges who decide almost unlimited issues of child custody, divorce, alimony, child support, dividing payments for expensive summer camps and private school, arranging complex visitation schedules that include vacations and travel plans, determining custody and payments for the care of family pets, paying for private tutors and therapists, dividing endless lists of marital property, apportioning value in retirement accounts and stock options, and even deciding control over frozen embryos. The assigned judges often provide scheduling conferences, settlement conferences, mediations, and pretrial hearings to resolve discovery disputes, and then ultimately the trials may be allowed to take up multiple days of court time. These are not the courts for the poor.

The courts for low-income families are IV-D courts, in which the focus is singularly directed toward ordering and enforcing child support obligations; much of the money is actually owed to the government rather than to the children. These courts for the poor are often not even courts. Rather, the impoverished parents are diverted to separate tribunals with fact finders who are often jaded from high caseloads and usually not real judges, with titles such as "hearing officers," "commissioners," "masters," or "friends of the court." The rooms are often overflowing and chaotic. Lawyers are rarely present, other than those representing the interests of the agency. Parents often attend in work clothes, having been forced to take unpaid time off their low-wage jobs. After waiting hours to be processed as if in a crowded assembly line, their cases are decided in minutes, sometimes less.

History of the IV-D Child Support Program

Child support initially had nothing to do with supporting children. Rather, the obligation grew from old English poor laws and early American laws known as "bastardy acts," which were enacted to protect towns from unwed mothers and their children, who were considered "illegitimate." Such laws regarding unwed mothers developed from broader English poor laws, which sought to punish individuals who were experiencing poverty. One such law from 1535 included punishment for the crime of being poor by whipping, banishment, cutting an ear off, and ultimately execution: "A valiant beggar, or sturdy vagabond, shall at the first time be whipped . . . and if he continues his roguish life, he shall have the upper part of the gristle of his right ear cut off; and if after that he be taken wandering in idleness, or doth not apply to his labour, or is not in service with any master, he shall be adjudged and executed as a felon."[1]

Early American child support obligations were modeled on the English laws, with states authorizing counties and towns to treat unwed parents like criminals. For example, Maryland's Bastardy and Fornication law of 1781 required incarceration of unwed mothers until they paid security to indemnify the county against any potential expenses for their children or until they named someone as the father, who paid the security.[2] Meanwhile, as poor unwed mothers were jailed to force payments to the county, a separate form of child support began to emerge in the courts. For married parents who could afford the process, the courts gradually began to recognize and order support obligations for the benefit of children and payable to the custodial parents.[3]

Thus, two systems of child support emerged in America. One developed as a court service available for financially better-off parents who were seeking divorce and to determine how to distribute family property and divide financial obligations for the benefit of children.[4] The other system was used to punish underprivileged families, especially those with children labeled illegitimate, who were prosecuted by local government agencies.

The development of this forced system was racially and economically targeted. As described in more detail in chapter 8, while the system was deeply harmful to poor White families, it devastated Black families; it developed alongside and was entangled with laws that treated all children of enslaved parents as illegitimate and post–Civil War laws and practices that continued the forced separation of Black parents from their children. This penal system developed into the current IV-D child support system and the factory-like IV-D courts.

After American states established their versions of bastardy acts, the federal government broadened the punitive measures, including policies that forced families apart.[5] The welfare program at the time, called Aid to Families with Dependent Children (AFDC), virtually banned fathers from living in the households receiving benefits. Several states created "man in the house" rules that disqualified families from aid if a man was found residing in the household, including making midnight raids to enforce the requirements.[6] The welfare rules were highly racialized, often targeting Black families and fueled by stereotypes of impoverished fathers as deadbeat dads and mothers who were often labeled "welfare queens," encompassing a disturbingly incorrect and racist view that an "AFDC mother is African American, urban, lazy, and a 'bad mother' who gets pregnant to obtain more AFDC benefits."[7] Even after AFDC was converted to the current TANF program, with propagandized goals of encouraging two-parent families, the requirements actually still do the opposite.

Congress enacted the current Title IV-D child support program in 1975, providing federal funding to the states for forced child support system requirements that still exist today: poor mothers applying for public aid are forced to "cooperate" in establishing paternity, forced to sue the fathers for child support, and simultaneously forced to assign child support rights to the government to repay any costs of the public assistance.[8] Just like the early bastardy acts and poor laws, the primary goal of the IV-D program at its creation was not to help poor children but to punish the families and indemnify the government against the children's expenses. Then, almost as an afterthought in the last minute of the legislative process, Congress decided to also make child support services available to parents who were not receiving welfare and thus not required to sign over their child support to the government.[9]

Most people are unaware of this history or the different systems of child support. When most people think of child support, they think of something helpful and only intended to benefit children. However, for millions of impoverished parents and children forced into the IV-D system, the reality is often the reverse.

Harm Caused by the IV-D Program

The breadth of the IV-D child support system is immense, with a disproportionate impact based on income and race. The IV-D system pulls in more than 14.3 million children in a year, approximately 20 percent of all the children in the United States.[10] Most of the families are poor, and the percentage of Black families pulled into the system is more than twice that of Black individuals in the overall population.[11] When custodial parents are poor, the noncustodial parents are usually also poor, with studies indicating that more than 70 percent of the national IV-D child support debt is owed by parents with annual incomes of $10,000 or less.[12]

Child support can be an important benefit when the payments are properly established and directed to help the custodial parents and children. However, even in cases where the child support is provided to children rather than taken by the state, improper order amounts and punitive enforcement tactics can cause significant harm, especially for low-income families. Therefore, courts are supposed to carefully consider the circumstances of parents and children, seeking a delicate balance of establishing child support orders that obligors have the ability to pay and only ordering the use of enforcement mechanisms when that is in the best interests of the children. If courts are financially incentivized to maximize orders and collections and to use overly harsh enforcement tools rather than solely making decisions based on the children's best interests, harm results. In a 2019 Abell Foundation report by Vicki Turetsky, the former commissioner of the Federal Office of Child Support Enforcement explains the harm in Baltimore: "[T]he evidence is clear: higher orders and tougher enforcement will not increase collections when the barrier to payment is poverty. It does no good, and in fact, it does harm. . . . Unrealistic child support policies and practices entangle poor African American men and their families in poverty and have become a destabilizing force in the Baltimore community. Child support orders set beyond the ability of noncustodial parents to comply push them out of low-wage jobs, drown them in debt, hound them into the underground economy, and chase them out of their children's lives."[13] Further, when payments are owed to the government rather than provided to the children, the orders and enforcement actions always cause harm. Across the country, more than $23 billion in such IV-D child support debt is owed to the government rather than to children.[14] In California, 40 percent of the total state child support debt is owed to the government.[15]

The IV-D program uses child support as a government-owed debt in multiple ways. When a custodial parent needs health care through Medicaid, the parent is often required to pursue "medical support" against the other parent, with the payments taken to repay the government's cost for Medicaid.[16] Also, when struggling custodial parents temporarily need welfare assistance, states again force the parents into child support proceedings. Choice available to other parents is stripped from impoverished mothers, as they are forced to identify the fathers and then to sue them for child support.[17] In addition to being forced to give up the payments to recover government costs, the mothers may have several concerns about participating in child support proceedings. A mother may be fearful of the father retaliating through custody litigation. She may not want to establish paternity to name the father, concerned about domestic violence or other circumstances in which she believes she and the child are better off without the father in their lives. Or she may have hopes of maintaining a good relationship with the father, both for her and the child, but the forced child support enforcement tactics will tear the fragile families apart.

Because noncustodial fathers pulled into the IV-D system are often also poor, they do not have the ability to pay unrealistic order amounts, and large arrearages quickly accumulate. As courts use punitive enforcement tools, the harm worsens. Fathers lose their jobs after their arrest for child support contempt. Truck drivers or construction workers who need to drive as part of the job—to make money to try to pay child support—face license suspensions. Fathers who help drive their children to school and doctor's appointments are no longer able to do so. Struggling fathers encounter court orders garnishing 65 percent of their wages for child support, losing the ability to afford rent or other expenses or to purchase needed items for their children. The fathers face criminal records resulting from nonsupport proceedings and driving on suspended licenses, making it even harder to find jobs. The child support debt is reported on the fathers' credit reports, blocking their ability to obtain loans to make ends meet. Young mothers and fathers may initially have a good relationship and hope to improve their co-parenting or to work toward living together, but the IV-D child support mechanisms will pit the parents against each other. Children pulled into the system often lose contact with their fathers as relentless court-ordered enforcement actions drive the parents apart.

Ultimately, we are all harmed. The IV-D program has caused poor noncustodial parents to further retreat from their families and leave legitimate employment, reducing tax payments and increasing economic instability in low-income jurisdictions and increasing crime, as the parents see no choice but to seek sources of money in the underground economy.[18]

Further, child support is also converted into a government debt through foster care. If a juvenile court removes $hawn from his home, the court will likely issue a support order against his mother under the rationale of repaying the foster care costs. While $hawn is pulled into foster care, his mother will be desperately trying to get her son back, confronted with the many challenges of being poor and seeking to overcome barriers in the hopes of reunification. When a court orders government-owed support payments, along with punitive enforcement actions, the mother's struggle for economic stability can be derailed.[19] A report from the Orange County, California, Department of Child Support Services, reviewing its own operations, confirmed such harm and concluded that enforcement actions in foster care cases also hurt the parents' credit scores and thus undermined their reunification struggles in several ways: they decreased the parents' ability to obtain housing, to set up basic utilities like water and heat, to obtain work due to credit checks, to obtain necessary loans, and to purchase a car necessary for work.[20] Further, courts often consider the payment of support as a requirement before allowing child reunification, effectively using children as collateral for the court-ordered debts. Then, if $hawn's mother falls behind as she seeks to overcome her other difficulties as well, some states will even terminate parental rights solely because of the debt.[21] Even if all the harm is ignored, the administrative costs of enforcing government-owed child support against impoverished families in Medicaid, welfare, and foster care cases are greater than the resulting payments.[22] The Orange County report found child support orders against parents in the foster care system to be financially harmful to the state, because "[f]or every dollar expended, only 27 cents is collected," and that cost-effectiveness analysis only considers the costs to the child support agencies, not the additional costs imposed by operations of courts and child welfare agencies.[23]

THE UNCONSTITUTIONAL COURT CHILD SUPPORT BUSINESS

Next this section uncovers how all this harm is monetized. Like the foster care agreements exposed in the previous chapter, courts are entering interagency contracts to generate revenue from children and families pulled into the IV-D child support system.[24] Often the same children and their families can be processed through both strategies.

Like IV-E foster care, the IV-D child support program provides federal funds that are intended for child support agencies. However, the courts again have developed contractual arrangements to obtain the money for themselves. State child support agencies are supposed to provide child support services. The federal government provides IV-D child support funds intended to help the agencies. And juvenile and family courts are supposed to conduct hearings to ensure that agency decisions and actions are guided by the best interests of children and their families. Again, independence between the courts and agencies is crucial. But also again, the courts are contracting away their independence to turn child support into business operations.

Federal law does not allow IV-D funds to be used for the costs of judges.[25] So to make money from child support hearings, the courts created a work-around to bypass the prohibition. State courts around the country developed vast systems of "IV-D courts" to hold hearings conducted by court officials who are not actually judges, but rather "magistrates," "judicial masters," "referees," and so on. These officials handle most of the judicial work of the IV-D child support hearings, but they issue "recommendations" rather than court orders. Such recommendations are later signed into an order by an actual judge through what is often virtually an automatic process.

Philadelphia's system illustrates this machinery. An annual report for the city's family court system shows that IV-D child support cases are first scheduled for "establishment conferences" before "conference officers." If no agreement is obtained, the cases are next scheduled for hearings before "quasi-judicial support masters," who prepare a "proposed order," and only then can a parent try to file "exceptions" to appeal the master's recommendations to a judge.[26] Because most parents don't have lawyers, such appeals are rare. Doing the math from data in the annual report, more than thirty-one thousand IV-D child support proceedings were filed in one year in Philadelphia's family courts, with only 3.7 percent of those cases being heard by a judge.[27] In such a process, the judges are cordoned off from the IV-D courts, and the justice system can contract to generate IV-D revenue by processing impoverished children and parents through the child support business operations.

The contractual strategies vary, such as in states like Ohio and Maryland, where the child support agencies are essentially buying court officials, and other states like Pennsylvania and Michigan, where the courts have usurped the child support agency function. However, although the approaches differ in structure, the results are the same: court systems are choosing to violate constitutional and ethical requirements to generate revenue from children and the poor. Like the foster care contracts, details are again buried and obfuscated in contract and budget documents. The details can be dense at times, but it is important to piece together the contractual stories of how state courts have built their child support industries. Our first stop is Pennsylvania.

Pennsylvania

The Pennsylvania family courts (Domestic Relations Sections) developed an expansive strategy to generate child support revenue, contracting with the state human service agency for the courts to take over the county child support offices.[28] Thus the courts—in addition to being courts—have also become the child support agencies.

Reading through the intergovernmental cooperative agreements, the violations of constitutional and ethical requirements are almost too many to list. Starting on the first page, the intergovernmental-branch takeover is expressed in direct terms: "[T]he Domestic Relations Section (DRS) or equivalent child support division of a family court will function as the local Title IV-D agency in its county."[29] Were it a criminal court, the result of this arrangement would be that the court functions as the prosecutor and policing agency, investigating and initiating charges against a defendant, and then the court functions as the court, holding a trial to review its own actions and to rule on its own criminal complaint. The more criminal investigations the court initiates, the more criminal complaints the court files, and the more rulings of criminal liability the court issues, the more money the court makes. Returning from the criminal court analogy to child support, the terms of the agreements detail how the courts have contracted to carry out the executive branch prosecutorial/enforcement functions of conducting child support investigations, preparing complaints, motions, and numerous other punitive enforcement requests—for the courts to review themselves and rule on their own filings.[30] The courts are even contractually required to petition themselves "for contempt sanctions," which can result in the courts ordering incarceration after ruling on their own petitions.[31] The result could not be a more direct afront to the US Supreme Court's directive that "no man can be a judge in his own case, and no man is permitted to try cases where he has an interest in the outcome."[32] As Justice Hugo Black explained, "[F]air trials are too important a part of our free society to let prosecuting judges be trial judges of the charges they prefer."[33]

Reading further, we see that the courts have contractually agreed to prioritize cases where child support is owed to the state when the parents receive public aid.[34] And the contract also requires courts to prioritize and increase order establishment and collections against impoverished families whose children are removed into foster care for "enhancement of child support revenues."[35]

Such a structure already destroys the separation of powers doctrine and due process requirement of judicial impartiality, and the contracts go further still. While the courts take control of local child support agency functions, they simultaneously submit to control by the statewide executive branch. The courts are contractually required to provide the state agency with access to "all books, documents, papers, financial transactions, or other records which are pertinent to the functions of the DRS [domestic relations court] under this agreement."[36] Further, the contract creates a "DRS Memorandum process" through which the state agency ultimately directs the process of issuing binding memoranda that control the actions of the courts.[37] The state agency also has "full discretion in deciding to conduct performance audits" and can suspend payments to the courts when their performance is not to the agency's liking.

Moving deeper still into the contract, the violations continue. Through the terms of the agreement, the courts are already improperly financially motivated to enter and enforce child support obligations to claim IV-D funds. Then, although incentives are the opposite of impartiality, the contract provides the courts with additional "incentive payments"—through which the math expands the constitutional and ethical violations exponentially. Fully ten pages of the contract are devoted to mathematical details of these bonus payments that the courts can fight over depending on their "performance" in entering and enforcing the orders. The contract explains that each court "is entitled to earn a portion of the incentive monies" paid to the state agency by the federal government, and that the court's "share shall reflect its relative score for each category of performance."[38] The courts are thus contractually redirected from pursuing justice toward incentives to maximize money, focused on using vulnerable children and families rather than helping them. First, an equation incentivizes courts to enter as many child support orders as possible, regardless of whether the orders help or harm the children and their parents: "The support order performance level for a DRS [court] for a FFY [fiscal year] is determined by dividing the number of court orders for support by the number of cases in the DRS caseload."[39] Thus, the more orders issued by the courts, the higher the courts' "performance level," the more money the courts can potentially make. Once the child support orders are entered, a similar equation incentivizes the courts to enforce the payments through any means possible, again regardless of possible harm.[40] Another equation gives the courts more money for issuing more paternity orders, even when the custodial mothers may not want paternity established due to threats of domestic violence or other concerns. And yet another equation financially rewards the courts for pursuing collections of past-owed child support arrearages owed mostly by impoverished parents, much of which is owed to the government rather than to children.

In fact, layered over each court performance equation is an alarming incentive over the incentives: the courts' incentive payments are doubled when they order and enforce child support that is taken from children and directed to the state agency. In the following quoted contract language, the court is given two times the incentive to enforce collections in "current assistance" or "former assistance" cases, in which the children have been pulled into foster care or the parents received public assistance, as opposed to cases in which child support is owed to the custodial parents and children: "The DRS collections base for a fiscal year is equal to two times the sum of the total amount of support collected for current assistance cases plus two times the total amount of support collected in former assistance cases, plus the total amount of support collected in never assistance cases in the fiscal year, i.e., 2 x (Current Assistance collections + Former Assistance collections) + all other Title IV-D collections."[41] Thus, of all the potential cases appearing before the courts, the judges are incentivized at twice the amount to use court resources and enter orders and enforcement actions on behalf of state-owed support debts, through a cost recovery process that causes deep harm to impoverished children and families.

Unfortunately, we are not done yet. Buried even further in the contracts is an actual contingency fee arrangement in which the courts take a cut of payments they order and collect from poor children and families needing Medicaid. If the courts enter and enforce orders requiring parents to pay back the state cost of Medicaid, the courts take 15 percent of the collections: "[A] 15 percent incentive shall be paid based on actual medical support payments collected by the DRS in TANF, IV-E, and Non-TANF Medicaid cases, representing reimbursement of title XIX Medicaid expenditures."[42]

Then, in a combination of both symbolic and actual harm, another performance equation encourages the courts to focus on "cost-effectiveness" in ordering and enforcing as many payments as possible, as quickly and cheaply as possible.[43] The courts are thus encouraged to rush parents and children through a factorized process and to engage in expedited and harmful collection practices rather than deliberately serving justice in the best interests of children.

COOPERATIVE AGREEMENT UNDER
TITLE IV-D OF THE SOCIAL SECURITY ACT

This intergovernmental cooperative agreement is entered into by and between the Pennsylvania Department of Human Services (DHS) and the Domestic Relations Section (DRS) of the Court of Common Pleas and County Commissioners of ___SOMERSET___ County.

TABLE OF CONTENTS

FIGURE 2. Pennsylvania Department of Human Services, Interagency Cooperative Agreement with Domestic Relations Section of the Court of Common Pleas and County Commissioners of Somerset County. *Source:* https://contracts.patreasury.gov/Admin /Upload/331135_4100070496_201510201057.pdf.

Finally, in something akin to a group wrestling match of ethical abdication, the contractual incentive process concludes with pitting all the courts against each other in a fight for the money. Once calculated, each court's incentive payments are pooled together, and the individual courts are contractually required to compete against each other on the same performance criteria to claim their percentage of the pooled funds: "The incentive payment for a DRS for a fiscal year is equal to the total DRS incentive payment pool for the fiscal year, multiplied by the DRS incentive payment share for the fiscal year. The DRS incentive payment share for a fiscal year is the incentive base amount for the DRS for the fiscal year divided by the sum of the incentive base amounts for all of the DRSs for the fiscal year."[44] However, despite all of this, the contracts include an incorrect assertion, like a falsely exaggerated advertising claim of a company product: "Independence of the Judiciary Guaranteed."[45]

Michigan

Michigan courts also developed a large child support enterprise, creating their own internal child support enforcement departments, called the Friend of the Court Bureaus (FOCs).[46] All the actions by FOCs are "performed under the direction and supervision of the chief judge," who appoints "referees" to hold hearings for an FOC in establishing and enforcing recommended child support orders.[47]

Again, the courts are violating constitutional and ethical requirements for money. The courts contractually create their internal FOC departments to take on the executive branch function of initiating and enforcing child support actions against litigants (who are usually poor), and then the actions initiated by the courts are ruled upon by the courts, all so the courts can obtain IV-D child support revenue.[48] Also, similar to the other state examples, the courts agree through the contracts to be monitored and overseen by the statewide executive branch human services agency.[49]

The lure of the money is apparently powerful, as some of the Michigan courts have engaged in almost mafia-like tactics in pursuing the revenue. For example, reports regarding the Ingham County FOC highlighted the use of warrants and arrests—even working with the sheriff's office to arrest a defendant at his own wedding and arresting a defendant's mother in retaliation after she filed a harassment report about the sheriff.[50] One of the court FOC officials, supporting the hard-line tactics, referred to a quote by mobster Al Capone: "You can get so much more with a smile and a gun than with just a smile."[51]

Alarmingly, such harsh practices are financially encouraged because both the courts and their law enforcement partners can make money from the arrests. Courts will "assess the costs of issuing a bench warrant," and then "[h]alf the bench warrant costs collected . . . are deposited into the Friend of the Court 215 Fund and half is paid to the law enforcement agency that executes the warrant and makes the arrest."[52] Then, apparently as part of an intimidation strategy after making money through the arrests, some of the court FOCs hold their child support hearings at the county jails.[53]

Furthermore, as in Pennsylvania, the Michigan courts also pursue incentive funds, through which they can receive greater amounts if they meet "performance" goals in issuing judicial orders and enforcement actions. The Michigan Supreme Court's FOC publishes a news-like resource of child support information called *The Pundit*, which highlights one of the FOC office's overt efforts to increase the incentive funds. The story is wrapped around a photo-graphic of money, hanging on a clothesline, and begins with a plea: "In these tough economic times, courts are financially strapped. Friends of the court must meet performance measures in order to maintain and increase funding and to protect against reductions because of decreased local revenue."[54] The story then describes an initiative by the Genesee County FOC, in which the court offered its own additional incentivized competition to staff. The court divided its FOC staff into teams, who were then lured by prizes of flextime to compete in increasing their child support orders, collections, and arrest warrants, all with the goal of increasing child support incentive payments for the court. $hawn and his mother are the target to earn the prize: "FOC employees were split into teams and, as an additional personal incentive, FOC Director . . . agreed to bring back previously terminated flex-time for the three top winning teams. . . . The overall focus of the friendly competition was to help employees learn more about the various functions of the FOC and, ultimately, in that same manner, encourage employees to do their part to increase incentive payments."[55]

Also as in Pennsylvania, the Michigan courts are financially encouraged by the contracts to pursue impoverished children and families when support payments are assigned to the government rather than to the children, receiving twice the federal incentive payments for such cases. Then the state adds its own contingency fee payment as an additional incentive, providing the courts with 3 percent of all collections on those cases in which support is assigned to the state.[56] Further, the courts can receive more contractual contingency fee payments, obtaining a 15 percent cut of collections when the courts enter and enforce "medical support" orders requiring impoverished parents to pay back the state cost of Medicaid. A letter from the director of the Michigan FOC encourages state judges to pursue the contingency fee, listing the amount at over $1.4 million in one year.[57]

Then the Michigan courts are additionally incentivized by even more contingency fees in foster care cases. Analogous to the concerns detailed in the previous chapter, if the courts remove children from their homes, they can issue orders against the impoverished parents to reimburse the costs of care, allowing the courts to get a cut of any money collected. The contract explains that "[t]he court has the authority and the responsibility for collecting the cost of care or service for all minors served by the court or placed by the court with the state" and then that "the court may retain 25 percent of the amounts collected as a result of court-ordered reimbursement for Child Care Fund expenditures."[58] Moreover, for those children the court orders removed from their homes who are eligible for IV-E foster care funds, the court is also incentivized by receiving at least 25 percent of those IV-E funds.[59]

Ohio

In Ohio, the courts took a different approach by contracting to convert judicial officers into child support mercenaries. Through the contracts, the courts sell the services of judicial magistrates and other court personnel to the state child support agency as "units of service." The court magistrates then carry out enforcement and conduct hearings at the beck and call of the agency that bought them, with the courts only getting paid if they adhere to the agency's monitoring of contractual performance standards.[60] In just one year of these contracts, the Franklin County juvenile court made over $1.2 million, the Lucas County court made three-quarters of a million, and the Cuyahoga County juvenile and family court made over $7.3 million—and the courts make millions more from children and impoverished families across the state.[61]

Such a judiciary-for-hire arrangement wreaks havoc on the separation of powers and judicial independence upon which this country was founded. As the Supreme Court in *U.S. v. Will* made clear: "A Judiciary free from control by the Executive and the Legislature is essential if there is a right to have claims decided by judges who are free from potential domination by other branches of government."[62] The opinion describes the importance of financial independence of the judiciary, quoting Alexander Hamilton from the *Federalist*, no. 79: "In the general course of human nature, A POWER OVER A MAN'S SUBSISTENCE AMOUNTS TO A POWER OVER HIS WILL [capitalization in original]."[63] Also, the Supreme Court looked back to similar concerns in the American colonies, where protections for judicial independence initially existed until they were thwarted by the English king (the executive branch):

> Originally, these same protections applied to colonial judges as well. In 1761, however, the King converted the tenure of colonial judges to service at his pleasure. The interference this change brought to the administration of justice in the Colonies soon became one of the major objections voiced against the Crown. Indeed, the Declaration of Independence, in listing the grievances against the King, complained:
> "He has made Judges dependent on his Will alone, for the tenure of their offices, and the amount and payment of their salaries."
> Independence won, the colonists did not forget the reasons that caused them to separate from the Mother Country.[64]

But have we now forgotten?

The constitutional violations also go beyond the executive branch's purchase of judicial magistrates and staff. The child support agencies also control the courts' actions through IV-D contract performance standards. The standards clarify that only court orders and hearings requested by the child support agency "are being purchased under this contract" and then dictate the courts' actions in the content of their orders, the speed at which orders are issued, the process of court proceedings, and even the scheduling of court hearings.[65]

A contractual performance review process further undermines the courts' independence. Documents from county commissioners' meetings show that the child support agency reviewed the Cuyahoga County juvenile court negatively—almost like the review of an overwhelmed factory line worker—for not processing child support orders fast enough, pressuring the court to increase its productivity: "The Juvenile Court continues to take steps to address the multiple issues that are impacted by delayed docketing and processing of filings. The Juvenile Court representatives that come to the contractual meetings have been cooperative and expressed a desire to improve the productivity of the Court."[66]

Further, applying the analysis from chapter 2, the contracts also violate the due process impartiality requirement because the courts are financially incentivized in ordering and enforcing the child support obligations. The courts are supposed to decide whether to enter orders, and how and when to enforce those orders, based only on the best interests of the child. However, regardless of resulting harm, the courts are financially encouraged through these deals to order as many child support obligations as possible and engage in as many enforcement efforts as possible, so the courts can charge their hourly rate. As in the aforementioned performance review, the courts are incentivized in their "productivity" not for justice, but for money. In fact, in documents from Cuyahoga County, the child support agency blatantly explains that "this contract is based upon the production of Child Support Court Orders produced."[67] Similarly, the Holmes County Juvenile Court's IV-D contract notes that the "unit of service" contractually purchased by the agency is "[t]he filing of a Judgement Entry/Order in CSEA initiated cases."[68] The court is literally selling court orders.

Such explicit violations of impartiality are intertwined with the separation of powers violations and are an abdication of judicial ethics, which require that judges must "uphold and promote the independence, integrity, and impartiality of the judiciary, and shall avoid impropriety and the appearance of impropriety."[69] Every judge who serves within these financially incentivized contractual structures arguably violates these ethical principles.

Maryland

Turning to similar contracts in Maryland, I pause here again to first consider the case of Mr. Harvey, a hardworking father from Baltimore who was one of my clients when I was a legal aid lawyer.[70] Mr. Harvey initially did not have custody of his children, but he started caring for his oldest daughter after her mother died, and then he took custody of his other three children when their mother faced difficulties. At the same time, he also took in a fifth child that was not his daughter but the half-sister of one of his daughters.

Mr. Harvey was struggling to raise five children while working for the city as a landscaper, making about $11 per hour, when the Baltimore child support agency started pursuing him. The agency had previously established a government-owed support obligation when the mothers needed public assistance but had not taken enforcement actions against Mr. Harvey until after the children began living with him. He tried to convince the agency that it was harming the children, hurting his ability to support them, reducing his credit rating and hopes to get financing for a family home, and curtailing his hopes to possibly save a little money to help the children. However, the child support office, which was then run by MAXIMUS, Inc., refused to stop the collection efforts.

I helped Mr. Harvey file a motion requesting suspension of the enforcement actions, but during the hearing an employee testified they would not cease enforcement because doing so "would potentially harm the numbers that show the local enforcement office's collection rate."[71] After the court denied his motion, I helped Mr. Harvey appeal. In appellate briefs, the child support agency cited the old Maryland Bastardy Act in arguing that the main purpose of child support and paternity laws is to protect the public from the burden of "illegitimate" children and to increase state revenues. Unfortunately, the Maryland Court of Special Appeals agreed and issued a decision concluding that the MAXIMUS contract in running the child support office could be "expected to increase revenues for the State" rather than benefit the impacted children.[72] The appellate court explained its unfortunate reasoning: "The record in this case suggests that one of [the child support office's] financial incentives was measured by its 'collection rate' with respect to child support arrears. . . . The legislature, in enacting [the privatization pilot project], undoubtedly understood that when a private company undertakes to collect monies owed to the State, its success in doing so may benefit both the company and the State. Although this financial incentive may work to the detriment of a debtor like Harvey, as well as his children, it also may work to the benefit of the State's citizens as a whole."[73] Thus, the court allowed the fiscal interests of the company and state agency in turning child support into revenue to take precedence over the welfare of the children. Some years later, the head of Maryland's child support agency at the time of Mr. Harvey's appeal would become a vice president at MAXIMUS.[74]

I did not realize at the time of Mr. Harvey's case that the Maryland courts are also contracting to generate revenue from child support. In fact, the Maryland courts go further in their IV-D revenue efforts than Ohio's courts do. Some individual county courts in Maryland, as well as the entire statewide Administrative Office of the Courts, have entered such contracts: "Each year the Maryland Judiciary enters into a 'Cooperative Reimbursement Agreement' (CRA) with the Maryland Child Support Enforcement Administration (CSEA)" and as a result, "[t]he Judiciary receives several million dollars each year under the CRA."[75]

Again, the courts' contractual arrangements violate the separation of powers and due process requirements, as well as judicial ethics. The intended role of the judiciary in child support proceedings is to review the actions of the child support agency and consider facts and arguments provided by the parents and the agency, then issue orders that are only guided by the best interests of the children. Instead, the executive branch child support agency in Maryland is contractually hiring the courts—including buying the services of the judicial magistrates—before which the agency appears.

In contract documents received through state freedom of information act request, the Maryland judiciary is described as a "provider" to the executive branch agency and subservient to control of the agency. The contracts thus turn the principle of judicial review of agency actions on its head, with the courts agreeing to supervision and review by the agency so they can generate revenue from the children and families. The three-year child support contract with the Administrative Office of the Courts is worth almost $30 million to the Maryland courts, which does not include the amounts from contracts with individual county court systems.[76] So the financial incentive is strong.

The contract reveals that the courts have agreed they "shall be subject to the supervision of the DEPARTMENT OF HUMAN SERVICES (DEPARTMENT) to include the Child Support Administration (CSA) [capitalization in original]."[77] The contracts further require that agency supervision of the courts "will consist of but not be limited to compliance reviews, case record reviews, statistical analysis, audits, monitoring of operational systems and procedures and any other reviews deemed necessary by CSA [the child support agency]."[78] Also, the agency "reserves the right to impose penalties [upon the courts] for failure to meet the terms and conditions of the Cooperative Reimbursement Agreement, including, but not limited to performance standards, performance goals, and reporting requirements."[79] The courts are also required to review and adjust existing child support orders and order parents to pay medical support "in a manner consistent with the DEPARTMENT's policies and directives."[80] The agency even controls how the courts can hire court personnel.[81]

The courts' submission to contractual supervision, control, payment, and punishment by the executive branch agency—all so the courts can make money from children and the poor—directly undermines the separation of powers, impartiality, and ethics.[82] As we look to documents in other state court systems, variations of these child support contracts continue to appear.[83] And the injustice enterprise unfortunately continues to grow beyond the courts. The next chapter uncovers how prosecutors have also joined the revenue operations, using the populations they are supposed to serve.

CHAPTER 4

Prosecuting the Poor for Profit

While our courts are meant to be the arbiters of justice, the enforcement of justice is entrusted to state and local prosecutors, probation departments, and numerous forms of police and sheriff's offices. The structure and division of responsibility in these agencies vary across the country, often in somewhat of a patchwork fashion. However, although inconsistently organized, the power of the enforcement arm is consistently immense. Thus, the enforcement agencies are supposed to operate under ethical and constitutional requirements similar to those of the courts, including impartiality and the separation of powers.

Within the enforcement arm of justice, prosecutors and attorneys general carry a sacrosanct role as attorneys "for the people." Under the *Model Rules of Professional Conduct*, the official comment regarding the "Special Responsibilities of a Prosecutor" begins by explaining that "[a] prosecutor has the responsibility of a minister of justice and not simply that of an advocate," and "[t]his responsibility carries with it specific obligations to see that the defendant is accorded procedural justice."[1]

The vast power and responsibility of prosecutors requires strict adherence to ethical and constitutional obligations, or vast harm results. Robert H. Jackson—who served as the US attorney general in 1940, was appointed to the US Supreme Court in 1941, and served as chief US prosecutor in the Nuremburg trials from 1945 to 1946—gave a speech in 1940 at the second annual conference of US states attorneys that included this cautionary advice: "The prosecutor has more control over life, liberty, and reputation than any other person in America. His discretion is tremendous. . . . While the prosecutor at his best is one of the most beneficent forces in our society, when he acts from malice or other base motives, he is one of the worst."[2] The "base motives" warned against by Jackson include financial motives, because one of the greatest lures from the path of justice is money.

Unfortunately, Jackson's advice is often lost in contractual language. Prosecutors and attorneys general have joined the courts in the unconstitutional business of monetizing children and impoverished adults through foster care and child support contracts.[3] Further, such contractual strategies are in addition to the prosecutors' efforts to generate more revenue through their ruthless pursuit of fines and fees—often against the same vulnerable litigants.

When operating under these strategies, rather than being ethically true in providing justice for the people, prosecutors' offices are using the people to serve themselves.

PROSECUTORIAL FOSTER CARE REVENUE

As in the courts' contractual deals, uncovering and deciphering the prosecutorial revenue strategies requires sifting through troves of state and county documents, including budget reports, agency materials, audits, minutes from county commissioners' meetings, and lengthy contract documents. To begin, the Michigan human services agency wrote a letter to the state legislature about using county prosecutors to make money from child removals. Strikingly, the letter explains that contracts with the prosecutors' offices are intended to use children's abuse and neglect proceedings to generate revenue, as "fund enhancements": "DHS now has 46 contracts for the title IV-E cost sharing agreements with county Prosecuting Attorney (PA) offices. The PA contracts are fund enhancements for the counties and do not impact state revenues. Federal regulations permit a title IV-E administrative claim to be made for the activities of a PA office in the representation of DHS staff in child abuse and neglect hearings."[4]

Looking further into Michigan's records, a resolution from the Oakland County Board of Commissioners describes the financial benefit, illustrating how such a contract is focused on making almost half a million dollars in IV-E foster care revenue without any additional staff:

WHEREAS the contract will be funded through Title IV-E pass through funds; and . . .

WHEREAS the existing staff at the Prosecutor's Office that currently represent the DHS will continue to do so under the contract, and no new staff or position changes are required; and . . .

WHEREAS the financial benefit to the County will be revenue receipts to the County without requiring any additional staffing or additional commitment of resources by the County, and . . .

BE IT FURTHER RESOLVED that Oakland County is projected to receive maximum revenues of $497,665.50 for the contract beginning the date of DHS signs the agreement.[5]

Reading through an example contract from Muskegon County reveals that the Michigan prosecutors' offices are financially motivated to cause more poor children to be removed from their homes. Following is the formula for the prosecutors' payments provided in the contract:

Monthly payment = actual expenditures incurred x county reimbursement rate

The county reimbursement rate is determined by the federal IV-E administrative cost reimbursement rate (50%), multiplied by the percentage of IV-E eligible children in out-of-home care in the Contractor's county.

The penetration rate is defined as the percentage of IV-E eligible children in out-of-home care in the county served by the Contractor.[6]

Deciphering the math, the formula provides increased payment depending on the percentage of impoverished (IV-E eligible) children in out-of-home care (the "penetration rate"). Thus, if the prosecutors' legal representation of the child welfare agency results in more poor children being removed from their homes, the reimbursement rate will be higher, and the prosecutors' offices can receive greater payments.

Next, turning to Wisconsin, the state human service agency similarly contracts with prosecutors (district attorneys) for representation in child welfare cases, again targeting IV-E foster care funds. A review of agency materials uncovers that district attorneys' offices are not only generating revenue from impoverished children pulled into the child welfare system, but are financially incentivized to seek termination of parental rights. The prosecutors are instructed that their representation of the child welfare agency shall include "diligent pursuit of termination of parental rights."[7] Then the district attorneys are informed that they can receive a higher payment rate when pursuing termination of parental rights (TPR) proceedings compared to court hearings that might lead to reunification:

> The net rate of IV-E reimbursement for legal services contracts varies depending on the type of activity. For CY 2021, expenses will be reimbursed for allowable expanded legal services at the following rates:
>
> - Children in Need of Protection or Services (CHIPS) orders, placement of children in out-of-home care, and court hearings on permanency plans at a net rate of twenty-seven percent . . . ; and
> - Termination of Parental Rights (TPR) and adoption related orders and legal services at a net rate of thirty-eight percent.[8]

The Milwaukee District Attorney's 2021 budget documents reveal the financial incentives in operation, indicating that "[w]e have a contract with the State of Wisconsin which covers the cost of our entire TPR unit," and thus explains its desire to "[c]ontinue the successful operation with the state Division of Milwaukee Child Protective Services of the Termination of Parental Rights (TPR) Speedy Resolution project."[9] Digging further, the extent of the motive becomes clearer. Two budget charts list the expenses "for the salaries and fringe benefits of any grant-funded Assistant District Attorney ("ADA")," that are "offset with state and federal grant revenue."[10] Reviewing the charts, for 2021 the cost of the district attorneys under the contract in child welfare cases ("DCF CHIPS TPR Contract") is listed at $892,975 and resulting revenue at $1,471,792, a difference of $578,817 that equates to a profit margin of almost 40 percent.[11] Such profit is more than five times greater than the average profit margin for all US companies, which is 7.9 percent, according to data from the NYU Stern School of Business.[12]

Other states use similar interagency IV-E foster care contracts that create financial incentives for prosecutors, revealed in minutes from county commissioners' meetings. For example, the commissioners in Green County, Ohio, approved "the IV-E contract between Job & Family Services and the Prosecuting Attorney."[13] The commissioners in Potters County, Texas, list an action item for approval of the "Title IV-E Legal Services Contract" with the County Attorney's Office.[14] Commissioners' meeting documents from Wasco County, Oregon, uncover another interagency contract that explains "Oregon District Attorneys may claim Title IV-E reimbursement," and—as in Michigan—the district attorneys are informed that their offices can receive more money when more impoverished "IV-E eligible" children are removed from their homes: "The net amount of Title IV-E reimbursement for legal services is based on the federal Title IV-E administrative cost reimbursement rate of 50% multiplied by the percentage of Title IV-E eligible children in out-of-home care in Oregon."[15]

Further, like the courts, prosecutors' offices sometimes hire private revenue contractors to help maximize the money. The prosecutor's office in Ingham County, Michigan, contracts to obtain both foster care IV-E revenue and child support IV-D revenue, and sought help in claiming the funds: "Ingham County Prosecuting Attorney's Office wished to engage their consultant Maximus, Inc. in the preparation and billing for the Title IV-D and Title IV-E in order to maximize the eligible reimbursement to the Prosecutor's Office."[16]

PROSECUTORIAL EXPANSION OF
THE IV-D CHILD SUPPORT FACTORY

Even broader in scope than their foster care contracts, prosecutors' offices are also entering interagency agreements to generate child support revenue from children and families. Again, the contracts create financial motives that violate ethical and constitutional requirements. Prosecutorial decisions about whether to initiate and enforce child support obligations, and how to enforce the obligations, are supposed to be guided purely by considerations of justice and the best interests of children. However, the contracts financially encourage prosecutors to pursue child support orders and punitive enforcement mechanisms against impoverished parents, even if they are harmful.

Pausing to consider the processing path for $hawn, both the juvenile courts and prosecutors can generate IV-E foster care revenue by removing $hawn from his home and then using him in an apparatus of administrative cost claiming and revenue consultants to maximize the money. Then the courts and prosecutors generate even more revenue by ordering and enforcing support payments against $hawn's impoverished mother—and thus harming her ability to reunify with him—moving $hawn along the conveyor belt with an even larger apparatus of enforcement mechanisms and more administrative cost claiming and revenue contractors.[17] Next, through interlinked contractual incentives, the prosecutors may be incentivized by yet more IV-E funds to seek the permanent termination of his mother's parental rights, and the prosecutors may simultaneously use the government-owed child support—which they are also incentivized to pursue—as one of the legal grounds for seeking the termination. And this processing path does not yet include the revenue efforts of probation departments, sheriffs, and police departments, described in the chapters to come.

A child in $hawn's circumstances becomes collateral in a vicious child support revenue cycle. The more support obligations are prosecuted, adjudicated and enforced, the more IV-D revenue is generated for the prosecutors and the courts, and the more difficult it is for $hawn's mother to get him back home unless she can climb out of the mounting court-ordered government debt before her parental rights are terminated.

Ethical and Due Process Violations by the Prosecution Business

The financial incentives in the foster care and child support contracts are precisely the type of "base motives" warned against by Justice Robert H. Jackson, and they lead to a continual flow of ethical and constitutional violations. Consider Missouri, where county prosecutors make money through interagency child support contracts by agreeing to meet numerous performance standards, including required speed and percentages of cases pursued, and are pressured to seek and obtain criminal nonsupport convictions against the parents.[18] As one of the contractual responsibilities, the prosecutors are required to provide the state agency with quarterly reports of their statistical success in obtaining criminal nonsupport convictions against struggling parents who have fallen behind on child support.[19] Compare this incentive to Jackson's admonitions regarding prosecutorial ethics—including his caution against a focus on "statistics of success"—in another excerpt from his 1940 speech:

> Your positions are of such independence and importance that while you are being diligent, strict, and vigorous in law enforcement you can also afford to be just. Although the government technically loses its case, it has really won if justice has been done. . . . Any prosecutor who risks his day-to-day professional name for fair dealing to build up statistics of success has a perverted sense of practical values, as well as defects of character. Whether one seeks promotion to a judgeship, as many prosecutors rightly do, or whether he returns to private practice, he can have no better asset than to have his profession recognize that his attitude toward those who feel his power has been dispassionate, reasonable and just.[20]

Jackson's advice is unfortunately ignored in the Missouri contracts, and other states include similar incentives, such as the Ohio IV-D contracts, which also require prosecutors to provide monthly reports of their statistics in prosecuting child support cases.[21]

As prosecutors turn from justice to focusing on statistical and moneyed incentives, harm results. In addition to harm from the overuse of harsh civil child support enforcement mechanisms, including license suspensions, credit reporting, garnishing 65 percent of any meager wages, and even attaching unemployment and workers' compensation benefits, the criminal records from prosecutions increase the barriers that low-income parents face in obtaining decent employment. Also, if the parents are incarcerated on the charges, they lose their jobs and can't pay any support whatsoever, and the localities pay a significant cost for the incarceration.

Harm from the contractually incentivized punitive tactics can reach a point of cyclical nonsense, such as a *Kansas City Star* news investigation about a daughter in Missouri who actually paid her own back child support owed by her sickly and impoverished mother, to help keep her mother from being locked up. The story explains: "If [the mother] misses payments, the county can lock her up for six months. . . . For about four-and-a-half years, . . . she was employed. The child support payments were garnished from her paychecks. But over the years, health problems, including emphysema and bulging discs, have hindered her ability to work consistently."[22] Thus, the investigation describes that "[s]ome months, when [the mother's] emphysema makes it too difficult to go to work, or she doesn't land enough day labor jobs, she comes up short on her 20-year-old daughter's child support," and "[s]o her daughter helps pay it."[23] And this is just one story of the sheer ridiculousness of harm. In this state where prosecutors are encouraged to pursue criminal nonsupport cases through the interagency contacts, the news investigation uncovered how striking the resulting numbers statewide in Missouri are: "Last year across the state, nearly 3,000 people were charged with criminal nonsupport," making it "the 10th most common offense for new prison sentences."[24]

The gist of the relevant ethical and constitutional due process requirements is both commonsensical and crucial: prosecutors and attorneys general are supposed to be impartial in the pursuit of justice. Simply put, financial incentives must not be part of the justice equation. However, the prosecutors' offices are signing child support contracts to provide financial rewards to influence prosecutorial decisions and actions, even payouts that are called "incentive payments."

The contractual incentives conflict with required impartiality in prosecutorial decisions, sometimes called the "neutrality doctrine."[25] Although not as strictly applied as in judicial decisions, ethical requirements of impartiality in the exercise of prosecutorial discretion are intertwined with constitutional due process. Forty years ago, the Supreme Court explained in *Marshall v. Jerrico, Inc.* that the constitutional impartiality requirement applies to prosecutors, cautioning that like judges, "[p]rosecutors are also public officials; they too must serve the public interest," and that "[a] scheme injecting a personal interest, financial or otherwise, into the enforcement process may bring irrelevant or impermissible factors into the prosecutorial decision and in some contexts raise serious constitutional questions."[26]

In *Marshall*, the case involved the prosecution of child labor violations and potential financial incentives through the resulting receipt of fines. The Supreme Court concluded that "here the influence alleged to impose bias is exceptionally remote" because there was no realistic possibility that the prosecutors' judgment could be "distorted by the prospect of institutional gain as a result of zealous enforcement efforts."[27] In reaching its conclusion, the court noted that the fines amounted to "substantially less than 1% of the budget" of the department and distinguished the facts from the due process violations in the *Ward* and *Tumey* cases (discussed in chapter 2): "Unlike in *Ward* and *Tumey*, it is plain that the enforcing agent is in no sense financially dependent on the maintenance of a high level of penalties. Furthermore, since it is the national office of the ESA, and not any assistant regional administrator, that decides how to allocate civil penalties, such administrators have no assurance that the penalties they assess will be returned to their offices at all."[28]

In contrast, the prosecutors' interagency foster care and child support contracts exposed in this chapter do not fall within the narrow range of permitted financial payments as in *Marshall*. Rather, these contracts include direct financial incentives that are substantial, the money is directly pursued for the prosecutors' offices, and sometimes the prosecutors are even profiting individually. For example, the Portage County Prosecutor's Office in Ohio explains that its "criminal child support enforcement unit" is totally funded by money it obtains from the IV-D child support contracts: "A criminal Child Support Enforcement unit locates and criminally prosecutes "deadbeat" parents with large child support arrearages. This unit is fully funded by Federal Title IV-D funds. The criminal division is staffed by a total of eleven Assistant Prosecutors, six investigators, and clerical support staff."[29]

The Lane County District Attorney's Office in Oregon explains that the office is dependent on the contractual funds ("grants"): "This

$1,538,552 grant is continuing, a 66% reimbursement of eligible expenditures spent on enforcing/establishing child support payments, plus 'Incentive' payments for exceeding specific benchmarks."[30] In Calhoun County, Michigan, the "IV-D Cooperative Reimbursement Contract" has been worth more than $550,000 a year for the prosecutor's office, plus incentive payments, which amounts to over 20 percent of the office's operating costs.[31] The statewide Texas Attorney General's Office has estimated receiving over $382 million in one year in federal child support funds, which amounts to over 30 percent of the office's total funding.[32]

In addition to the contractual motives to prosecute and enforce child support orders in a manner that increases IV-D child support revenue, some prosecutors' offices are further influenced by additional "incentive payments" on top of the IV-D payments.[33] And as described in the previous chapter, the incentive payments financially encourage obtaining court orders and using punitive enforcement mechanisms regardless of harm; the incentives are increased for prosecuting government-owed support payments against low-income parents. Illustrating the moneyed mindset, a presentation by the Minnesota Department of Human Services, which references IV-D contracts with prosecutors, provides a visual of a salivating smiley-face emoji with large dollar signs for eyes, to encourage seeking the incentive payments, along with the directive: "Improve Measurements to Maximize Incentives—Get More Money!"[34] Similarly, the Texas Attorney General's Office previously bragged that its Child Support Division (CSD) has led the way in chasing the incentive payments: "The CSD received more than $71.4 million in federal incentive payments in FY 2014—the most of any state in the nation in the latest federal reporting period. Texas has been the top recipient of federal incentive payments every year since federal FY 2006."[35]

As another example, the Lake County "IV-D prosecutor" in Indiana describes the incentive payments as "gravy."[36] The Indiana Prosecuting Attorneys Council is an independent state judicial branch agency, which has used a training slide presentation titled "Prosecutor's Budgets."[37] The training lists child support incentive payments as a key revenue stream, showing the amount at over $31 million in incentive fund accounts, over a third of which is directed to county prosecutors' offices.[38] Further illustrating a focus on pursuing money and power rather than justice, the council training asserts principles of power to increase prosecutor's budgets: "Nobody gives you power, real power you take!" The presentation even gives model examples of Michael Corleone, the infamous fictional mafia leader from the *Godfather* movies, and J. R. Ewing, the fictional ruthless oil tycoon from the TV show *Dallas*, and quotes Dirty Harry from the movie *Magnum Force*.[39] Also, the Indiana prosecutors are advised to "know your opponent," who is described as the county council and commissioners; the Prosecuting Attorneys Council states "Power of Money. Control" and exclaims:

Make it hard to say NO!
- No = Pain
- Cause Council to feel pain
- If they say no—Public Safety Suffers and they caused the suffering[40]

Several other states also encourage prosecutors to pursue these IV-D incentive payments through interagency contracts.[41] Further, not only do the prosecutors' offices benefit from the incentive payments, some counties have also rewarded individual prosecutors directly with the payments. For example, MAXIMUS provided Indiana counties with a presentation about using the child support incentive funds for "incentive bonuses" and salary supplements.[42] For prosecutors specifically, MAXI-MUS assured the counties that "any bonus paid to them can be paid 100% from incentive funds."[43]

Prosecutorial Separation of Powers Violations

In addition to violating ethics and impartiality, the prosecutor's inter-agency revenue contracts destroy the separation of powers. For example, both the family court in Muskegon County, Michigan (as described in chapter 3) and the prosecutor's office entered interagency contracts to generate child support revenue through impoverished litigants, then went further, combining to generate the money more efficiently.[44] "In 2012, Muskegon's prosecuting attorney and chief judge determined that the public in Muskegon County would be better served by having their offices combine resources to provide in one location the services that were formerly provided separately."[45] Although intended to be two sepa-rate branches of government, "the Muskegon County Prosecutor's Office Child Support Division was moved into the Family Court and became the Muskegon County Family Court Establishment Division."[46] Despite this being unconstitutional, the county explained its hopes that combining the court and prosecutor's offices as one agency/office would become the national model.[47]

Texas's Unconstitutional Child Support Two-Step

The Texas Attorney General's Office has gone even further in the money chase and resulting constitutional violations, taking control of the entire state child support agency and then of the courts that adjudicate the child support cases. First, the Texas legislature designated the Attorney General's Office (AG) as the statewide IV-D agency, allowing the office to reap millions in child support revenue each year from vulnerable families.[48] Then, through an intertangled two-step dance termed a "cooperative agreement," the AG's office has hired the "child support courts," including directly paying the salaries, benefits, and perks of the judges and court staff, and the AG can review and control the courts' performance.[49]

Reading through the agreement, obtained through a state public records act request, we see that the AG contracted with the Texas Supreme Court's Office of Court Administration to create a statewide court system for expedited processing of IV-D child support cases. The courts are described as subservient, listed as "sub-recipients" of federal child support funds paid by the AG's office to the courts—but only if the courts meet performance standards that are reviewed by the AG's office.[50] The contract allows the AG to issue findings regarding its concerns with court performance that can force the judges to implement corrective action, and the AG can also require the courts to participate in its workgroup in which the AG evaluates associate judges.[51] If the courts fail to implement corrective action as required and overseen by the AG, the AG's office can withhold payments to the courts.[52]

The AG's resulting contractual and financial power over the Texas child support courts is vast, directly undercutting Alexander Hamilton's caution that the power over a person's subsistence is the power over their will. The contract is worth up to $39 million for the courts.[53] Through the agreement, the AG's office pays virtually every cost for the judges, including but not limited to their salaries, merit pay, service awards, cash advances, parking costs, training and travel expenses, and costs of supplies.[54] The AG also pays the judges' retirement and health insurance benefits and even pays the judges' "bar dues and Family Law Section dues payable to the State Bar of Texas," as required for the judges to be licensed to practice law.[55] In exchange, the contract requires the judges and AG's office to act in adherence to child support revenue maximization goals that are included in the contract and in a Texas statute: "The presiding judges and the Title IV-D agency shall act and are authorized

COOPERATIVE AGREEMENT BETWEEN
THE OFFICE OF THE ATTORNEY GENERAL OF TEXAS
AND
THE OFFICE OF COURT ADMINISTRATION

Agreement Number: 20-C0018

1. **INTRODUCTION**

    1.1. **Parties**

    This Agreement (the "Agreement") is entered into by and between the Office of the Attorney General of Texas (the "OAG"), as the Title IV-D Agency for the State of Texas, and the Office of Court Administration (the "OCA"), as the entity for the State of Texas that employs Associate Judges and Administrative Assistants for expedited Title IV-D Cases. In this Agreement, the OAG and the OCA may be referred to individually as (a "Party") or collectively as (the "Parties").

FIGURE 3.Cooperative Agreement between the Office of the Attorney General of Texas and the Office of Court Administration, Agreement No. 20-C0018, effective September 1, 2019, to August 31, 2024. *Source:* On file with author.

to take any action necessary to maximize the amount of federal funds available under the Title IV-D program."[56]

Considering the Texas structure under a constitutional separation of powers lens, the lens is shattered. The AG's office is part of the executive branch. Serving in the crucial role of the state's top legal adviser and law enforcement agency, in addition to its role as the state child support agency, the AG must strictly adhere to the pursuit of impartial justice for vulnerable litigants.[57] The courts, in turn, are supposed to independently and impartially review the AG's actions—again solely incentivized by justice. However, though the interagency contract, the AG's office gained contractual and financial control of the judicial branch to churn the children and impoverished adults through punitive child support operations with a goal of maximizing revenue rather than justice. Rather than the Texas branches of government independently seeking justice, they have joined in the pursuit of making money from the poor.

Hawaii Attorney General's Office Follows Texas's Unconstitutional Lead

Hawaii has followed Texas's lead, with a twist. The Hawaii Attorney General's Office has also taken over the role of statewide IV-D child support agency but uses a different structural approach to violate the separation of powers doctrine.[58] Rather than contracting with the courts, the Hawaii AG's Office has usurped the judicial branch function by essentially creating its own internal child support courts. First, the AG's office claimed the same power and jurisdiction as the courts: "Notwithstanding any other law to the contrary, the attorney general, though the agency and office, shall have concurrent jurisdiction with the court in all proceedings in which a child support obligation is established, modified, or enforced." [59] With this power, the AG established an internal "office of child support hearings" and even appoints and commissions its own judge-like hearing officers, who have virtually all the power of actual judges. [60]

As a result, the Hawaii AG's office initiates and enforces child support petitions in its role as the child support agency, and the office then appears in its prosecutorial role before itself in its judicial role for its own appointed hearing officers to rule on its own contested cases—and to issue orders with "all the force and effect of a final order or decree of the circuit court." [61] And the point of this unconstitutional process is money: the Hawaii AG's budget estimates show that resulting IV-D child support revenues plus incentive payments amount to over 15 percent of the AG's total budget. [62]

As in Texas, the separation of powers violations spur further due process and ethical violations, as independence and impartiality are abandoned. The Hawaii AG's office can efficiently process children and parents to maximize IV-D funds, acting as both enforcement agency and court, and is financially encouraged in both roles to make decisions that increase incentive payments. [63]

Unfortunately, such unconstitutional structures have received little attention. Two state supreme courts, in Montana and Minnesota, struck down less egregious examples of executive branch IV-D child support agencies usurping judicial functions as violating the separation of powers doctrine—without even considering the due process violations—but those cases are more than twenty years old. [64] Meanwhile, unconstitutional IV-D business operations continue across the country and have grown, largely unchecked, as courts and prosecutors continue to flout the Constitution and merge their revenue-driven operations.

PROSECUTORS PROFITING FROM FINES AND FEES

Prosecutors' contractual foster care and child support operations are often in addition to their efforts to generate revenue by enforcing fines and fees against the poor. Prosecutors join in these financially incentivized fines and fees strategies with our courts, discussed in chapter 1, and with our probation and policing departments, discussed in the chapters that follow. The practices violate the constitutional requirements of impartiality even more and further undermine Justice Jackson's call for seeking purity in prosecutorial ethics.

As an example, district attorneys in Alabama obtain up to 70 percent of their total office budgets from enforcing and collecting fines and fees. As Alabama courts shut down during the onset of the COVID-19 crisis, like court systems across the country, the intrinsic harm in the district attorney funding structure was uncovered. When the lower courts halted proceedings, they could not keep ordering fines and fees against the poor, and the district attorneys' offices could not use the courts to generate revenue in collecting those fines and fees, so the offices faced concerns with possible layoffs.[65]

A local news investigation explains that the state only provides about 30 percent of district attorney budgets, and most Alabama counties do not provide additional funds, so the prosecutors' offices make up the bulk of their budgets by enforcing fines and fees.[66] In an interview conducted as part of the investigation, the Montgomery County district attorney asserted that money from collecting fines and fees is "'a horrible source of revenue for the criminal justice system . . . [b]ut that's the way historically it's been done.'"[67] The district attorney for Autauga and Elmore Counties "called the state's method of funding DAs 'gimmicky' and 'the most messed up (stuff) I've seen'" and complained that the state "didn't raise sales taxes, they didn't raise income taxes, they didn't raise the property tax, and we're left with the system we have now."[68] The investigation recognizes that the revenue strategy disproportionately harms impoverished individuals and falls "heaviest on African-American communities" and describes a 2018 survey by Alabama Appleseed of residents burdened by the court debt: "[N]early 83% said they had given up food, rent, car payments or child support to pay debts," "[n]early half said they had been jailed to pay court debt," and "44% said they used payday loans to address it."[69]

If $hawn lives in Covington County, Alabama, a 30 percent "collection fee" is added on top of the court-ordered debts against his mother, and then 65 percent of that amount is directed to the district attorneys, 25 percent of the spoils goes to the court, and 10 percent goes to the county general funds.[70] If $hawn lives in Iowa, the state's county attorney offices are motivated by obtaining 5 percent of fines and fees collections.[71] If $hawn lives in Ohio, in addition to the courts using him to maximize IV-E foster care and IV-D child support funds and the county prosecutors doing the same, the Ohio Attorney General's Office has become a statewide debt collector—likely impacting $hawn's mother—pursuing fines and fees, medical bills from public hospitals, and countless other state debts against the poor, to which the Attorney General's Office adds an additional 10 percent commission charge on all the collections to keep for itself.[72]

Unfortunately, these are just a few of countless examples, as prosecutors' offices across the country seek revenue from harm. The next chapter looks to the numerous revenue practices of the probation wing of the factory.

CHAPTER 5

The Probation Business

The probation business is massive, processing almost 3.5 million adults under sentences of supervised probation, and with juvenile courts sentencing over 60 percent of youth in delinquency proceedings to probation each year.[1] Probation is supposed to be part of the solution to needed criminal justice reform, by diverting adults and juveniles from incarceration to a more humane individualized provision of supervised rehabilitation services and requirements. However, all too often probation has become a business in itself, contributing to injustice rather than transforming our systems toward justice. And like other parts of the injustice enterprise discussed in this book, the probation business has a disproportionate impact based on poverty and race.

As an example of the scope of this business, the Los Angeles County Probation Department brags that it is "the largest probation department in the nation with more than 6,600 employees providing services for 57,000 adult probationers and more than 12,000 juveniles with an annual budget of $852 million dollars."[2] As in the other components of America's justice systems, an inherent tension exists: Does the institution exist to serve vulnerable populations, or does it use the vulnerable populations in a business-like mindset to serve itself? James Baldwin described this tension in 1972: "Does the law exist for the purpose of furthering the ambitions of those who have sworn to uphold the law, or is it seriously to be considered as a moral, unifying force, the health and strength of a nation? . . . Well, if one really wishes to know how justice is administered in a country, one does not question the policemen, the lawyers, the judges, or the protected members of the middle class. One goes to the unprotected—those, precisely, who need the law's protection the most!—and listens to their testimony."[3] Unfortunately, the self-serving motives of our foundational justice systems are winning out.

TO SERVE OR TO USE?

Probation departments form a key component of the enforcement arm of justice, with as broad an impact as prosecutors, possibly greater. However, justice reform efforts have considered probation departments with a less critical lens and often as part of the solution to hyper-criminalization and mass incarceration, now adding a problem of "mass probation."[4] More than twenty years ago, the US Justice Department's Office of Juvenile Justice and Delinquency Prevention described the growth and breadth of juvenile probation: "Through its popularity and the broad array of duties and services it performs, juvenile probation has the power to affect decisionmaking and service delivery at every stage of juvenile justice processing."[5] By 2020 the result had become a "plight of young people placed on probation by juvenile courts, where they are more likely to be trapped in a cycle that makes it virtually impossible to escape further involvement in the justice system."[6]

Juvenile probation officers are among the first and last justice officials involved in determining $hawn's fate as he is processed by the system. Well before an initial court hearing is held, the probation officers are powered into operation. The officers conduct initial investigations, in some states they decide whether to file the complaint seeking juvenile charges, and they make recommendations directly to the court on how to rule. A probation officer decides whether $hawn should be immediately placed into a detention center while waiting for an initial court hearing, arranges and provides the "supervision" of $hawn before the court, and decides whether $hawn is cooperative or not. The probation officer monitors $hawn at home, at school, and pretty much anywhere else at any time, and can perform and observe drug tests. In some states, the officers have the power to arrest, and some carry visible guns. Imagine $hawn's level of anxiety as he is brought into court, where the probation officer is present to watch whether he speaks and acts as directed before the officer also testifies and makes recommendations to the judge. After court, the officer continues to monitor $hawn and has discretion to add more restrictive and punitive supervision requirements or more drug tests, monitoring $hawn's communications, conducting curfew checks, partnering with school officials and checking $hawn's grades, recommending and collecting payments of court fines and fees, forcing $hawn into unpaid community work programs and then overseeing his work, deciding to install an electronic monitor on his ankle, and more. Throughout this process, the probation officer holds the power over whether to recommend that $hawn be further detained or be allowed to go home; to decide between placement alternatives; and to threaten revocation of probation, resulting in $hawn being jailed or sent to an out-of-state detention camp. In some states, the probation officer can even decide whether to initiate the termination of $hawn's mother's parental rights. The probation officer has power over how long $hawn stays on probation and decides when to finally tell the judge that the terms of probation have been met.[7]

Probation officers are often poorly trained, poorly monitored, poorly paid, overworked, and used as a branch of factory worker foot soldiers in the business of monetizing vulnerable adults and children.[8] Under such conditions, with minimal oversight and preloaded with such an immense breadth of power, it is unfortunately not surprising that probation officers often abuse their power. For example, in a Wyoming case that went up to the state's supreme court, a conviction was upheld regarding a juvenile probation officer who tried to bribe a child's mother. The officer first "suggested her son might be taken away from her until he reached the age of twenty-one and she could be charged with abandonment if she moved out of Wyoming," then indicated that she could pay him "'persuasion money' to make things better for her son."[9]

The Los Angeles Probation Department has been the subject of repeated reports about its abuse of power. By 2013, oversight by the US Department of Justice Civil Rights Division had been ongoing for several years after findings that the LA Probation Department's "camps" violated the due process rights of youth by failing to protect them from harm.[10] Then, in a report by the county's own Office of Independent Review (OIR), illegal drug use and lying were found to be so widespread in the probation department that "policies that we identified as most acutely deficient or in need of clarification" included that probation officials should not use illegal drugs and that they must be honest.[11] The Probation Department even had to issue a directive on "employee honesty" to clarify that honesty is a necessary policy and specifically listed a concern with dishonesty by probation officials in "court reports or any other document in the course of their duty."[12] In the same OIR report, an example is provided of misconduct by a juvenile probation officer overseeing children placed in detention:

> A detained minor in a juvenile hall was observed receiving food and special privileges including access to staff offices, from one of the more experienced officers who was the staff shift leader in the module. . . . Other minors found this minor to be physically intimidating. On one occasion, the sworn employee instructed this minor (Minor 1) to strip another minor's clothes off, put him in a suicide gown and remove all his personal items from the room. While the subject employee was present, Minor 1 threatened the second minor that he would be harmed if he "snitched." The second minor was supposed to be on heightened one-on-one supervision by staff as a possible self-harm risk.[13]

Concerns continued. By 2018 the California Department of Justice, then headed by Attorney General Xavier Becerra (later appointed by President Joe Biden in 2021 as secretary of the US Department of Health and Human Services), started further investigations and filed a legal complaint because the Probation Department "has endangered youth safety," including using "excessive and inappropriate physical and chemical use of force."[14] As a result of the complaint, a settlement agreement was reached in January 2021 in which the Probation Department agreed to "a wide range of corrective actions" and to be overseen by an independent monitor.[15]

In multiple states, numerous juvenile probation officers have been criminally charged with sexual abuse and other offenses involving minors under their supervision.[16] And those are only the cases in which the abuse was reported. For example, in El Paso, Texas, a juvenile probation officer was convicted for his role in a forced sex-trafficking ring involving underage girls operating in four states—including targeting girls placed into an "academy" for troubled youth, the type of facility that also profits from vulnerable children, as described in chapter 7.[17] Imagine the pressure that $hawn could be under to do whatever a probation officer wants, as the officer threatens to harm him or to place him in an out-of-state detention center if he does not comply.

PROBATION DEPARTMENTS PROFITING FROM FOSTER CARE AND CHILD SUPPORT

In addition to such instances of abuse of power by individual probation officers, entire probation departments are using their power to join the business operations of courts and prosecutors, signing similar interagency contracts to generate revenue through impoverished children and their families. Again, details parsed from budget reports, contract documents, and audits tell the story.

In Orange County, California, audit documents describe the steps of how juvenile probation departments make millions from IV-E foster care funds. First, a probation department signs a contract with the state foster care agency, an "Interagency Operation Agreement to claim Title IV-E costs."[18] Then the probation department can claim foster care funds when using its power to recommend that children should be removed from their homes. Further, the audit describes how the departments can also obtain IV-E revenue by labeling and processing children as foster care "candidates": "Administrative costs are claimed for activities related to cases where a minor is considered a 'reasonable candidate' for foster care. To determine reasonable candidacy, Probation identifies the factors that will require removal of the minor from the home unless they are satisfactorily resolved."[19] Through this process, the departments are incentivized to keep children like $hawn in probation under constant threat of removal from their homes, with virtually limitless intrusive supervision, monitoring, and punitive controls. If a probation officer simply fills out a form to periodically assert that $hawn should be considered a foster care candidate, the commodification can continue: "There is no maximum length of time a minor may be considered a reasonable candidate; however Probation is required to document in the case record the reasons the minor is a reasonable candidate every six months."[20] Probation officers can also carry out threats and move $hawn back and forth from his home and out-of-home placements. If the processing continues, the revenue continues.

In a slide presentation used as part of training for California probation departments, the probation officers are encouraged to put detailed negative information in their periodic write-ups about children, because negative assessments are what keep the children in probation and labeled foster care candidates. For example, one of the training slides provides an example of a case note labeled as "bad" because it indicates the probation officer visited the child and made the conclusion "all okay."[21] A "good" example case note suggests that even though the child is doing well in school, the probation officer should list that the child could see a substance abuse counselor and should describe the child as making "minimal progress in resolving family issues."[22] If all is okay, then the money stops, which apparently is not okay.

The Orange County audit document further describes the revenue claiming process. The "Probation Department records the allowable costs necessary for the administration of the foster care program by compiling claimable administrative expenditures."[23] Next, the "Probation Department utilizes a cost allocation plan to identify the appropriate administrative costs applicable to the Title IV-E program." The audit provides a list of several costs that the probation departments can claim to obtain the revenue from children, even creating data and reports about the children and then claiming the costs of creating such data and reports:

(i) Referral to services;

(ii) Preparation for the participation in judicial determinations;

(iii) Placement of the minor;

(iv) Development of the case plan;

(v) Case reviews, case management and supervision;

(vi) Recruitment and licensing of foster homes and institutions;

(vii) Rate setting;

(viii) A proportionate share of related agency overhead; and

(ix) Costs related to data collection and reporting.[24]

In just one year of processing children through this system, the Orange County Probation Department generated over $5.7 million in IV-E foster care revenue.[25] Orange County, Los Angeles County, and several other California counties hired the same revenue maximization consultant used by multiple courts and prosecutors, JBI, to help the probation departments increase revenue.[26]

Probation departments in other states have established similar contractual arrangements. The Texas Juvenile Justice Department entered such an interagency contract for its probation departments to generate foster care revenue, with a value of up to $10.5 million.[27] As explained in chapter 2, the Texas judges are also interlinked with the process, because the county probation departments are run by a juvenile board comprised of judges. The Hidalgo County Probation Department explains that the contractual motive is to generate revenue when removing poor children from their homes and placing them in the types of residential facilities detailed in chapter 7: "State agencies were mandated by the 73rd Legislature to maximize the use of federal funds. The Texas Juvenile Probation Commission (TJPC) studied the IV-E Program and considered it as a possible benefit to juvenile probation departments across the State of Texas. TJPC aimed at accessing these federal funds in order to increase the amount of placement funds available to juvenile probation departments."[28] Thus, the probation department explains that the point of the contract is to benefit itself financially from child removals.[29] As in California, some of the Texas juvenile boards also contracted with JBI to help maximize the money.[30]

Documents from other states also illustrate how probation departments use children for revenue.[31] The Michigan Supreme Court's Judicial Institute put together required training for its juvenile court probation officers and caseworkers, with an emphasis on pursuing IV-E and pretty much any source of money they can obtain from children and their parents. The training includes a section that directs a businesslike focus on money and efficiency, titled "Why Consider Funding When Developing a Case Plan?":

> While the needs of the child should determine case planning, tight budgets require the court to utilize all possible resources to fund programs. While the Child Care Fund, the General Fund, and IV-E funding are key to probation, intensive in-home care programs, and out-of-home placements; the court must also pursue such things as restitution, community service, allowable fines and costs, parental reimbursement, income tax intercepts, adoption subsidy, social security benefits, veteran's benefits, and private insurance. Each staff member of the family division of the circuit court is responsible for the success of the system. The court must be both effective and cost-efficient.[32]

As probation departments are financially incentivized in processing children, the probation officers can be contractually required to initiate terminations of parental rights. For example, the interagency agreement used in Indiana details how the probation officers must make recommendations about terminating parental rights within fifteen months of children being removed from their homes and placed under the supervision of the probation department.[33] Similarly, for children under contractual probation supervision in California, a state rule requires: "Whenever a child has been declared a ward and has been in any foster care placement for 15 of the most recent 22 months, the probation department must follow the procedures . . . to terminate the parental rights of the child's parents."[34] The time limits are imposed to continue the receipt of IV-E funds, and the chase for the money leads to high numbers of terminations even though many children do not want their parents' rights to be terminated, and many are not adopted but instead rendered legal orphans. Over about a ten-year period, the California system terminated parental rights over almost eighty thousand children. Texas, also under statewide interagency contracts with its county probation departments, terminated the rights of the parents of more than ninety-one thousand children during the same time period.[35]

Next, turning to New Jersey, the probation departments work under the direction of the courts to make money from impoverished families through IV-D child support proceedings. The strategy starts with the judiciary, in which the Administrative Office of the Courts contracts with the executive branch state child support agency.[36] Then the county family courts run their own probation divisions, which are required under the contract to act as the local child support enforcement offices, so the courts and their probation divisions can generate revenue from child support. Like the concerns exposed in chapter 3 and 4, such an arrangement violates constitutional and ethical requirements. The court probation divisions are financially incentivized to initiate more enforcement actions, even when these are harmful to the children and families. Further, the structure creates a child support business wherein the probation divisions—which are part of the courts—carry out agency child support enforcement actions that are reviewed by the courts, with the courts incentivized to rule in favor of their probation divisions.

Further, the New Jersey court probation divisions also provide probation supervision to children pulled into the juvenile justice program through delinquency proceedings.[37] So if $hawn lives in New Jersey, the same court probation division may be supervising him and making recommendations against his return home, while simultaneously generating revenue by pursuing child support against $hawn's mother while he is removed from his home. These unconstitutional deals turn a profit. The New Jersey judiciary was receiving over $120 million per year in IV-D child support revenue as of 2020, including through contracts for its probation and family court services.[38]

MORE PROBATION BUSINESS MONEY: FINES AND FEES, WORK PROGRAMS, AND PRIVATIZATION

In addition to processing children through contractual foster care and child support operations, the probation business uses children and the poor to make money in multiple other ways. Counties and cities also enlist their probation departments to generate revenue by charging and enforcing millions in fines and fees, by overseeing their supervisees in unpaid work programs, and by contracting with for-profit companies.

Unconstitutionally Extorting Fines and Fees from Children and the Poor

Along with the efforts of courts and prosecutors, probation departments play a big role in pursuing seemingly unending fines and fees against vulnerable children and adults, again with disproportionately racialized targeting and harm.[39] For example, in Pennsylvania the court probation departments have their own "collections enforcement units" that are "mandated to enforce the collection of court ordered fines, costs, probation fees, and restitution" for both adults and juveniles.[40] Georgia went further and enacted a structure for the sole purpose of using the power of probation to extract money from the poor, as the state legislation requires: "'Pay-only probation' means a defendant has been placed under probation supervision solely because such defendant is unable to pay the court imposed fines and statutory surcharges when such defendant's sentence is imposed."[41]

The pursuit of fines and fees revenue converts probation into a pyramid-like scheme of inescapable harm. In addition to collecting the initial court fines and fees, probation departments charge their own additional monthly fees for their probation services. Further, the probation officers also enforce numerous conditions of probation, such as frequent drug testing, mandatory classes, attending therapy, and wearing electronic ankle monitors, all of which add substantial fees owed by the probationer.[42] If probationers fall behind on payments, they are charged additional fees and interest. A Harvard study found that "[i]n places like Rhode Island and parts of Georgia, if a person on probation has already paid for and attended several sessions of a court-ordered class, but then misses a few classes because they are unable to pay, they are required to start the program from the beginning and pay for each session again."[43] Further, the study found that "in parts of Idaho, the providers of the classes decide how many sessions a person on probation needs," and "these providers sometimes keep people in their programs longer to extract more money from them."[44] The probation departments may also seek assistance from private debt collectors, with yet additional fees added for private collection.

In several states, probation departments will even treat full payment of all the charges as a condition of probation, in mafia-like extortion that threatens the bondage of incarceration if payments are not made. For example, Michigan courts direct their probation officers that for anyone placed on probation, "any fines, costs, and assessments ordered shall be a condition of that probation."[45] Several states also give probation officers the power to arrest, used when the officer decides a condition of probation has been violated. Thus, "if a person misses a single payment, the probation officer can arrest or have the person arrested."[46] Also, if the probationer is unable to make payments, the probation officer may repeatedly ask the court to extend the period of probation. So in some states without limits on extensions, "people can be kept on probation for decades simply for nonpayment."[47]

In addition to trapping impoverished individuals in debt and the harm of supervisory probation, the probation business also directly undermines democracy by restricting the right to vote. As of 2020, over half of the states will not allow individuals to vote before completing a criminal sentence, including completing the term and conditions of probation.[48]

Like the practices of courts and prosecutors in prior chapters, the financial incentives of the probation business violate the due process requirement of impartiality. The US Supreme Court has repeatedly recognized that the strict rule of impartiality prohibits financial motives that create both actual bias in tribunals and circumstances that create the possibility of bias, which "would offer a possible temptation to the average man."[49] The impartiality requirement imposes this "stringent rule" not only on judges, but on anyone acting in a "judicial or quasi-judicial capacity."[50] In *Harper v. Professional Probation Services, Inc.*, the US Court of Appeals for the Eleventh Circuit held in 2020 that the strict impartiality requirement can apply to probation officers.[51] The court ruled that in a circumstance where "a private probation company earned a fee for every month that a misdemeanor offender remained under its supervision," the impartiality requirement was violated when the probation entity "unilaterally extended the duration of probationers' sentences, increased the fines that they owed, and imposed additional conditions of probation."[52] The same reasoning should apply in any state when county probation departments are financially motivated and provided with similar discretion.

Further, even in circumstances where probation departments are not acting in a quasi-judicial capacity, impartiality is still required in performing law enforcement functions. Although the same strictness of the test does not apply as in judicial decisions, a "scheme injecting a personal interest, financial or otherwise, into the enforcement process" can still violate due process when actual bias conflicts with impartiality, as is the case with the financial incentives of the probation business.[53]

Following this reasoning, a federal district court in Tennessee ruled in 2021 that the "neutrality requirement applies to officials performing quasi-judicial functions and those performing enforcement functions," and that "[p]robation or parole officers traditionally perform both types of functions."[54]

Also, in many jurisdictions where probation officers make recommendations to judges rather than technically making decisions themselves, those probation officers are often employees of the court, so the court is essentially reviewing its own recommendations and actions—raising concerns not only about due process, but also about separation of powers. Moreover, when probation departments collaborate with the courts to revoke probation because of the failure to pay the fines and fees, they may violate the Supreme Court's ruling in *Bearden v. Georgia* that requires an evidentiary finding regarding the probationer's ability to pay: "[W]ithout considering the reasons for the inability to pay or the propriety of reducing the fine or extending the time for payments or making alternative orders, the court automatically turned a fine into a prison sentence."[55]

Probationers Used as Free Labor: Work Programs and "Community Service"

In addition to extorting fines and fees, the probation business also extracts more revenue and savings by converting probationers into a free labor force. Many probation departments around the country oversee juveniles and adults in work programs. For example, the Kern County probation department oversees its Juvenile Court Work Program to carry out hard physical labor for county agencies and nonprofits, and "[t]he program is occasionally called upon by local politicians to aide in the cleanup of unlawful dump sites throughout the County."[56] The Missouri Department of Corrections explains that "Probation and Parole staff oversee the completion of more than 385,000 community service hours annually, which translates into nearly $3 million in free labor and services."[57]

Also, in addition to requiring children and impoverished adults to work for free, the probation departments actually charge them fees for doing so. For example, in Jackson County, Oregon, the probationers are used in a seven-day-a-week work crew that provides free labor "to other county departments with landscape maintenance and trash removal"; this "Community Service program requires a $50.00 sign-up fee followed by a $30.00 maintenance/monitoring fee each month thereafter," and "[a]n offender who is non-compliant and requires a formal complaint to be filed with the court, will be assessed an additional $100.00 enforcement fee."[58] In Westland, Michigan, the Probation Department's work program charges probationers $30 per day to participate.[59]

In 2019 UCLA's Labor Center and School of Law completed an important investigation into the use of these work programs in Los Angeles. The study uncovered alarming numbers, revealing that the county "operates a large-scale system of court-ordered, unpaid and unprotected labor ... that involves about 100,000 people and millions of hours of work each year."[60] According to the report, the mandatory community service programs "required people in Los Angeles County to perform an estimated 8 million hours of unpaid work over the course of a year—the equivalent of 4,900 paid jobs."[61] Like other strategies of the probation business, the forced labor programs have a disproportionately racialized impact: "People sentenced to mandatory community service appear to be overwhelmingly low-income people of color, who comprise a staggering 89 percent of those from traffic court."[62]

For-Profit Business Joins the Probation Business

Many county probation departments have shed any veneer of mission-driven restorative justice to cover their revenue pursuits, turning over their operations to private for-profit companies. Searching through minutes of county meetings, examples of the motive come to light, such as a 2015 court request to the Fulton County, Georgia Board of Commissioners: "Request approval to renew existing contracts—State and Magistrate Court, RFP #14RFP65898ACJC, Misdemeanor Probation Services with anticipated revenue in the amount of $1,460,900 with Judicial Correction Services, Inc. (Atlanta, GA) to provide supervision and case management services for misdemeanor offenders sentenced by Judicial Order in the State and Magistrate Courts of Fulton County."[63] Looking at that actual contract, the source of county revenue becomes clear in the "scope of work"—the pursuit of fines and fees:

a. Provide extensive misdemeanor probation management services for the Superior, State and Magistrate Court of Fulton County ...

f. Provide timely financial, offender and management reports

g. Aggressively collect fines, fees and restitutions due the County and victims ...

k. Enforce probation conditions . . . [which can include the required payment of the fines and fees]

l. Provide a schedule for remittance to the courts of all fines, fees and other costs due the courts . . .

o. Deliver monthly, written reports to the Court Administrator of Superior Court and the Chief Clerk of State Court, itemizing the amount each month collected in probation fees, fines, surcharges and other costs per judge and the number of probation violation warrants issued . . .

q. Plan to collect delinquent traffic citation fines.[64]

Under the terms of the contract, the company did not charge the county for its services but rather operated under an "offender-funded" model that charges individuals numerous fees for the probation services on top of the fines and fees collected for the courts. The contract document provides a fee schedule with a list of charges for the probation services, including $40 per month "Standard Probation Supervision," $40 per month "Intensive Probation Supervision," $15 per hour "Community Service Work Coordination," $15 per drug screen "Substance Abuse Detection," $12 per day "Electronic Monitoring," $8 per day "Remote Alcohol Monitoring," $20 per session "Domestic Violence Counseling," $25 per session "Anger Management," and $65 per session "Financial Responsibility."[65] The company, Judicial Correction Services, Inc., was purchased by Professional Probation Services, Inc., founded by Clay Cox, who served as a Republican in the Georgia House of Representatives in 2005–2010 and 2016–2018.[66]

Georgia has led the nation in the probation business, with courts putting one out of seventeen adults on probation—four times the national rate—and "[a]bout 80 percent of people on misdemeanor probation in Georgia are supervised by private companies."[67] An investigation by Human Rights Watch helped uncover the financial incentives in the industry, estimating that private probation companies collected almost $100 million in fines, fees, and restitution for Georgia courts in one year, with the companies pursuing at least $40 million in revenue for themselves from additional supervision fees.[68]

A growing number of lawsuits have challenged the use of probationers for profit. The Southern Poverty Law Center initiated a lawsuit against Professional Probation Services, Inc., in Alabama, leading to rulings by the US Court of Appeals for the Eleventh Circuit that the company violated the due process rights of probationers.[69] Also, multiple lawsuits have been filed by Civil Rights Corps, Equal Justice Under Law, and the American Civil Liberties Union (ACLU), resulting in successful settlements.[70] For example, Civil Rights Corps filed a class action lawsuit in Giles County, Tennessee, against two companies, Community Probation Services, LLC, and PSI Probation, LLC, including claims that the companies violated the Racketeer Influenced and Corrupt Organizations Act (RICO): "Defendants' conspiracy to extract as much money as possible from impoverished misdemeanor probationers through a pattern of illegal racketeering activity, including threats of arrest and jailing, physical confinement, and extended periods of supervised probation due to nonpayment of debts owed to the court and to the private companies."[71] Giles County officials agreed to a $2 million settlement of the lawsuit in 2021, including agreeing to end the use of probation companies.[72] However, as lawsuits have continued, private probation companies have continued to operate in several states. In Tennessee, "[w]hile the suit ends the reign of private probation companies in Giles County, 25 companies continue to supervise misdemeanor probationers in 19 other Tennessee counties."[73]

CHAPTER 6

Policing and Profiting from the Poor

The Arlington County Sheriff's Office seems to long for the past when describing its own history: "In colonial days in Virginia, the Sheriff was a formidable figure. Vested with as much dignity as their counterpart in England, this Officer of the County Court was the collector of public and parish levies, keeper of the County prison and public hangman. Acting as an arresting officer, they were required to physically lay hands upon the accused. They could use force, break down doors, commandeer anyone or anything—people, horses, boats—when pursuing a felon."[1]

It turns out, much of the past is still present. Police, sheriffs, marshals, and constables are not new participants in the injustice enterprise, with many of their current revenue strategies dating back to colonial times. The practices were highly racialized and harmful then, as they are now.[2]

Local law enforcement departments around the country employ numerous unconstitutional mechanisms to harvest resources from low-income residents, including contracts like those discussed in prior chapters to make money from child support and foster care, revenue maximization contracts for jailing undocumented individuals, profiting from executing warrants and "body attachments," financially incentivized evictions, seizing property in civil "forfeitures," claiming a percentage of collections, using privatized police companies, and even diverting funds intended to feed jailed inmates to the sheriff's coffers. As law enforcement agencies join the courts, prosecutors, and probation departments in revenue-driven processing of children and impoverished adults, the harm is immeasurable.

SHERIFFING FOR CHILD SUPPORT AND FOSTER CARE FUNDS

Police and sheriff's offices in several states are collaborating with the courts, prosecutors, and probation departments in their contractual revenue strategies. For example, chapter 3 uncovered how Pennsylvania family courts contracted to become the state's child support enforcement agencies so the courts can use low-income children and families to obtain federal IV-D child support revenue. Those courts in turn have contracted with local sheriff's departments to execute arrest warrants issued by the courts, along with other enforcement services, to further increase the IV-D revenue. Searching through the contract reveals that so much money is apparently flowing from the arrangement that the courts even give their own cars to the sheriff's departments to process the arrests.[3] Contractually incentivized, the sheriffs are eager to pursue the money, including frequent late-night "warrant sweeps" into the homes of struggling families. A story in the *Philadelphia Inquirer* provides an example, in which a father was arrested at his home at 4:00 a.m., taken from his sleeping daughter, held in a cell for several hours until his release, and forced to walk eight miles home in the cold: "[S]heriff's deputies were waiting impatiently in the cold February night. . . . 'They told me they were about to take down the door. . . .' His 5-year-old daughter was asleep upstairs. The deputies told him he'd better find a babysitter fast: He was under arrest."[4] The sheriff's office asserted the reason for the arrest was that the father "was a 'deadbeat' who owed $1,323.99 in child support."[5] However, like Mr. Harvey's circumstances described in chapter 3, this father had custody of three of his children, and "[f]or the fourth, child support had been deducted from his paycheck each week, until he switched from a temp agency to full-time work as a mason."[6] Thus, the news investigation explains: "He called the Montgomery County Domestic Relations Office to straighten out the transition—he couldn't appear in person, he explained, as he had to be at work, in part to earn money for child support. Instead, a warrant was issued for his arrest."[7]

Multiple other states use similar contractual arrangements through which sheriffs or police departments receive substantial child support revenue, including financial incentives to carry out arrests.[8] The more enforcement actions ordered by the courts, the more arrests by the sheriffs, the more IV-D money. For example, in Prince George's County, Maryland, the Sheriff's Department obtained more than $2 million in child support revenue in just one year.[9] Law enforcement departments in Michigan partner with the courts to divide up the money from child support arrests: "Half the bench warrant costs collected . . . [is] deposited into the [court fund] and half is paid to the law enforcement agency that executes the warrant and makes the arrest."[10]

As another example, multiple Florida county sheriff's departments contracted to generate revenue from child protective services investigations, allowing the sheriffs to obtain millions in IV-E foster care and TANF welfare assistance funds for themselves.[11] The investigations are not supposed to be criminal: the foster care agency function is normally carried out by social work professionals focused on serving the best interests of children and needs of the families rather than punishment. Thus, the contractual transfer of the responsibility to sheriff's offices creates risk that the investigations will be more criminally focused and revenue driven and could lead to unnecessary and harmful child removals. The Florida Department of Law Enforcement provides a history that describes the punitive focus of sheriffs: "The early sheriffs' duties encompassed many of the same areas of concern that modern day sheriffs are still responsible for. The early sheriffs were responsible for the maintenance of law and order, the collection of taxes from the serfs, and the maintenance of a jail, or in some cases a dungeon."[12]

This concern has largely been ignored because there is significant money to be made; a state legislative document shows how just six county sheriff's departments in Florida claimed more than $57 million through this practice in one year.[13] However, a 2021 news investigation illustrates that the concern should not be ignored. The *Tampa Bay Times* investigation first discusses two Florida counties hiring a private contractor to run their foster care agency operations, resulting in significant problems and harm.[14] The Pinellas County Sheriff announced a criminal investigation, asserting the contractor had made children stay in "deplorable" conditions.[15] But simultaneously, the sheriff's office was also operating as contractor, obtaining millions in revenue by investigating and then removing children—and placing them with the privatized foster care agency.[16] According to the investigation, the Pinellas County Sheriff's Office has the highest rate of child removals in the state.[17] And according to legislative records, the sheriff's office was making more than $11.8 million per year through the contract as of 2016.[18]

MODERN-DAY BOUNTY HUNTERS

In several cities, local law enforcement officials act like bounty hunters by pursuing a percentage of collections and fees for carrying out enforcement actions against the poor. Perhaps the most alarming example is New York City, which still uses city marshals, a throwback to the seventeenth century, and not in a good way: "They've been a fixture of New York life since 1655, when the region was a Dutch colony."[19] Although called city marshals, they are not city employees and receive no salary. But they wear badges and carry weapons, acting like hired guns appointed as independent contractors by the mayor. The marshals only need a high school diploma or GED. They enforce court eviction orders, collections of fines and fees, utility shutoffs, foreclosures, car repossessions, and more. The marshals are even given the power to seize bank accounts, garnish wages, and sell off personal property. They make their money by collecting numerous fees and "poundage," a term dating back to medieval times, through which the marshals take a contingency fee of 5 percent of their total enforced collections.[20]

Although they are paid nothing by the city, and in fact generate revenue for the city, wielding power is profitable for city marshals. Through private contractual arrangements with the mayor, the annual gross income of a city marshal in New York averages $1 million.[21] Yes, you read that correctly. Depending on how the marshals set up their operations, they have varying overhead expenses and are required to pay 4.5 percent of their takings back to the city, but even considering all their expenses, the marshals still make an average of $420,000 in net income. And the city generates an average of $47,000 in annual revenue from each marshal.[22]

The marshals usually thrive in bad times. They pulled in some of their highest revenues during the mortgage crisis and great recession of 2008.[23] Their incomes also skyrocketed as predatory lenders who charged over 400 percent interest made increasing use of court judgments and saw a profitable partnership with the marshals.[24] An investigation by *Bloomberg News* uncovered the practices of one such marshal, who made $1.7 million in 2017: "Barbarovich and a few others have become cogs in a debt-collection machine that has crushed thousands of small businesses. They use their legal authority on behalf of lenders who charge more than some mafia loan sharks once did."[25] Meanwhile, the owner of *Bloomberg News* reportedly appointed twenty marshals when he was mayor, including his own bodyguard, who "grossed $2.2 million [in 2017] and who has consistently grossed more than $1 million each year since 2010."[26] According to news reports, some New York City mayors have raised concerns about the marshals over the years, but all eventually fall in line with the lure of the money.[27]

Other cities and towns across America also use such a bounty hunter structure for their local law enforcement. City marshals in Louisiana profit from enforcing court orders against the poor, including taking 6 percent of collections.[28] The city of Alexandria, Louisiana, has a poverty rate of almost 25 percent, and the medium income is only a little over $22,000. With so many poor families to pursue, the Alexandria city marshal "pocketed more than $132,000 in fees and garnishments" in one year, in addition to his normal salary.[29] Massachusetts still uses constables who are appointed by town officials to generate revenue by enforcing court orders against impoverished residents.[30] Texas uses both constables and sheriffs, providing them with "commissions" up to 10 percent of the enforced collections.[31] And Texas goes big with its annual "Great Texas Warrant Roundup," a collaboration of the courts and law enforcement from more than three hundred jurisdictions aimed at generating revenue from low-income individuals for outstanding warrants because of their inability to pay fines and fees:

> "I've got officers out on the street knocking on doors, going to people's jobs, going to their school," Wichita Falls Municipal Court Administrator Stan Horton said. "They're going to pick them up and take them to jail."
> Ready or not, here they come, and you can't hide. The Texas Warrant Roundup has begun and they are taking all prisoners. And there's only one way around it. "I advise people to come on down or get online and make those payments."[32]

Further, several other states and counties use similar bounty hunter structures for their sheriff's departments, such as in Indiana, where a percentage of enforced collections is given both to sheriffs directly and to the sheriff's pension fund.[33] The city marshals in New York have competition from the city's sheriffs, who also chase down the same 5 percent "poundage" and other fees by enforcing judgments against the poor—and as a clear sign of the moneyed focus, the New York City Sherriff's Office has been established as a division of the city's Department of Finance rather than public safety.[34]

TO SERVE AND PROTECT?

When searching the mission and core values of most law enforcement departments, some similar variations will appear: to selflessly serve and protect those in need. For example, the Harford County Sheriff's department in Maryland based its code of ethics on the International Association of Chiefs of Police model and includes the following provision among similar requirements: "As a deputy, my fundamental duty is to serve mankind; to safeguard lives and property; to protect the innocent against deception; the weak against oppression or intimidation, and the peaceful against violence or disorder; and to respect the Constitutional rights of all to liberty, equality and justice."[35] Powerful words if truly followed. As with our courts, prosecutors, and probation departments, it is crucial that law enforcement offices create a structure wherein ethics and mission are paramount. If we in the justice systems lose our way, or if we strive for the right path but serve in a system that is structurally compromised, harm results. If we pursue money over mission, harm results.

Consider the policing role in evictions, and whether the mission just quoted is being served. As just one part of their financially driven enforcement strategies, local law enforcement departments are making money by evicting struggling individuals and families from their homes. An investigation by the *Bronx Ink* describes a typical day for a retired city marshal in New York: "It's 27 degrees Fahrenheit outside, and there are four inches of snow on the ground. He knocks on the door of a low-income Bronx apartment. A woman answers. He tells her he's a marshal. She's being evicted for not paying rent. The woman starts to cry. Her three children, ages 2 through 7, gather in the hall. Could you throw this family out on the street? If the answer is no, . . . [explains] a city marshal for nearly three decades, then you should find another job."[36] The *Daily Gazette* describes how a deputy sheriff in Schenectady County, New York, was "awarded the New York State Sheriffs' Association Civil Deputy of the Year Award for his work processing evictions." After single-handedly carrying out 774 evictions in one year, "he referred to the crowbar under his desk as 'the key to the city.'"[37] According to the executive director of the state Sheriffs' Association, "[t]he volume of evictions he's done is staggering," adding that "[i]t's a sad commentary on the economy, but it's also just a huge amount."[38] Hard times for the poor usually mean more money generated by the sheriff's department: "Evictions generate revenue for Schenectady County," and "the sheriff's department makes about $300,000 processing evictions each year."[39]

However, although hard times usually mean more profit under this bounty hunter structure, the circumstances of the COVID-19 pandemic turned things on their head—and in doing so, disclosed the inverted mission of law enforcement. When the pandemic spread across the globe and people were unable to work and pay rent, most US states began issuing temporary moratoriums on housing evictions, and courts temporarily halted legal proceedings. Similarly, the Centers for Disease Control and Prevention (CDC) issued a "Temporary Halt in Residential Evictions to Prevent the Further Spread of Covid-19."[40] If law enforcement offices exist to serve and protect those in need, then halting evictions and court proceedings in order to serve and protect vulnerable citizens in a time of crisis should align perfectly with the interests of the law enforcement offices. But protecting the vulnerable ended up harming the offices' financial self-interests. For example, in its 2020 annual report, the Sheriff's Office in Putnam County, New York, describes its annual revenue "generated in the form of service fees, mileage charges and poundage on monies collected on executions issued to enforce judgments" being cut almost in half: "The significant decrease in revenue was due to the Covid-19 restrictions placed on the enforcement of Civil Judgments by New York State Executive Orders."[41] Also, unable to pursue the poor as aggressively, multiple New York City marshals obtained large forgivable Paycheck Protection Program (PPP) loans that were intended to help small businesses struggling with the COVID-19 crisis.[42]

The conclusion is inescapable. If state and federal actions to protect vulnerable citizens conflict with the interests of law enforcement offices because the offices are profiting from doing harm to those vulnerable citizens, then such structure and revenue practices of law enforcement are in conflict with their missions and ethical codes. Which brings us to sheriff's sales.

MERCHANDISING POVERTY ON THE COURTHOUSE STEPS

When salespeople operate on commission, they are incentivized to sell more goods. To sell more goods, they need power to obtain more goods, preferably a diverse and valuable allotment. They also need a sales venue to best draw in a captive audience. What better way, then, to spur the fervor of hopeful buyers than a bidding war? Sheriff's sales are another relic from the time of America's founding, and the reasoning was the same then as it is now: to encourage the enforcement and collection of court-ordered debts, give power to seize property to someone with a badge and a gun, give them a cut of the sales proceeds, and do all this under the power and auspices of the courts and law enforcement agencies.

Sheriffs today wield the same power to seize and sell property that they have wielded for almost four hundred years. Once seized, the property is sold off to satisfy court judgments that the sheriffs are enlisted to enforce. As an incentive, countless jurisdictions still give sheriffs a percentage of the sales. Under current Virginia law, the state's sheriffs take a 10 percent commission "and . . . [their] necessary expenses and costs" out of the sale proceeds, the same percentage taken by sheriffs for enforcement actions when Virginia was still a colony.[43] In Louisiana, the sheriff's commission depends on the type of property: "For commission on sales of property made by the sheriffs, three percent shall be allowed on the price of adjudication of immovable property, and six percent shall be allowed on the price of adjudication of movable property."[44] In New Jersey, sheriffs obtain 6 percent of the first $5,000 in sales proceeds and 4 percent of any greater amount.[45] Variations exist across the country.

Through sheriff's sales, law enforcement offices turn from their mission of serving and protecting the vulnerable to profiteering from the vulnerable. And the practice has deeply discriminatory, dehumanizing, and harmful roots. In antebellum America, when sheriff's sales began, common listings of property being sold often included human names— because they were enslaved persons. The newspaper clipping shown here is from Mississippi's *Natchez Weekly Courier and Journal* of June 3, 1840. The image is part of a page that also includes the market's current prices for lard, molasses, tobacco, bacon, and cotton. If we could zoom out, we would also see several notices labeled "Runaway in Jail," such as the description of "a negro man calling his name Henry. . . . Said negro is of mulatto color, 5 feet 11 inches high, square built . . . has had the right hand injured by a gin and the left scared by a burn . . . said negro has been shot in the left shoulder."[46] Continuing to scan the page, we see even more notices of sheriff's sales to auction off human beings on the courthouse steps, for which the sheriff would claim his commission.

Such sheriff's sales of enslaved persons were disturbingly common events. Further, sheriffs also profited from directly inflicting intense physical harm. In the laws of Virginia compiled in 1694, sheriffs were paid for carrying out whippings and putting people in the pillory.[47] In 1758, when North Carolina was still a colony, the law provided payment to sheriffs for castrating enslaved persons: "Twenty shillings were to be paid to the sheriff for carrying out such castrations and £3 were allotted

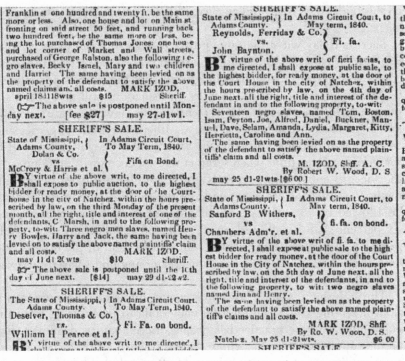

FIGURE 4. Clipping from *Natchez Weekly Courier and Journal*, June 3, 1840. *Source:* www.newspapers.com/image/248855080/.

'to defray the expence [*sic*] of the Cure, of such Slave Castrated.' Lastly, the act set at £60 the maximum compensation for executed slaves, those who died after being castrated, or slaves 'killed on outlawry, or in being apprehended when run away.'"[48]

Professor Thomas D. Russell uncovers stark details regarding the scope of sheriff's sales in an article in which he describes the business collaboration between courts and sheriffs to tap into profits from slavery: "The courts of South Carolina operated much like commission-merchant firms. Profit motivated the individuals who comprised the institutions. In firms, vendue masters—as commercial auctioneers were called in South Carolina—took a percentage of the sale amount as a commission. Fees also drove the work of sheriffs and other officials who conducted sales. Like auctioneers, they all worked on commission."[49] The current law in South Carolina continues a profiteering mindset in utilizing sheriff's sales: "When any sheriff or other officer shall take the lands, tenements, goods and chattels of any person whatsoever by virtue of any execution and the owner of such lands, tenements, goods and chattels shall not, within five days after such taking, satisfy the debt, damages and costs of the party issuing such execution, such sheriff or officer shall and may sell, by auction, the lands, tenements, goods and chattels so taken or so much thereof as shall be sufficient to satisfy the judgment for the best price that can be got for them."[50] Sheriffs and courts in the antebellum South developed business practices as "commission-merchant firms" to profit from slavery, and modern-day sheriffs and courts have evolved those practices into business operations to continue profiting from racial and economic injustice.

PROFITING FROM CIVIL FORFEITURES

Law enforcement agencies use an additional strategy to profit from seizing property—civil forfeiture—which is another relic dating back to medieval England and possibly even to biblical times.[51] In the United States, law enforcement offices expanded the strategy during the war on drugs in the 1970s and 1980s, with the promoted idea of seizing property related to suspected drug crimes as an additional deterrent.[52] However, rather than using this tool for crime deterrence and community well-being, police and sheriffs increasingly look to civil forfeiture as another means of making money from the poor.

To carry out this revenue strategy, law enforcement officers assert that they are investigating possible criminal activity and then seize cash, vehicles, personal possessions, and virtually any other type of property.[53] Once the property has been seized, the officers often team up with prosecutors, who help with a notice or complaint in the form of a civil proceeding against the property ("in rem") rather than against the person. To contest the takings, the owner of the property—who rarely has a lawyer—would need to overcome the intimidation and fear and file a claim against the law enforcement agency arguing that the agency acted illegally in seizing the property. Even if such intimidation is overcome, the owner then needs to figure out how to prepare and file the claim under the legally required format and specifications. Thus, not surprisingly, most civil forfeiture actions are uncontested. In those circumstances when the property owner is able to file a claim contesting the seizure of property, the law enforcement office need only establish a nexus between the property and some allegations of often unproven criminal conduct.[54] The sheriffs and police keep a large percentage of the takings, frequently sharing a cut with the prosecutors, and often without acquiring criminal convictions or even filing criminal charges.

The financial incentive in civil forfeitures is strong, from small towns to large cities. In Chicago, the police and sheriffs seized over $86 million in property from 2005 to 2015.[55] Digging through records of Buda, Texas, an "Interlocal Agreement" reveals how the small city police force partnered with other county police and sheriff's departments, the local prosecuting attorney, and even the Texas State University Police Department to broaden the scope of their takings and divide up the loot.[56] While Detroit continued to struggle with economic turmoil after the city filed bankruptcy in 2013, the city and county law enforcement agencies seized more than twenty-six hundred vehicles and collected more than $1.2 million in revenue from civil forfeiture over just two years.[57] A recent report by the Institute for Justice found that between 2002 and 2018, law enforcement in twenty states and the federal government reported over $63 billion in forfeitures.[58]

Much has been written about the misuse of civil forfeiture, and legal advocates have raised numerous legal challenges to current practices, including asserted violations of constitutional due process requirements and the Eighth Amendment prohibition against excessive fines.[59] In 2019 the US Supreme Court made clear in *Timbs v. Indiana* that the excessive fines clause applies to states, increasing the likelihood of ongoing legal challenges.[60] However, although the *Timbs* decision leaves the door open for more challenges to civil forfeitures in state courts, most individuals impacted by the practice cannot afford lawyers and are not appointed free lawyers because these are civil rather than criminal proceedings.[61] Thus, mostly unrepresented, low-income litigants have to go up against state prosecutors, many of whom are financially incentivized by the takings. The individuals have to somehow know the correct legal arguments to make, and even if they know to raise an Eighth Amendment excessive fines argument, they then need to overcome a difficult "disproportionality" test to convince the court that the seizure of their property is grossly disproportionate to the specific allegations of criminal infractions (even if the individuals have not been charged).

The ACLU and other organizations are also raising important legal challenges to civil forfeitures under the due process clause, similar to the analysis included in prior chapters regarding due process concerns with courts and prosecutors profiting from foster care and child support funds.[62] The ACLU argument is strong, that the impartiality requirement should be interpreted to clearly prohibit such financial incentives of both the prosecutors and law enforcement officers who seek to profit from civil forfeiture.[63]

Nonetheless, as legal challenges continue, police and sheriff's offices continue to use civil forfeiture as a tool to loot the citizenry. In response to advocacy efforts and news coverage, several states have enacted legislation to require more protections, and a handful of states have taken steps to eliminate civil forfeitures. However, even in states that have restricted the practice at the state level, the police and sheriff's departments often find an end run around the restrictions through the federal "equitable sharing" program.[64] For example, an investigation by St. Louis Public Radio examined practices by the Phelps County, Missouri, Sheriff's Department and found that "Phelps County deputies seized more than $1 million a year from cars on I-44," but the county, "like other jurisdictions, almost never files state criminal charges against those whose cash they seize, nor does it make big drug seizures during these stops targeting cash."[65] Although Missouri is one of the states that have enacted protective legislation, including requirements that in a criminal conviction seized property and proceeds are supposed to provide revenue to public schools, the St. Louis Public Radio investigation explains how law enforcement offices have bypassed the law:

> The off ramp that allows local police and sheriffs to detour around these legal requirements is the federal Equitable Sharing Program. It permits local law-enforcement agencies to turn over their civil asset seizures to the federal government, which then "adopts" them. The feds keep 20 percent for their trouble and return up to 80 percent to the local law-enforcement agencies.
>
> It's a legal way to wash away the strict state law requirements. The requirements of a criminal conviction and school funding do not apply. Instead, most funds are returned to local police who spend them.[66]

Further, like the use of other revenue strategies, law enforcement offices' use of civil forfeitures is often economically and racially targeted. An investigation into the use of civil forfeiture in South Carolina found that "[a]bout 65 percent of the people targeted for civil asset forfeiture in the state from 2014 to 2016 were black males in a state where African-American men make up just 13 percent of the population."[67] Also, "[t]he Nevada Policy Research Institute analyzed 346 forfeiture cases in 2016, and found that 66 percent of the forfeitures occurred in 12 (of 48) zip codes in Las Vegas: neighborhoods that are predominantly minority and low-income."[68]

Again, rather than focusing on their mission of serving and protecting vulnerable populations, law enforcement offices are targeting vulnerable populations as a source of revenue. In that unfortunate vein, we look back—to Ferguson.

FERGUSON, FINES, FEES, AND ARRESTS

When Michael Brown, an unarmed Black teen, was shot and killed by a police officer in Ferguson, Missouri, distrust of the police department was already high. As in many other cities and towns across America, the local court and police were teaming up to make money by issuing endless fines and fees and using arrest warrants to enforce the fines and fees. This collaboration has the feel of an assembly line, but it is really the reverse—more of a disassembly line, in which already struggling individuals are targeted and deconstructed for every possible penny. The numbers in Ferguson are staggering. In an excellent investigation, NPR journalist Joe Shapiro explains: "To understand some of the distrust of police that has fueled protests in Ferguson, Mo., consider this: In 2013, the municipal court in Ferguson—a city of 21,135 people—issued 32,975 arrest warrants for nonviolent offenses."[69] Racial disparity runs deep through the revenue mechanism: "African Americans accounted for 85% of FPD's traffic stops, 90% of FPD's citations, and 93% of FPD's arrests from 2012 to 2014."[70] Meanwhile, at the time, Black officers accounted for only 5 percent of the Ferguson police force.[71]

Further, in Ferguson and numerous other cities across the country, the municipal court is actually housed within the police department, presenting more than symbolic evidence of the business partnership between the courts and police. In fact, a 2015 US Department of Justice investigation found that the Ferguson Municipal Court staff reported directly to the chief of police.[72] The DOJ report uncovers the story of Ferguson, which is emblematic of stories that unfortunately continue across America, of lower-level courts and law enforcement teaming up to maximize revenue at the expense of justice: "The City has been aware for years of concerns about the impact its focus on revenue has had on lawful police action and the fair administration of justice in Ferguson," but the city "has disregarded those concerns—even concerns raised from within the City government—to avoid disturbing the court's ability to optimize revenue generation."[73] As the DOJ's complaint against Ferguson explains, "the court prioritizes the collection of fines and fees over the administration of justice," and "[t]he priority the court has placed on maximizing revenue directly contributes to the unlawful police practices."[74]

The story of Ferguson's revenue-driven partnership between the court and police—abdicating justice for money—is repeated in town after town across America, with incalculable harm. An excellent investigation by John Archibald at AL.com uncovered how the small town of Brookside, Alabama, used its police and courts to increase revenues from fines and forfeitures by "more than 640 percent and now make up half the city's total income," leading to more arrests and towed vehicles than the town has residents: "By 2020 Brookside made more misdemeanor arrests than it has residents. It went from towing 50 vehicles in 2018 to 789 in 2020—each carrying fines. That's a 1,478% increase, with 1.7 tows for every household in town."[75] The investigation further explains how in the quiet town with only fifty-five serious crimes over an eight-year period, the focus on fines and fees "grew the police department tenfold," so that "[b]y 2020 officers in the sleepy town were undergoing SWAT training and dressing in riot gear" and even "parked a riot control vehicle—townspeople call it a tank—outside the municipal complex and community center."[76] Money became the goal rather than justice: "Traffic tickets, and criminalizing those who passed through, became the city's leading industry."[77]

CONTRACTS TO TARGET UNDOCUMENTED INDIVIDUALS

Several sheriff's departments across the country have also tapped into another source of federal funds. If the sheriffs increase the number of undocumented individuals they detain and hold them in jail for at least four days, they can target greater revenue through the State Criminal Alien Assistance Program.

Again, many sheriff's departments hired JBI to help them make money through this process, giving the company a percentage of increased revenues, often 15 percent or more. As of 2012, the company was contracting "with more than 500 counties nationwide, including 26 in Georgia."[78] A 2016 contract with the sheriff's office in Lucas County, Ohio, gives JBI a 22 percent cut, and a 2020 proposed agreement with the Alameda County Sheriff's Office in California provides JBI with 18 percent of all revenues claimed over $205,763.[79]

FOOD PROFIT

Some sheriff's departments have even profited from inmate food, or lack thereof. Until state legislation halted the practice in 2010, Indiana sheriffs were allowed to increase their salaries through funds intended to feed prisoners. Before the change in state law, a news report explained: "The state of Indiana provides a per diem of $1.37 per meal, per inmate. If a sheriff can feed an inmate a meal approved by a registered dietitian for less than $1.37, the sheriff is entitled to pocket the difference."[80] Adding such food profit to revenue from warrant collections, the sheriffs' pay seemed without limit. For example, the sheriff in Marion County "managed to add more than $260,000 in tax warrant and meal money revenues to his $100,000 base salary."[81]

Sheriffs in Alabama have engaged in the same practice; outrage emerged after news investigations revealed that the sheriff in Etowah County pocketed $750,000 in surplus inmate food funds in just three years, which he reportedly used to buy a beach house.[82] After significant press coverage about the sheriff's personal use of money intended for prisoner food, the Alabama legislature passed a bill in 2019 that was described as restricting the practice. However, the specific text of the new law still allows the sheriff's offices to take a cut: "Monies deposited in the Prisoner Feeding Fund shall only be used for feeding prisoners except as provided herein. At the conclusion of each fiscal year, the sheriff may expend not more than 25 percent of the unencumbered balance in the fund on jail operation or for law enforcement purposes related to the operation of the office of the sheriff."[83] Further, apparently unhappy with only being able to take 25 percent, at least two counties, including Etowah and Marshall County, pushed forward local constitutional amendments by voter referendum to allow the sheriffs to ignore the state law and access all surplus food moneys to use for other sheriff's law enforcement purposes.[84]

PRIVATE POLICE

Following the revenue-driven mindset in law enforcement to its fruition, multiple states and cities have given full police powers to an increasing number of private police companies. The use of private police in America also has a long history, such as hired guns used to protect western saloons. Often unknown to the public, for-profit policing companies have not disappeared but have modernized and grown.

The National Union of Special Police Officers explains how states give the privatized police—often called "special police" or "company police"—the full statutory authority of government police officers.[85] For example, the union reports that in Washington, D.C., alone, "there are about 7,700 special police officers in the District, and about 4,500 of them are armed," and that the special police "have the same powers as a law enforcement officer to Arrest without a warrant for offenses committed within the premises to which his or her jurisdiction extends or outside the premises on a fresh pursuit for offenses committed on the premises."[86] One of the organizations operating private police in D.C. as a limited liability company (LLC) lists an office on K Street, an area known for lobbyists.[87] Although the "special police" in D.C. are granted the full powers of law enforcement by the city, an alarming court ruling concluded that the city could be shielded from liability for their actions: "We conclude that a special police officer, rather than being an agent of the District, has essentially the same status as an architect, a beautician, an engineer, or a physician."[88]

Several states, including Virginia, Kentucky, North Carolina, Maryland, Massachusetts, and others, have granted similar authority to privatized police.[89] The trend raises significant concerns about decreased accountability, less transparency, less training, possibly fewer constitutional protections—and overtly embracing a mission of profit rather than the public good.[90]

Mission matters. When public justice officials deviate from serving the common good, we have the potential to expose their failings in the hopes of truing their paths. If justice becomes an "LLC," the potential for trued mission can be lost.

DUE PROCESS VIOLATIONS

Through all these numerous revenue schemes, the policing branch of our justice systems follows the harmful, unethical, and unconstitutional path of our courts, prosecutors, and probation departments, systemically violating the due process requirement of impartiality. As explained in prior chapters, the Supreme Court made clear in *Marshall v. Jerrico, Inc.*, that the impartiality requirement applies in the law enforcement process, even if not to the same degree as in the courts themselves, that "[a] scheme injecting a personal interest, financial or otherwise, into the enforcement process" can violate the constitutional requirement.[91]

Now, more than forty years after the *Marshall* decision, federal courts have gradually started applying the crucial, commonsense reasoning that the due process impartiality requirement applies to law enforcement.[92] For example, the court in *Flora v. Southwest Iowa Narcotics Enforcement Task Force* concluded that the narcotics task force (comprised of law enforcement officers and county attorneys) violated due process impartiality when assets the officers seized for forfeiture partially funded the law enforcement departments.[93] Hopefully this trend will continue, and hopefully the due process requirements will be applied to any privatized police under contract with local governments, as well as to public officers. Otherwise, if the due process requirement does not apply to each component of our justice systems, then due process—and justice—will have no meaning.[94]

CHAPTER 7

Bodies in the Beds

The Business of Jailing Children and the Poor

While John Kelly was chief of staff for former president Trump, he was interviewed about the administration's zero tolerance and child separation policies for migrant families arriving at the border. When asked if it was "cruel and heartless to take a mother away from her children," Kelly responded: "The children will be taken care of—put into foster care or whatever."[1] It turns out, just three months before the interview, the administration had reportedly awarded a $50 million contract to a for-profit company to detain and house migrant children in a "temporary influx care facility" in Homestead, Florida.[2] Located on federal land next to a military base, the facility was exempted from state child welfare inspections.[3]

Although the inner workings of the operations were mostly shrouded in secrecy, attorneys gained access to investigate possible violations of what is known as the Flores Settlement Agreement, an agreement with the US government requiring minimum standards of care for detained migrant children. In their federal court filings, the attorneys included transcribed testimonials from countless children who were the source of profit. Two are provided here, identified by initials:

B.M.
Sometimes it's really hard having to stay here. A couple of girls since I've been here have been cutting themselves. That's why we're not allowed to bring pens or pencils into our bedrooms. We're only allowed to have clothes

and a few other things like a toothbrush and a hairbrush. I have spent a lot of time crying and the other girls too. When the other girls cry, I try to tell them that they should try to be patient, focus on where they are now and to not think about the future or getting out to their families. But that's hard to do.

A.B.
Sometimes when your friend is crying because they can't stand being here any longer you want to be able to give them a hug. But you can't because it's against the rules.[4]

After the initial $50 million contract in 2018, the contract to operate the Homestead facility was reportedly renewed for $222 million two months later and for another $341 the following year.[5] The company that ran the facility, Comprehensive Health Services, Inc., operated as a subsidiary of Caliburn International.[6] The Kelly connection? Before he joined the Trump administration in 2017, Kelly served on the board for DC Capital Partners, a private equity firm that owned Caliburn.[7] Then, after resigning from the White House in 2019, he joined the board of directors for Caliburn.[8]

The Homestead "shelter" is just one example of the countless types of facilities that have profited by warehousing vulnerable children and adults, the commodities that are often processed through the revenue-driven business operations described in previous chapters. In addition to using facilities to detain migrant children and families, government and private entities collaborate in revenue strategies using juvenile detention centers, youth residential and behavioral treatment centers, adult prisons, and jails. City and county governments, nonprofit entities, religious organizations, for-profit companies, and even larger private equity firms and real estate investment trusts all generate revenue from the various structures used to jail or "treat" children and the poor. And they all share a common commodification need: bodies in the beds.

The business model is a simultaneously simple and complex tale to tell. Simplicity lies in the industry's profit goal: maximizing the occupancy rate while minimizing the money spent on care, to maximize revenue and profit. Complexities enter the story through the several types of facilities, varied funding and revenue streams, applicable laws and regulations—or lack thereof—and numerous forms of government and private entities competing for the business opportunity. Seemingly endless stories of harm resulting from the business model can start to feel overwhelming, but we must be aware.

JUVENILE JAILS AS TOWN FACTORIES

When localities have struggled with lost jobs and reduced revenue as factories shut down or leave town, several local governments have looked toward youth as the future, in a different form of factory, one that withstands or even grows during economic turmoil: juvenile detention centers. Over the last two decades, an important national consensus has emerged about decreasing the population of incarcerated youth and shifting reliance from state juvenile correction facilities to more local community alternatives. However, many local governments still view detaining children as a means of economic development.

During the recession of 2008, Siler City in North Carolina was one of the countless small towns across America that was devastated by the economic downturn. A news investigation explains that when the town's largest employer, a poultry processing plant, announced it was closing, the town manager described the impact: "'We already have folks leaving our town,' [he] said," "[g]rocery stores, clothing stores, car dealerships—all will suffer," and "those who stay have less buying power."[9] However, the investigation reports that the town manager tried to stay positive and looked toward other economic opportunities, that he was "trying to look on the bright side" because "[a] new juvenile detention center for girls will bring 80 new jobs to town."[10]

A few years later, in 2011, the town of Jennings in Jeff Davis Parish, Louisiana, was competing with other towns to reel in a juvenile detention center after news spread that the state had set aside money to open a new facility.[11] A local news story describes how, like a small-scale version of the competition of states and cities fighting for Amazon's second headquarters, the parish hoped to woo the detention center to spur the local economy:

> In addition to providing some relief for area jails, which are often over-crowded with juvenile offenders, the facility would provide an economic boost for the home parish. The facility would bring along with it 100 permanent jobs and even more temporary construction jobs.
>
> "A hundred jobs is a lot of jobs in this market," said Fox. "We're going to give it our best shot. We're going to do our best to put everything in the proposal that they are looking for and we hope to be at the top of the list."[12]

Similarly, in 2017 the city of Chesapeake, Virginia, proposed a new juvenile correction facility, noting that "[m]ost importantly, this project will add 300 stable, well-compensated jobs to the Deep Creek section of Chesapeake," and that "[t]he Joint Juvenile Justice Center will also redevelop a City property on Military Highway and might spur private redevelopment investment."[13] In Maryland, a proposal for a new detention center explained that it's all about money and jobs: "An economic impact report by the Department of Business and Economic Development found that the design and construction of the Southern Regional Children's Center (SRCC) will generate $72 million for Charles County and surrounding counties, and beginning in 2017, the SRCC's operations will generate $61 million per year for Charles County and surrounding counties. . . . The economic impact report also found that at the peak of construction, the project will create an estimated 119 new jobs for the local economy and almost 300 new jobs once the facility becomes operational."[14] The analysis by Maryland's Department of Juvenile Services described its economic modeling, using a tool called IMPLAN, by comparing the jailing of children to a factory producing automobiles: "IMPLAN is an input-output model. It is based on data collected at the national level by the U.S. Bureau of Economic Analysis that accounts for every input into an industry that is required to create a specific output. So, if an industry is producing automobiles, the inputs for creating that product could be steel, plastic, glass, engineering services, transportation of goods to and from factories, electricity, etc. The creation of each of these inputs is also accounted for, as each input into one industry is an output from another."[15]

Further, in addition to focusing on boosting jobs and the surrounding economy, some local governments view juvenile detention centers as government revenue producers. For a county to turn its juvenile jail into a profit center, the judge, sheriff, or other county official running the facility will often market the service to other counties or to the state or federal government. For example, the juvenile court judge in Richland County, Ohio, proudly described his agreement with other county juvenile courts to jail their children: "My staff and I are pleased to assist our neighboring counties, many of which do not have a juvenile detention facility of their own. . . . In 2019, we generated $196,800.00 in revenue that supports the general fund."[16]

To make money, a county needs to pull enough children into its juvenile facility. According to an investigation by the *Victoria Advocate*, the county judge in Victoria, Texas, explained in 2018 that he "credited the juvenile detention center as a growing source of revenue for the county that helped to offset a decline in property values."[17] He expressed that the success was the result of the county's efforts to increase the population of children held in the facility: "Due to our work out there in improving trends, increasing populations, better payment rates, we were able to budget upward $450,000 in revenue at juvenile detention."[18] Similarly, as explained in the *Whitman County Gazette*, a county commissioner in Whitman County, Washington, expressed relief that after a discouraging beginning of the year for the juvenile jail in terms of its low occupancy, "because the juvenile center's population has increased and remained steady, the center is secure."[19] However, he also warned that they needed to keep jailing enough children to make ends meet: "[T]he juvenile center is losing $25,000 a month for every four juvenile inmates under the minimum number of 28 inmates it takes to keep the center financially stable."[20] Union County, New Jersey, was more aggressive, explaining in a press release that it was requiring a neighboring county to send a minimum quota of children to its juvenile facility: "Approval of the measure next Thursday would clear the way to finalize a two-year contract that could bring $2.1 million annually in additional revenues to Union County. Under the proposed terms of the contract, Hudson County would pay Union County $230 per day per juvenile detainee over the first year and $240 per day during the second year. The contract would guarantee that at least 20 juveniles be housed at the Union County facility."[21] The chairman of the county Chosen Freeholders (the term that New Jersey used for county commissioners until 2021) expressed approval of the arrangement: "This is an example of good governmental policy that would maximize the revenue potential of an asset the County has in our newer Juvenile Detention Center."[22] The additional revenue was icing on the already existing profit cake, because the county juvenile detention center had been pulling in over $1 million in annual revenue since 2009 under a contract providing ten beds for the federal government to detain migrant children.[23]

Thus, even as a national effort has helped to reduce the overall number of incarcerated children in state correctional facilities, a shift toward more local placements has led to juvenile facilities continuing to be an economic lure in local cities and towns. Looking again to Victoria, Texas, the county's chief juvenile probation officer explained that "[t]his trend toward more local, community-based facilities brought more funding and more kids to the Victoria County juvenile detention center," because "state lawmakers were intent on decreasing the number of kids and teenagers in state-run facilities."[24] Again, when local communities build or expand juvenile detention facilities, they need bodies in the beds. As an attorney with the Texas Criminal Justice

Coalition explains, "[W]hat tends to happen is when you build additional detention facilities and you expand capacity, those beds tend to get filled."[25]

PROFITING FROM JUVENILE RESIDENTIAL "TREATMENT" CENTERS

Considering the national desire to reduce placement of children in state juvenile prisons, private entities realized a window of opportunity in the growing "troubled youth" industry. Both for-profit and nonprofit companies grew business operations that still detain impoverished children, but with benevolent-sounding names such as camps, farms, villages, residential treatment centers, behavioral health centers, campuses, and academies. There is no universal terminology, but policy experts commonly use residential treatment centers (RTCs) as the catchall term. Resulting from the money chase, most of these "residential" settings are now private. According to data from the US Department of Justice (DOJ) Office of Juvenile Justice and Delinquency Prevention (OJJDP), while private companies run about 20 percent of juvenile correctional facilities, they have taken control of two-thirds of RTCs.[26]

As companies view children like $hawn through a lens of dollar signs, an all-too-frequent combination of low-quality care and punitive practices can result in harm. Children pulled into the juvenile justice systems have already encountered significant trauma in their lives, and even short-term detentions and out-of-home placements can inflict even greater trauma—or worse.

These mostly privately run RTCs are supposed to be less like juvenile prisons. However, the OJJDP reports that "more than 70 percent of youth in RTCs are in locked facilities."[27] The RTCs are supposed to provide better care and services, but a 2018 study "found that long-term secure facilities were more likely than RTCs to offer mental health and substance abuse services."[28] The RTCs are supposed to be less punitive in their treatment of children, but the OJJDP reports that 82 percent of the facilities used seclusion or restraint.[29] The reason? If juvenile facilities reduce the cost of care by reducing quality of care, children are cheaper to detain. And if the facilities reduce the need for more highly trained staff by instead controlling the children with seclusion and restraints, the children are cheaper still. More children. Lower costs. More money.

"So Much Money"

Cornelius Frederick died after he was "restrained" on April 29, 2020, by seven staff members at Lakeside Academy, an RTC in Kalamazoo, Michigan. According to news reports, "[t]he Black 16-year-old wanted to be a therapist when he grew up, to give back to the foster care system that had raised him."[30] After he tossed a piece of a sandwich in the cafeteria, "[a] staff member responded by tackling Cornelius to the ground, and then, for 12 minutes, as Cornelius struggled and gradually grew still, seven men who worked for Lakeside held him down, some putting their weight on his legs and torso."[31] After he went limp, a video showed Cornelius lying on the floor unconscious as staff looked at him, and a news report explains "[a]fter staff released him, no one called 911 for 12 minutes, and for an additional 15 minutes no one started life saving measures, the state said."[32]

Investigations indicate Cornelius suffered cardiac arrest as he was pinned to the floor, and the county medical examiner declared his death "homicide by a result of 'restraint asphyxia.'"[33] Several children witnessed the events, and when the Lakeside facility announced Cornelius's death, more than twenty-five children "escaped" and ran away.[34] According to a news report, a nearby homeowner encountered a fifteen-year-old boy looking for protection: "The boy ran straight to my house for protection and was screaming and crying that they just killed somebody right before his eyes."[35]

The Lakeside Academy, a program of Lakeside for Children, held itself out as a nonprofit, but it hired a for-profit company to run the facility: "That company, Sequel Youth and Family Services, LLC, has for years faced allegations of mismanagement and abuse at the facilities it operates in multiple states."[36] An attorney for Cornelius expressed his frustration with the profit motive: "The privatization of these facilities that are run for profit and institutionalized children who have no choice in the matter are being treated as commodities and not as human beings."[37]

Jay Ripley cofounded Sequel Youth in 1999. In a 2015 interview, reported by *Reveal News*, Ripley described his decision with his mentor, James Hindman—who was the founder of Jiffy Lube—to transition from the oil change business to juvenile treatment centers:

> After their oil change business was taken over by another company in the early '90s, the two men hatched a plan to start a new venture. The idea was to run juvenile treatment centers and to make a profit doing it. . . .

At the time, reform schools were usually run either by the government or as charities. So they visited one in Pennsylvania to see how it worked. And when they saw the accounting ledger.[38]

Ripley indicated amazement that the facility "made so much money," describing his response to his mentor: "And I'm like, 'Jim, I think this is a good business. I'm not that smart, but I think this is a pretty good business.'"[39]

They decided to seek children from government foster care and juvenile justice agencies. As Ripley explained, "We focused on public pay because we figured kids are always going to have issues and they're always going to get in trouble, and again, the government has to figure out a way to take care of them."[40] Thus, he described the flow of children through the business enterprise: "'It's really like drinking from a fire hose.'"[41] Ripley also explained his view that "the reason that we can make that profit is if you control your staffing level."[42] Sequel pitched similar themes to potential investors, such as a 2017 investor presentation in which the company highlighted its "capital efficient business model" and "low operating expenditures," and how it was "well-positioned with regard to industry valuation drivers" including a "[f]ocus on attractive at-risk adolescent market."[43] Through the strategy, Sequel grew its operations into nineteen states, with forty-two states and US territories sending children to the company facilities as of 2017.[44]

News investigations would later point to inadequate staffing as one of multiple concerns with Sequel facilities. For example, a local news investigation in Ohio "found that inadequate staffing has been part of the criticism of what former residents and staffers alike say led to problems at places like Sequel Pomegranate where children were exposed to violence—or in some cases—abuse."[45]

Profiting from Public Funds

Companies like Sequel discovered a seemingly unending cash flow by tapping into federal and state funding streams, converting government aid for vulnerable youth into revenue and profit. The potential government aid sources vary depending on the type of facilities, the services provided, and the way the children are obtained, and the companies encounter complex eligibility and regulatory frameworks in their pursuit of money. As an investor presentation by Sequel explains, "significant barriers to entry" exist for organizations seeking to make money from juvenile facilities due to "[h]igh regulatory hurdles, state and federal law complexity."[46] However, for those companies that navigate the requirements, the barriers to entry can reduce competition and lead to a potential steady flow of children and profit.

. Clarinda Academy, a juvenile facility in Iowa that was structured as a nonprofit but contractually operated by Sequel, provides an example of targeted funds. In its "schedule of expenditure of federal awards," the academy listed funds from federal adoption assistance, the Social Services Block Grant, the US Department of Agriculture's School Breakfast and National School Lunch Program, and federal IV-E foster care funds—among others.[47] Further, the academy's financial report explains that "[p]rogram service revenue consists principally of amounts billed to state and county governments nationwide under the terms of agreements to provide program services at per diem rates," with the state payments adding up to over 96 percent of the academy's total revenues.[48] Such state government payments, in turn, are often funded in significant part by the states obtaining federal aid for the children. In addition to the funding listed in the Clarinda report, companies that operate juvenile facilities often seek to profit from several other forms of government aid, including Medicaid funds intended for care and treatment, school-based Medicaid funds intended for the educational needs of disabled students, state education funding, children's Social Security Supplemental Security Income benefits, the Substance Abuse Prevention and Treatment Block Grant, and so forth.

When the mission shifts from maximizing care to using government aid to maximize profit, harm often results. According to news reports, Sequel indicated plans to close its operations at the Clarinda Academy in 2021 after allegations of abuse and sexual assault: "The Clarinda Academy, a youth facility in southwest Iowa that has been the focus of multiple investigations into alleged abuse and rape of troubled teens, is shutting down."[49] The *Des Moines Register* explains: "For years, numerous serious allegations of excessive restraint, assault and sexual abuse—including allegations of forcible sodomy and rape by staff members—had been reported to police at Clarinda Academy," as well as reports of "staff slamming children to the ground and injuring them" and keeping "several children for weeks at a time in a suspension room."[50]

While companies seek to profit from children and their government aid funds, the referring state agencies and courts are often profiting from the children as well, as described in previous chapters—a distorted public-private partnership in the monetization of children. For example, just as the Ohio Juvenile Courts and Texas probation departments use children in strategies to obtain revenue from IV-E foster care funds, the courts and probation departments may then place the children in juvenile facilities that also profit from IV-E or other government funds.

As an additional complexity and potential financial incentive, two of the larger government funding streams often used for juvenile facilities, Medicaid and IV-E foster care funds, are structured as matching grant programs. In a state like Alabama, where Sequel has operated facilities, the state has benefited from about a 72 percent match rate, meaning just $28 of state spending triggers $72 in federal funds, which can be leveraged as revenue for county agencies and used to provide payments to juvenile facilities. In 2021, "Alabama Disabilities Advocacy Program filed an immediate jeopardy complaint" against one of the Alabama facilities, "Sequel Owens Cross Roads, a psychiatric residential treatment facility for girls under the age of 21."[51] The complaint alleged that the "Huntsville-area facility used violent and illegal restraints against the girls, most of whom are in foster care, and that one employee strangled a resident."[52]

Profiting from False Claims

As companies maximize revenue from government aid, they risk violating the Federal False Claims Act, a law that was originally "enacted in 1863 by a Congress concerned that suppliers of goods to the Union Army during the Civil War were defrauding the Army."[53] States enacted similar laws, so under both state and federal statutes a person or company can be liable if they knowingly submit false claims for government aid. The false claims acts provide authority to the respective governments to pursue perpetrators of fraud, and private individuals with inside information can file "qui tam" actions on behalf of the government.

In addition to false claims for services that were never provided, the government has also challenged false claims for federal aid when the care is "grossly substandard." As the DOJ warns, "[o]perators who bill Medicare and Medicaid while failing to provide essential services or bill for services so grossly substandard as to be effectively worthless will be pursed for false claims."[54] The same theory of liability can be applied to claims for IV-E foster care funds or other government aid by juvenile facilities providing substandard care.

Due to inconsistent and insufficient oversight, much is unknown about the practices of juvenile facilities in claiming government funds. The lack of information presents a barrier to false claims act proceedings unless a company insider bravely decides to come forward to file a qui tam action. Nonetheless, even with these barriers, juvenile facilities have been subject to multiple complaints. For example, Universal Health Services (UHS) is another large company that operates behavioral health and psychiatric facilities across the country, including residential facilities for children.[55] In July 2020 UHS agreed to a $117 million settlement with the DOJ and multiple states' attorneys general to resolve eighteen false claims act lawsuits. According to the settlement agreement, the claims resulted from multiple allegations: "(i) admission of beneficiaries who were not eligible for inpatient or residential treatment, (ii) failure to properly discharge beneficiaries when they no longer needed inpatient or residential treatment, (iii) improper and excessive lengths of stay, (iv) failure to provide adequate staffing, training, and/or supervision of staff, (v) billing for services not rendered, (vi) improper use of physical and chemical restraints and seclusion; and (vii) failure to provide inpatient acute or residential care in accordance with federal and state regulations."[56] The settlement included a corporate integrity agreement requiring an independent monitor, but the state and federal governments agreed not to exclude UHS from participating in Medicaid or other federal programs, thus allowing the company to continue profiting from government aid.[57] This was not the first settlement of a false claims act lawsuit with UHS. In 2012 the federal government and the Commonwealth of Virginia also settled a false claims act lawsuit with UHS regarding its operations of a juvenile residential facility: "Under the settlement, UHS and its subsidiaries ... agreed to pay $6.85 million to the United States and the commonwealth to settle allegations that they provided substandard psychiatric counseling and treatment to adolescents in violations of Medicaid requirements, falsified records and submitted false claims to the Medicaid program."[58]

Similarly, the DOJ settled a false claims lawsuit against CRC Health Corp. (CRC), another large company that operated juvenile facilities. CRC "agreed to pay $9.25 million to the federal government and the State of Tennessee to settle allegations that CRC knowingly submitted false claims by providing substandard treatment to adult and adolescent Medicaid patients" at a residential treatment facility with units for both adults and juveniles called the New Life Lodge.[59] The settlement resulted from a lawsuit brought by an insider whistleblower who worked in the facility's billing department and was motivated to help the children because she also grew up in state custody.[60] According to a news investigation by the *Tennessean*:

The 20-page complaint . . . states that New Life billed TennCare [Medicaid] for patients who had been discharged or sent home for trial home visits. It also charges that New Life misled TennCare and billed for services that were not covered.

[The whistleblower] recalled being instructed to order cots, which were then used to enable New Life to admit more patients than it was authorized to care for under its state license. . . . On another occasion, she said in the interview, she found 12 patients sitting on the floor outside the nurses' station because they were sick and needed medication but the office was closed.[61]

Investigations by the *Tennessean* also indicate a lawsuit had been filed against CRC in 2012 by a woman who alleged in the complaint that her grandson "died after being administered a powerful antipsychotic drug without being properly monitored by medical personnel, . . . the third New Life Lodge patient to die within a 15-month period."[62] At the time of the false claims lawsuit settlement in 2014, CRC was owned by Bain Capital, a private equity firm that was cofounded by Senator Mitt Romney. Less than a year after the settlement, CRC was purchased for $1.2 billion by Acadia Healthcare.[63]

In Florida, the state settled a false claims lawsuit in 2016 with yet another company that operated juvenile facilities, Youth Services International (YSI), founded by James Hindman. Jay Ripley, who later helped to found Sequel Youth & Family Services, had managed YSI's juvenile justice division until 1995.[64] A local news report describes Florida's Department of Juvenile Justice "ending the company's contracts," which "came after criticism of the firm by local communities and a whistleblower lawsuit alleging, at least in part, that YSI made false claims about providing services, and even food, to juvenile offenders."[65] An investigation by the *Miami Herald* into a YSI facility in Palm Beach County reported that staff set up fights between the children and bet on them, among other disturbing allegations: "Teens said there were maggots in the food—and barely enough of it. The youths wore threadbare and filthy clothing. They lacked soap, toothpaste, deodorant, socks. The medical care was lousy, toilets overflowed and the buildings were crumbling. Officers choked and punched them. For discipline and diversion, workers organized fights among the detainees. And sometimes they bet on them."[66]

The Unknown

Perhaps the most concerning facts regarding juvenile facilities are how much we don't know and the obfuscated nature of what we do know.

The OJJDP explains that facilities are allowed to pick their own classification and self-report their own data under a haphazard system—if we could call it a system—in which there are not even standard definitions of classifications: "[T]he lack of standard definitions has contributed to inconsistencies and challenges in the oversight of these programs, as individual programs can select their own classification."[67]

Further confusing things, much of the data relied upon by the OJJDP comes from the Census of Juveniles in Residential Placement (CJRP), which is limited by its reliance on the facilities' self-reporting data regarding children in their care. Not all facilities respond to the CJRP, and there currently is no way to easily verify if those who do respond are responding accurately. The facilities are asked to report information about children who were sent to them from juvenile delinquency proceedings, which does not consider that many of the same facilities also hold children who are "referred" from child welfare/foster care proceedings. Also, "CJRP does not capture data on youth in adult prisons or jails or those placed in facilities used exclusively for mental health or substance use treatment or for dependent children."[68]

Unconstitutionally and Harmfully Hiding behind Religion

Under the veil of religion, even less is revealed. Multiple states allow facilities that claim a religious affiliation to avoid licensing requirements and oversight. For example, a Mississippi law exempts facilities from licensing requirements by simply operating "under the auspices of a religious institution."[69] The law has effects. The *Daily Journal* reported an investigation into runaway children from Summit's View Ranch for Boys, which claimed the religious exemption, and the deputy sheriff's incident report stated: "I asked the boys why they ran away and they told me that they felt safer in the woods on their own than they did at the ranch."[70] The last name of the ranch's founder is Lovely. A former staff member was interviewed by the *Clarion-Ledger*:

> Tomlinson said he once saw Lovely reprimand a child in front of other boys by forcing him to stand on a table in the kitchen. As Lovely berated the boy, he took a mop from the restroom that was used to clean up urine and rubbed it in the teen's face, he said.
>
> In another incident Tomlinson described—and was corroborated by a former student also interviewed by the Clarion Ledger—a teen was handcuffed for days to a ladder in the gym. The boy slept on the floor and was provided a bucket to relieve himself in.[71]

After more allegations found their way out of the religious veil, multiple lawsuits were filed.[72] According to the *Clarion-Ledger* investigation, ten juvenile facilities in Mississippi are exempt from CPS licensing but are still registered with the health department, and "there are an unknown number of other children's homes in Mississippi whose names are not on file with the Health Department, allowing them to operate without any state oversight."[73] And Mississippi is not alone. An investigation by *NBC* and *Dateline* in 2021 found that in twenty-three states, juvenile facilities that label themselves as religious boarding schools "do not even have to tell their state education department that they exist."[74]

A juvenile facility's religious claim should not be a false shield. As a Missouri state legislator explained in support of a bill seeking increased oversight of such facilities, "I can't find any scriptures in the Bible that would say that it's OK to physically or sexually abuse children, to starve them as means of punishment, to withhold medication, to deprive them of sleep, to force them into manual labor."[75]

Even after the US Supreme Court's decisions siding with religious organizations, a textualist reading of the Constitution not only allows but arguably requires the licensing and regulation of juvenile facilities claiming religious affiliation. The Constitution's establishment and free exercise clauses require that "Congress shall make no law respecting an establishment of religion, or prohibiting the free exercise thereof." In cases challenging the application of state laws and regulations to religious organizations, the Supreme Court has made clear that only laws that are not neutral and generally applicable will be subject to strict scrutiny judicial review. In the 1993 decision *Church of the Lukumi Babalu Aye, Inc. v. Hialeah*, the court explained that "[i]n addressing the constitutional protection for free exercise of religion, our cases establish the general proposition that a law that is neutral and of general applicability need not be justified by a compelling governmental interest."[76] Chief Justice John Robert's opinion regarding COVID-19 restrictions in *Roman Catholic Diocese of Brooklyn v. Cuomo* (2020) relied on that same principle: "Because the challenged restrictions are not 'neutral' and of 'general applicability,' they must satisfy 'strict scrutiny,' and this means that they must be 'narrowly tailored' to serve a 'compelling' state interest."[77] Following this reasoning, state regulations and licensing requirements for juvenile facilities—whether they are called RTCs or boarding schools—do not need to exempt religious organizations in order to be neutral and generally applicable. In fact, the state laws that provide preference to religious organizations through licensing and regulation exemptions are the provisions that raise constitutional concerns.

In 1961 the Supreme Court unanimously ruled in *Torcaso v. Watkins* that Maryland's requirement for a person holding public office to state a belief in God violated the establishment clause. Justice Hugo Black did not mince words in his opinion: "We repeat and again reaffirm that neither a State nor the Federal Government can constitutionally force a person 'to profess a belief or disbelief in any religion.' Neither can constitutionally pass laws or impose requirements which aid all religions as against non-believers, and neither can aid those religions based on a belief in the existence of God as against those religions founded on different beliefs."[78] In another unanimous decision in 1968, the Supreme Court held in *Epperson v. Arkansas* that a state law forbidding public schoolteachers from discussing evolution violated the establishment clause. Justice Abe Fortas could not have been clearer in explaining that the clause "mandates governmental neutrality between religion and religion, and between religion and nonreligion."[79] Thus, if state law exempts juvenile facilities that claim religious affiliation from licensing or regulations that apply to secular juvenile facilities, the neutrality requirement is arguably violated.

The Profit in Nonprofit Juvenile Facilities

There is not much "non" in nonprofits when the organizations focus on revenue over mission. So, in the chase for money, a question can arise: If the leaders of an organization claim a nonprofit status, are those individuals ethically driven by a true charitable mission, or are they using the harm experienced by others as a financial opportunity while avoiding taxes?

Some organizations operating juvenile facilities have structured themselves as nonprofits but hired a for-profit company to run the facilities. For example, the Lakeside Academy—where Cornelius Frederick died—was a program of Lakeside for Children, which claimed nonprofit status. On the organization's 990 form filed in 2019, a tax filing required by the IRS for tax-exempt nonprofit organizations, Lakeside lists $13,614,872 in total revenue for the year, $13,253,878 coming from government grants.[80] Then, in terms of expenses, Lakeside lists zero compensation or salary to the organization's officers or employees but lists $12,963,518 paid to Sequel Youth & Family Services.[81] So Lakeside paid over 95 percent of its total revenue to the for-profit company that operated the juvenile facility. Sequel used this collaboration with other nonprofit organizations as well. An investigation by *American Public Media* explains that Sequel teamed up with nonprofits to obtain children placed from California, "one of Sequel's most lucrative clients," because "California law requires that any facilities housing children from the state be 'operated on a nonprofit basis only.'"[82] Another investigation, by the *San Francisco Chronicle and Imprint*, found that Sequel's arrangements with nonprofits resulted in the company receiving about half of the children that California sent to out-of-state facilities between 2015 and 2020: "This practice has allowed Sequel to skirt California's mandate that the campuses be nonprofit, and collect public funds that, as a for-profit company, it alone would not otherwise be eligible to receive."[83] Only after the news reports did California decide to pull the children back out of Sequel-operated facilities and bring the children back to their home state.[84]

Such examples raise questions of accountability, not only for nonprofits using for-profit companies to run their facilities, but also for the state and local governments knowingly sending children into such arrangements. Also, the examples call for investigations to determine if False Claims Act and tax code violations may be occurring, and whether nonprofits that are profiting from vulnerable children—including organizations that claim religious affiliation—should lose their tax-exempt status.[85]

Further, concerns can still arise about nonprofit juvenile facilities that do not contract their operations to for-profit companies, such as the Wordsworth Academy in Philadelphia. In 2016 the Pennsylvania Department of Human Services revoked Wordsworth's license, explaining that "[t]he Department's decision to revoke your license is based on your failure to comply with the Department's regulations and gross incompetence, negligence and misconduct in operating the facility."[86] An incident report attached to the revocation letter provides a brief description of the death of a child, referred to as Child #1. According to the report, three staff members entered the boy's room looking for an iPod: "During the restraint, according to Staff Member B who was holding the legs of Child #1, Staff Member A was observed throwing punches at the ribs of Child #1." Children who were in the hallway "overheard Child #1 yelling 'get off me, I can't breathe' and then everything went silent."[87] An investigation by the *Philadelphia Inquirer* provides more details about the death of Child #1, David Hess, a Black seventeen-year-old "who suffered from profound mental illness."[88] According to the investigation, David was not the first child subjected to violence at Wordsworth: "In the last decade, at least 49 sex crimes have been reported at Wordsworth, including 12 rapes and 23 accounts of sexual abuse, an Inquirer and Daily News investigation has found."[89]

While incidents like this were occurring at Wordsworth, a private nonprofit, Community Behavioral Health (CBH), was supposed to be overseeing Philadelphia's facilities, like Wordsworth, and approving payments of government funds. CBH reportedly "funneled about $6 million a year in state and federal money to Wordsworth to care for a steady stream of young people at an average cost of $326 per day."[90] According to the *Philadelphia Inquirer*, CBH "continued to write those checks even after it learned of serious problems at the facility, including sexual assaults."[91] It wasn't until after David Hess was killed that Wordsworth's license was revoked.

Yet another nonprofit organization, Public Health Management Corporation (PHMC), then announced its plan to acquire Wordsworth. PHMC describes itself as "a regional public health institute . . . [w]ith more than 350 programs in 70 locations," and both runs its own programs and is the parent company to smaller nonprofits.[92] In its announcement, PHMC explained that "[a]s part of the acquisition, Wordsworth will reorganize its financial affairs under Chapter 11 of the Bankruptcy Code."[93] According to the *Inquirer*, an attorney for sexual assault victims at Wordsworth expressed concern that "if this bankruptcy and acquirement is used to rob the victims of compensation for the poor treatment that they've received through Wordsworth."[94] And the attorney hired for the bankruptcy proceedings was candid: "'PHMC would never do this if they were going to be exposed to potential unlimited liabilities,' McMichael said. 'They wouldn't touch it with a 10-foot pole. Nobody else would either. That's why a bankruptcy is necessary.'"[95] Illustrating the interconnections, after the bankruptcy proceedings and acquisition were completed, CBH—the nonprofit organization that is supposed to oversee payments to PHMC and behavioral health facilities across the city—announced it was hiring a senior director from PHMC to serve as its new CEO.[96] Meanwhile, although also a nonprofit, PHMC provided its CEO over $1.2 million in annual reportable and other compensation as of 2018, according to the organization's IRS 990 form.[97]

Next, while harm at Wordsworth Academy was coming to light, yet another private nonprofit, Devereux Advanced Behavioral Health, had been operating juvenile facilities in Pennsylvania and other states for decades.[98] A 2017 story in *Main Line Today* described a transformation in leadership and business mindset at Devereux that had started twenty-three years earlier, focused on controlling costs and spending:

> In 1994, Devereux's board of directors recruited Robert Kreider, a well-known economic guru and co-CEO of Fairmount Capital Advisors who'd just strengthened Main Line Health System by refinancing the debt of individual hospitals. Kreider launched an investigation of Devereux's finances, and the news was shocking. The organization was overextended on finances, debt and human resources. . . .
>
> Debt refinancing, asset allocation and credit ratings are brain food for Kreider. He gets animated when expounding on them, and his financial gymnastics resulted in one undeniable bottom line: By the end of 1995, Devereux was on economically solid ground.[99]

In more excellent journalism by the *Philadelphia Inquirer*, a 2020 investigation uncovered a history across multiple states: "At least 41 children as young as 12, and with IQs as low as 50, have been raped or sexually assaulted by Devereux staff members in the last 25 years, an Inquirer investigation has found."[100] Also according to the *Inquirer*, "DHS said it has received 254 reports of suspected child abuse and neglect on Devereux's three Chester County campuses from Jan. 1, 2018, to Nov. 16, 2020."[101] Philadelphia's Department of Human Services (DHS) and CBH had reportedly provided about $20 million to Devereux in 2019 and 2020, including for foster care and residential treatment services. After these revelations, DHS and CBH initiated a safety review and removed fifty-three children from some Devereux facilities, but other contractual foster care services with Devereux were continued.[102] Reading through Devereux's listing of senior management shows that its senior vice president and general counsel previously "spent 23 years as chief counsel for the Department of Public Welfare" (later named the Pennsylvania Department of Human Services).[103]

PRIVATE EQUITY FIRMS, REAL ESTATE INVESTMENT TRUSTS, AND LARGE-SCALE CORPORATE PROFIT FROM JAILING CHILDREN AND THE POOR

The companies get bigger, as does their cash. Structured as private equity firms, real estate investment trusts, or other corporate entities, large companies buy up other companies that run prisons, immigrant detention centers, juvenile facilities, behavioral health treatment centers, halfway houses, electronic monitoring, and so forth. The companies frequently change hands in lucrative deal after lucrative deal, buying and selling beds—with barely a mention of the vulnerable humans in them—with investor presentations about "occupancy rates," profitability, acquisition strategy, cost control, tax avoidance, and market growth. Again, the companies need bodies in the beds to make money. And the larger the companies, the more bodies are needed.

GEO Group, Inc., traded on the New York Stock Exchange as GEO, is one of the largest companies that owns and operates adult and juvenile correctional facilities. In its 2020 annual report filed with the Securities and Exchange Commission (SEC), GEO describes the scope of its operations in the United States, Australia, South Africa, and the United Kingdom: "As of December 31, 2020, our worldwide operations included the management and/or ownership of approximately 93,000 beds at 118 secure and community-based facilities, including idle facilities, and also includes the provision of community supervision services for more than 210,000 individuals."[104]

In 2012 GEO restructured itself as a real estate investment trust (REIT), a structure originally established by former president Dwight D. Eisenhower to allow individuals to invest in commercial real estate without needing to own the real estate.[105] REITs eventually caught the attention of organizations that one wouldn't normally associate with being a real estate company: large corporations like Sabra Health Care REIT, Inc. purchased nursing homes across the country—which like GEO purchased prisons, detention centers, and juvenile facilities to generate revenue from incarcerating children and adults.[106] Why the REIT structure? As GEO explains in its 2020 SEC filing, "The Company's effective tax rate differs from the U.S. statutory rate of 21% primarily due to a zero tax rate on earnings generated by the Company's REIT operations."[107]

GEO recognizes that it competes not only with other companies but with the very government entities with which it seeks contracts: "We compete directly with the public sector, where governmental agencies responsible for the operation of secure services, processing services, youth services, community-based services and reentry facilities are often seeking to retain projects that might otherwise become a public-private partnership."[108] GEO also recognizes that it needs those government entities to send children and adults to facilities to increase its "utilization rates": "[W]ith respect to our contracts that have no fixed-price payments, we are highly dependent upon the governmental agencies with which we have contracts to utilize our facilities. Under a per diem rate structure, a decrease in our utilization rates could cause a decrease in revenues and profitability."[109] Dependent on utilization rates, GEO was significantly impacted by COVID-19: "[T]he spread of COVID-19 has resulted in lower occupancy at a number of our facilities and programs beginning in late March and continuing throughout 2020 into 2021 and is therefore expected to continue to result in lower full year revenues."[110]

GEO has been the subject of multiple lawsuits and investigations. For example, the DOJ completed an investigation in 2012 into the Walnut Grove Youth Correctional Facility (WGYCF) in Mississippi, which the DOJ reports had been contractually operated by GEO since 2010.[111] A federal judge entered an order in March 2012 approving the settlement and consent decree of a class action lawsuit regarding the facility and included this conclusion: "The sum of these actions and inactions by WGYCF, WGDA, the State, the Department of Corrections, GEO and Health Assurance, L.L.C., paints a picture of such horror as should be unrealized anywhere in the civilized world."[112] The judge expressed concern that the violations and harm were ongoing: "As of the date of the hearing, according to testimony, management has done nothing to address staffing issues. WGYCF has allowed a cesspool of unconstitutional and inhuman acts and conditions to germinate, the sum of which places the offenders at substantial ongoing risk."[113] Then, in April 2012, soon after the "federal court ordered sweeping changes," as NPR explains, the "news broke that GEO would be out as manager of its three Mississippi prisons by July," including the Walnut Grove juvenile facility.[114]

In another example, a federal securities class action complaint was filed in 2020 alleging that GEO "made false and/or misleading statements and/or failed to disclose," that "GEO Group maintained woefully ineffective COVID-19 response procedures," and that "those inadequate procedures subjected residents of the Company's halfway houses to significant health risks," among other allegations.[115] Also, a *Mother Jones* news investigation asserts that "a series of lawsuits filed in federal courts from Washington to Georgia" include "allegations of coercive labor practices inside for-profit immigration detention centers run by GEO and its main competitor, CoreCivic," claiming that the companies "that operate the detention centers are violating minimum wage, unjust enrichment, and antislavery laws by coercing detainees to work for free, or, in some cases, $1 per day."[116]

Leading up to the 2020 elections, a *Washington Post* investigation found that "GEO Group officials gave six-figure donations to Trump's election campaign and inaugural committee" and "have spent millions on lobbying the administration."[117] On January 26, 2021, six days after he was sworn in, President Joseph Biden issued an executive order directing that "[t]he Attorney General shall not renew Department of Justice contracts with privately operated criminal detention facilities" and included the following policy statement:

> More than two million people are currently incarcerated in the United States, including a disproportionate number of people of color. There is broad consensus that our current system of mass incarceration imposes significant costs and hardships on our society and communities and does not make us safer. To decrease incarceration levels, we must reduce profit-based incentives to incarcerate by phasing out the Federal Government's reliance on privately operated criminal detention facilities. . . .
>
> The Federal Government also has a responsibility to ensure the safe and humane treatment of those in the Federal criminal justice system. However, as the Department of Justice's Office of Inspector General found in 2016, privately operated criminal detention facilities do not maintain the same levels of safety and security for people in the Federal criminal justice system or for correctional staff. We have a duty to provide these individuals with safe working and living conditions.[118]

GEO released a statement the same day that the executive order was issued, asserting that "President Biden's Executive Order is a solution in search of a problem."[119]

In addition to buying prisons and detention centers, large companies have also profited through buying and selling RTCs. For example, Acadia Healthcare Company, Inc. is traded on the NASDAQ and explains in its SEC filings that it "develops and operates inpatient psychiatric facilities, residential treatment centers, group homes, substance abuse facilities and facilities providing outpatient behavioral healthcare services," and as of "September 30, 2020, the Company operated 582 behavioral healthcare facilities with approximately 18,300 beds in 40 states, the U.K. and Puerto Rico."[120]

One of Acadia's acquisitions involved CRC Health Group, a company that was founded in 1995 with The Camp Recovery Center in California. According to an article in *Behavioral Healthcare Tomorrow*, the buyer of the "camp," Barry Karlin, "was barely 40, living in the lofty air of high-tech entrepreneurship, and savoring his slice of success in America," and "knew nothing of addiction treatment, outside of what he had stumbled across in the press."[121] The article explains that when "a colleague told him that a chemical dependency facility in Northern California might be for sale," Karlin "uttered the reply that will forever be his punch line. 'I asked him, 'What kind of chemicals do they manufacture?'"[122] After that purchase, "[w]ith the contacts and reputation he built in technology and venture capital (one of his former companies established navigational systems now routinely installed in luxury automobiles), Karlin brought with him uncommon access to financing."[123]

In 2002 the private equity firm North Castle Partners acquired an ownership interest in CRC through a "nationwide roll-up strategy."[124] In 2006 Bain Capital finalized an agreement to acquire CRC for $720 million, "which provided more than 3x equity return for North Castle."[125] An article in *Fortune* about Bain's acquisition of CRC describes what a roll-up strategy means in the world of private equity; it had been used in the waste management and funeral homes business, and then was applied to profiting from vulnerable children: "In the handbook of private equity investing techniques, few make more intuitive sense than the 'roll-up.' Borrow some money, buy up small players in a fragmented industry, cut costs, find synergies, juice profits, increase multiples, pay down debt, and sell at a profit. Financial operators have done it well in waste management, funeral homes, and advertising."[126] With Bain ownership and money, CRC reportedly purchased more facilities and companies, including Aspen Education Group, which itself had already acquired several "troubled teen" facilities.[127] According to the *Fortune* article, CRC "proceeded to go on a shopping spree," and although purchases slowed during the financial crisis, CRC "resumed its buying binge" in 2011.[128] Then, in 2014, Acadia Healthcare reached an agreement to purchase CRC from Bain Capital for $1.2 billion.[129]

Illustrating connections in the industry, the private equity firm Altamont Capital indicates that after Jerry Rhodes left his role as CEO of CRC, he became an operating partner.[130] In 2017 Altamont acquired a majority stake in Sequel Youth and Family Services, the company discussed in detail earlier.[131] Altamont reports that Rhodes joined Sequel's board of directors.[132]

In the background of the buying and selling of juvenile facilities, lawsuits and investigations reportedly followed CRC through its various owners, including a 2012 investigation published in *Salon* regarding concerns at multiple CRC facilities.[133] For example, Oregon required two Aspen Education facilities to close in 2009, and "investigators found nine cases of abuse and neglect at Mount Bachelor Academy in central Oregon, including incidents of 'sexualized role play,' in which young patients were allegedly forced to do lap dances during therapy sessions."[134] The *Salon* investigation reports that "[c]ourt documents and ex-staffers also allege that such incidents reflect, in part, a broader corporate culture at Aspen's owner, CRC Health Group," and that "[l]awsuits and critics have claimed that CRC prizes profits, and the avoidance of outside scrutiny, over the health and safety of its clients."[135]

Further, CRC reportedly agreed to a settlement of Medicaid fraud claims in 2014, agreeing "to pay the state of Tennessee and the federal government $9.25 million over allegations that it provided substandard substance abuse treatment and overcharged the state's Medicaid system."[136] A DOJ press release describes a 2019 settlement agreement in which CRC's new owner Acadia agreed to pay "$17 million to resolve allegations of a billing scheme that defrauded Medicaid" in CRC facilities in West Virginia.[137] An article in the *Santa Fe New Mexican* in 2020 discusses more lawsuits and how the state child welfare agency revoked the license of an Acadia-owned juvenile facility: "Allegations against the residential treatment center for troubled youth were horrific: numerous suicide attempts, fights that injured both staff and kids, sexual abuse of children as young as 7."[138]

Across the country, a business model seems to permeate operations of prisons, detention centers, and the numerous forms of residential treatment facilities, whether run by for-profit, nonprofit, or religious organizations—or the many government-run facilities that strive to operate more like businesses. More bodies in the beds. Lower costs. More money. Such a business model, paired with minimal oversight, has led to harm. And absent reform, harm will continue. In 2007 the managing director of the Forensic Audits and Special Investigations Unit with the US Government Accountability Office (GAO) provided congressional testimony regarding juvenile residential treatment facilities, testimony that is not easy to read: "Moving on to the results of our work, we identified thousands of reported cases of death and abuse at these programs. Sources of these allegations include HHS, state agencies, the Internet and pending and closed civil and criminal lawsuits. Allegations include physical, emotional and mental abuse. Examples of abuse include: youth being forced to eat their own vomit; denied adequate food; being forced to lie in urine or feces; being kicked, beaten and thrown to the ground; and being forced to use a toothbrush to clean a toilet and then forced to use that toothbrush on their teeth."[139] The 2007 testimony also included haunting foreshadowing: "It seems the only way staff could be convinced that these kids were not faking it was when they stopped breathing or had no pulse."[140] Over fifteen years later, the money—and the harm—continue to flow.

CHAPTER 8

Racialized Harm of the Injustice Enterprise

America's founding was paradoxically framed with words of equal justice but built from racial and economic injustice. Now, the commodification of inequality—which began on the backs of enslaved persons—permeates America's justice systems.

Racial and economic inequalities are inextricably intertwined in the profiteering used by each of our foundational institutions of justice. Vulnerable children and adults of every demographic are impacted, throughout America's cities, towns, suburbs, mountains, farmland, and everywhere in between. But the operations of the injustice enterprise have a starkly disproportionate racial impact.

With that lens of understanding, this chapter reflects on how racial injustice fuels the machinations of the machine. Imagine sounds of the factory, the steadily disrupted hum of destructive production, with ancient and unending repetition.

"BOY BURGLAR": REVISITING THE RACIAL HISTORY OF THE SHELBY COUNTY JUVENILE COURT

Chapter 1 briefly introduced the business operations of the Shelby County Juvenile Court in Memphis, Tennessee. Here we look back to that court's beginning in 1910 as an example of the racially unequal foundation that underlies juvenile justice systems across the country.

The *Tennessee Historical Quarterly* published a history of the court that described a punitive and discriminatory structure at its inception. The judge could "sentence the children brought before him to serve on the city rock pile (the county 'workhouse'), or bind them over to the criminal courts," and "built-in inequities and biases" were stark: "There was a significant relationship between race and offense, and between race and disposition. Blacks were far more likely to be referred to the court for delinquent offenses. Whites, in contrast were about twice as likely to be referred for dependency and neglect and status offenses. This reflects a prevailing view in Memphis and elsewhere that black youths and their behavior were more often viewed as 'criminal' than their white counterparts."[1] Further, while White children were more frequently sent to reform and industrial schools for the goal of rehabilitation, many Black children "were simply handled by the adult system and sentenced to prison, or they were handled informally by the police, e.g., 'curbstone justice.'"[2]

In 1914 the court moved into a larger building "[s]oon to be known as the 'White Juvenile Court,'" including the detention center, school, gymnasium, and an outdoor playground and garden—but only for the White children. The court processed and jailed the Black children across town: "The Colored Detention Home was a small, one story building in the southern part of the city," and "the building was described as 'an old house, badly equipped, its sewer connection in the back yard.'"[3] With this history, the *Tennessee Historical Quarterly* included and described an aged photograph from the collections of the Memphis and Shelby County Public Library: "A four-year old child, described as 'boy burglar,' stands in front of the Colored Detention Home."[4] The photograph, provided by the library, shows the child clinging to what appears to be a worn stuffed animal.

Digging deeper into historical records, we find more details of how the juvenile court treated Black youth separately, and inhumanly so. During this time, the National Child Labor Committee was conducting broad investigations of child welfare across multiple states. In 1920 the report *Child Welfare in Tennessee* was published.[5] The report provides disturbing facts about the Shelby County Juvenile Court, including a description of the separate detention center for Black youth.

The 1920 report explains that "[t]he Memphis court now operates two detention homes, one for white and one for colored children."[6] Regarding access to education during the time of imprisonment, "[t]he

FIGURE 5. Child standing in front of "Colored Detention Home," Memphis, Tennessee, ca. 1910. *Source:* Memphis and Shelby County Room, Memphis Public Library & Information Center, Scruggs Collection.

white children attend the Mary B. West Special School in the detention home building under the teachers furnished by the city board of education," while the Black children were "entirely deprived of schooling during their period of detention."[7] The report takes us on a verbal tour through the separate facilities, starting with the Detention Home for White Children: "A large waiting-room made attractive with growing plants and pictures. . . . The remodeling of the second floor of the building has been so skillfully planned . . . all furnishings are of good quality and cleanliness, the sunshine pouring into every room and the spirit of friendliness which pervades the place make the detention home attractive. . . . Each dormitory has its own bathroom. . . . The supply of gowns and bed linen is adequate and the beds are comfortable."[8]

Then we travel across the city, as the report explains: "In striking contrast to the accommodations provided for the white children are conditions of the colored detention home. A five-room flat on the second story of negro tenement house in a particularly undesirable neighborhood has been converted into a detention home by the simple process of barring the doors and windows."[9]

Moving into the building, we find the holding space for Black youth and encounter a group of six children huddled together in the dark, including six- and seven-year-old boys:

> [O]pening on the hall by a heavily grated door is a small room used as the boys dormitory. The one window is protected by cross-bars of iron at least two inches wide, which so effectively cut off the light that on a sunshiny day one could not see across the room clearly enough to tell that six little negroes were huddled before the open fireplace. Two of the boys present on one occasion when the home was visited were little fellows of six and seven, both dependent children who were locked into this dark room with four older delinquent boys and were released only at meal-time. They had absolutely no provision for recreation.[10]

Leaving the room, we find the only facilities available for the children, shared by the boys and girls: "Next to the shabbily-equipped kitchen was a dark, ill ventilated bath-room, with one tub, and in a separate closet, a foul-smelling toilet, which was the only provision for the boys and girls, dependents and delinquents and attendants."[11] And walking out the back door, "[t]he back porch, which might have offered a breath of fresh air to the little children, was used for the storage of coal."[12]

This detention home was apparently considered better treatment of Black youth than in other Tennessee counties. Although a new state law at the time discouraged placing children in adult prisons, the law was largely ignored, especially for Black children. Thus, for the Black youth who were not detained in detention homes with conditions such as those in Memphis, they were often processed into adult prisons and jails. The report explains that several counties in Tennessee did not separate the children from the adult prisoners, and one county used its asylum to detain children. The 1920 report also provides a description of juvenile detention in Chattanooga: "The situation as regards detention, however, is not absurd, but tragic. Although the special act forbids the detention of children in a 'jail or detention station with other prisoners,' the provision of a proper place of detention is optional and in the nine years since the organization of the court, no place but the jail has been made available. One hundred and seventy-two children under 16, according to the jail register, were during 1919 incarcerated for periods ranging from one to 150 days. They occupied the same cell-blocks and at times the same cells with adult criminals."[13] Of the 172 children incarcerated with adults during this one year in Chattanooga, 122 were

Black children (over 2.4 times the number of White children), as young as eight years old.[14]

Further, in addition to the vastly unequal detention facilities and disproportionate treatment of Black children like criminals, the juvenile courts also processed the children through the adjudication system unequally. For example, although almost half of those brought before the Shelby County Juvenile Court were Black children, the report explains that the court devoted three times the number of days and amount of time to resolving the cases of White children: "Court sessions are held regularly four times a week. Saturday morning is reserved for colored cases; Tuesday, Wednesday and Friday mornings for the white."[15]

Fast forward to 1994. Nina Bernstein, who would become a renowned journalist with the *New York Times*, completed an investigation of the Shelby County Juvenile Court and published an excellent piece for the Alicia Patterson Foundation, "Misery Funds a Legal Fiefdom."[16] As part of the investigation, Bernstein was given a tour of the court's detention center by the chief probation officer. During the tour she encountered a small Black boy, and she provides a written image of his circumstances and treatment: "Behind the locked door of a shelter unit in the detention wing, the tour stumbles on a child. He is a small black boy in drab detention clothes with a look of desolation beyond grief." When "[a]sked his age, he holds up eight fingers."[17] After the tour, the staff explained the boy "is a foster child with a speech impediment, dyslexia and 'periods of outrage.'"[18] The boy's story of trauma and path to a juvenile jail continues. After an ice storm caused a power outage at his foster home, "the foster mother said he had to leave the house and the boy became distraught" so "she took him to the nearest police precinct."[19] Bernstein explains how the police and juvenile court system responded to the boy, who was in a moment of understandable trauma, by criminalizing him: "'He was crying and screaming—he wanted his brother,' police officer Ruth Hawkins recalls. 'He wouldn't talk to us. He was out of control.' Officers arrested the sobbing eight-year-old for disorderly conduct, she says, and took him as a delinquent to juvenile detention."[20]

Fast forward again to 2019. Journalists from the *Daily Memphian* were allowed to tour and photograph the Shelby County Juvenile Court and then published an image of a small young Black child, sitting alone in the detention center's small library, head down and thin arms pulled inside his orange shirt, hidden but exposed, with words in the form of an order hovering over him on the wall above a large symbol of a sheriff's badge: "Attitude is Everything."[21] Similar to the child encountered by Bernstein, and the child one hundred years earlier when the court was founded, he was apparently struggling with trauma and clinging to himself, as "burglar boy" clung to his stuffed animal. The child in the photograph could be $hawn.

A few years before the photograph published in the *Daily Memphian*, the juvenile court asserted in its 2012 annual report that it was "known throughout the nation for its innovative efforts" and that many of its initiatives were "models for other programs in Tennessee and across the nation."[22] However, the US Department of Justice's (DOJ) Civil Rights Division also issued a report in 2012, after a multiple-year investigation, finding that the court's "administration of justice discriminates against Black children," "fails to provide constitutionally required due process to children of all races," and "violates the substantive due process rights of detained youth by not providing them with reasonably safe conditions of confinement."[23] As a result, the DOJ initiated an oversight agreement requiring numerous improvements and ongoing monitoring. But soon after the Trump administration took control, an investigation by *MLK50* found that the Shelby County juvenile court judge, mayor, and sheriff had joined in writing to the new attorney general, Jeff Sessions, requesting the end of DOJ monitoring.[24] Sessions, who had already made clear his opposition to federal oversight that sought to redress civil rights concerns in state justice systems, readily agreed.[25]

The due process monitor entered a final report in 2018, expressing concern that "the structure of the Juvenile Court of Memphis and Shelby County remains deeply flawed enabling a culture of intimidation that undermines due process," and that "[t]he abrupt termination of oversight . . . failed to recognize that Juvenile Court has actively resisted compliance with the word and the spirit of the Agreement and is likely to result in the Court reverting to prior practices."[26] As an example, the monitor described how the judge controlled children's attorneys.[27] The University of Memphis School of Law had created a Children's Defense Clinic, but after "the airing of a podcast where the Clinic Director expressed concerns about the conditions of confinement in the juvenile detention center, the juvenile court judge responded by instructing the Panel Coordinator to stop assigning cases to the clinic."[28] According to the report, the judge emailed the dean of the law school and the president of the university, complaining that the clinic director "maligned me directly on a podcast and tweet," arguing that he had "no input" into who was hired for the clinical position, and that "[t]he school's inability to discipline its staff is mystifying."[29] The monitor's report also provided copies of internal emails using derogatory language, including an email from the court's chief legal officer that referred to the clinic director by asking "Did she spend her Christmas break with the Stepford Wives? I may barf."[30]

A core finding of the original 2012 DOJ report was that "Black children are disproportionately represented in almost every phase of the Shelby County juvenile justice system." In the 2019 "state of the court" address, the juvenile court judge celebrated the end of DOJ oversight, declaring "mission accomplished" and describing his court as a "model court."[31] However, also in 2019, an investigation by the *Memphis Flyer* explains how the juvenile court transferred more children into the adult criminal justice system than any other county in Tennessee, and almost 96 percent were Black children, an even greater racially disproportionate impact than at the court's beginnings.[32] Further, the court's 2019 data showed that almost 90 percent of those placed in detention were Black children, and almost 90 percent of the most common juvenile charges were against Black children.[33] According to the *Daily Memphian*, the former DOJ oversight settlement coordinator explained that "I don't think it is a surprise to anybody" that "[a]t best, nothing's changed and at worst it could be getting worse."[34]

Meanwhile, Shelby County's juvenile court judge was elected treasurer of the National Council of Juvenile and Family Court Judges in 2018, with the organization calling him a trailblazer in his home state.[35] And the organization elected him president in 2020.[36]

Then, three years after the juvenile court asked the Trump administration to end DOJ oversight, the county's Juvenile Justice Consortium issued a report in 2021 about ongoing concerns at the court, including due process, safety, and racial disparities.[37] The *Memphis Commercial Appeal* reports that the county's commissioners voted to request the DOJ to reevaluate the court's practices.[38]

Model court? The court had made a similar proclamation of success in 1973, as a history of the court in the *Tennessee Historical Quarterly* explains: "In the annual report of 1973 it was written that the goal to make the juvenile court a 'model court' has 'been fully realized.'"[39] Going all the way back to the court's beginning in 1910, we find a similar assertion: "In the opinion of local supporters and visiting notables, this court was a model juvenile court."[40] But the historical account of the court's activities in 1910 describes pervasive inequality.[41] The disproportionate racial impact of the court's practices in 1910 presents concerns similar to those raised by the DOJ more than a hundred years later. And similar concerns are found in juvenile justice systems across the nation.

RACIAL INJUSTICE FUELS THE INJUSTICE FACTORY

Earlier chapters uncovered details of the contractual arrangements in which justice systems are commodifying vulnerable children and their parents. This section examines how those systems disproportionately target children of color and their families as the resources used in the revenue machines. The resulting operations harness power from both civil and criminal justice systems, already built on foundations of structural inequalities—and accelerated with the lure of money into continuously intertwined racialized harm. In the words of Cedric J. Robinson, who developed the concept of "racial capitalism" in 1983, "it could be expected that racialism would inevitably permeate the social structures emergent from capitalism."[42]

Juvenile Courts Monetizing Youth of Color

First we revisit Ohio, where juvenile courts developed a contractual business model now followed in multiple states by straddling and combining the criminal side of juvenile justice with the civil side of child welfare. Michele Alexander skillfully and devastatingly portrays the deep structural racism underlying America's criminal justice system impacting both juveniles and adults in *The New Jim Crow: Mass Incarceration in the Age of Colorblindness*.[43] Professor Dorothy Roberts provides equally excellent and groundbreaking accounts exposing the structural racism and harm in America's child welfare system in *Shattered Bonds: The Color of Child Welfare* and *Torn Apart: How the Child Welfare System Destroys Black Families—And How Abolition Can Build a Safer World*.[44] America's foundational justice institutions are now generating revenue from the harm of both systems.

As a brief reminder, the Ohio juvenile courts created interagency contracts through which the courts take on the foster care agency role. If the juvenile courts exercise their judicial power and rule that children are delinquent or unruly, the courts can then shift into their agency role and generate IV-E foster care revenue through the children; the courts then act like courts again to review their own actions. The more children are adjudicated delinquent, the more potential foster care revenue is generated. And most of those targeted are Black children.

Consider Cuyahoga County, which includes Cleveland. According to state records, the Cuyahoga County juvenile court accumulated $4 million in IV-E revenue reserves resulting from this strategy in 2017, and the court was adding about $1.5 million a year in IV-E revenue from the children as of 2019.[45] Although Black individuals account for about 30 percent of the population in Cuyahoga County, court records show that 75 percent of those processed and adjudicated by the juvenile court as delinquent or unruly are Black youth.[46] Also, a review of the data shows that the disparate impact increased from intake to court disposition. At the point of intakes/charges, about 70 percent of those charged were Black youth, compared to 22 percent White youth. And at the stage of court dispositions/rulings of delinquency and unruliness, about 75 percent were Black youth, compared to 17 percent White youth.[47] Similarly, the Summit County juvenile court was obtaining more than $1.1 million a year through this strategy as of 2015.[48] White individuals comprise almost 80 percent of the total population in Summit County. However, although the court records do not provide the racial breakdown regarding delinquency actions, the court's annual report lists that Black and "Bi-racial" youth accounted for over 70 percent of children held by the court in juvenile detention.[49] Pulling back from the individual counties to look at statewide data, a 2019 Ohio report explains that "[r]elative to the population, White youth outnumber African-American youth 5:1." However, "[w]hen examining state data, which includes jurisdictions with varied population sizes and racial and ethnic composition, African American youth are nearly 6 times more likely to be arrested than white youth," and "African-American youth are 3.44 times more likely to be referred to juvenile court."[50]

Looking to Louisiana, where juvenile courts use IV-E revenue strategies similar to those in Ohio, youth of color are again disproportionately targeted. For example, a 2019 report indicated that "[y]outh of color in Calcasieu Parish were referred to juvenile court at rates three times higher than that of white youth," that Black youth in Jefferson Parish "are overrepresented at every contact point" in the parish's juvenile justice system, and that "[e]ven though Black youth made up only thirty-three percent of the population [in Jefferson Parish], they represented sixty-nine percent of all youth referred to court."[51]

The racialized commodification continues into juvenile probation departments. Probation departments are sometimes run directly by the juvenile courts and sometimes operated independently under the state juvenile justice agencies, but the revenue-driven and racialized search for child commodities is the same. As detailed in chapter 5, the scope of the probation industry is vast. The following descriptions are just a few examples of how probation departments' revenue strategies disproportionately impact youth of color.

Georgia's Department of Juvenile Justice, which includes juvenile probation services, created its own Office of Federal Programs and Revenue Maximization Unit with the goal of using children to maximize revenue from federal aid.[52] Through this "Rev Max" initiative, juvenile probation officers are required to use the children to try to establish eligibility for IV-E foster care revenue. Further, the agency will also use the children to maximize Medicaid revenue.[53] And if the children are disabled or have deceased parents and thus are eligible to receive disability or survivor benefits, the agency will take control of the children's money and then will take most of the children's funds.[54] Within this system focused on maximizing revenue from children, the impact on Black youth is devastating. A 2018 report regarding "disproportionate minority contact" in Georgia's juvenile justice system explains that "African American youth were at greater risk of being referred to the juvenile justice system as compared to White youth almost every year for which we calculated a [relative rate index] and for almost every county." The report provides details on how Black youth are targeted at increasingly disproportionate rates at each stage, in which they are more deeply pulled into the juvenile justice system:

> Statewide, African American youth make up 34% of the at-risk youth population. The magnitude and frequency of disproportionate contact that African American youth have with the juvenile justice system increases their portion of the population to 60% of those referred and 62% of cases petitioned. The proportion of African American youth who are deeper in the juvenile justice system jumps again to 71% of those confined and 67% of those committed to DJJ.[55] While the portion of African American youth increased at outcomes further into the system, the White youth population decreased.

The same trend continues in other states. The Florida, Texas, Arizona, California, Missouri, and Nebraska (among several more states) juvenile justice and probation systems are also financially incentivized to use children to claim IV-E foster care revenue, and they all disproportionately target youth of color. In Florida, although Black children account for about 21 percent of the juvenile population, data from the state's Department of Juvenile Justice shows that Black children are subjected to over half of juvenile arrests, over 58 percent of "secure detention," and over 60 percent of sentences to "residential commitment."[56] In

Texas, Black youth "experienced the largest rate of disproportionate contact with the juvenile justice system at the moment of arrest, diversion, and detention," and "Hispanic minorities also purportedly experienced a higher rate of arrest, diversion, and detention than white juveniles."[57] Although Black individuals account for only about 5 percent of the population in Arizona, the state "has almost four times as many Black children in jail compared to white kids," and state data shows disproportionate impact in various stages of the juvenile justice system against Black, Native American, and Hispanic or Latino youth.[58] A 2021 California study uncovered a devastatingly alarming statistic: half of all Black and Native American children in California have been subjected to child protective services investigations during their childhoods.[59] Further, a 2020 study explains that Black youth represent only 6 percent of the total youth population in California but 36 percent of youth committed to the Department of Juvenile Justice. Also in California, Black youth are 7.7 times more likely to have a petition filed in juvenile court, 5.1 times more likely to be referred to probation, and 31.1 times (no, that is not a typo) more likely to be committed to the department compared to White youth.[60] A state report regarding "disproportionate minority contact" in Missouri "has determined disproportionality exists at every contact point" of the juvenile justice system, and the city of St. Louis reports that "Black children are nearly five times as likely as white children to be referred to juvenile court."[61] And reports in Nebraska show that Black, Native American, and Hispanic or Latino youth face significant overrepresentation in multiple stages of the state's juvenile justice process.[62]

The trend continues across the country. In fact, during a national trend in which the overall number of juvenile delinquency cases has declined since 2005, the proportion of delinquency cases involving Black youth has increased.[63] The statistics—and the moneyed business operations of juvenile justice systems—are lined up against Black children and other children of color.

IV-D Child Support Factory Monetizing Harm to Black Families

America's child support policies are built on racial and economic injustice. From the importation of the English poor laws to the development of bastardy acts and the discriminatory label of illegitimacy, America's justice systems surrounding families embraced deep structural inequalities at our country's beginning. The early practices targeted impoverished children and their parents, were often punitive toward poor White families, and were even more uniformly devastating to Black families. The disproportionate harm continued through the racialized evolution of intertwined child support and welfare policies, including "man in the house" rules, and the demonization of "deadbeat dads" and "welfare queens."

Today, the structural injustices continue. And as laid out in prior chapters, America's foundational justice systems are contractually profiting from the harm.

Bastardy Acts, Poor Laws, and Race

The poor laws and bastardy acts in the early American colonies (and then states), described in chapter 3, developed alongside the laws enforcing slavery and discriminatory treatment of the free Black population. The early laws sought to discourage impoverished parents from having children born out of wedlock, using harsh punishments such as forcing parents to indemnify towns for the financial burdens of their "illegitimate" children. The first child support obligations began from this punitive framework.

The early colonies and states applied the poor laws and bastardy acts to both Black families and White families, but free Black families were targeted much more harshly, and enslaved families inhumanly so. As described by William P. Quigley, "The entire legal apparatus was used to establish and enforce the enslavement of blacks," and "[t]his included the poor laws."[64] While children of White families were considered illegitimate only if born outside of recognized marriages, all children of enslaved parents—whether married or not—were considered illegitimate. In colonial Virginia, the 1705 Act Concerning Servants and Slaves provides an example of how the children and parents were treated:

> [I]f any woman servant shall have a bastard child by a negro, or mulatto, over and above the years service due to her master or owner, she shall immediately, upon the expiration of her time to her then present master or owner, pay down to the church-wardens of the parish wherein such child shall be born, for the use of the said parish, fifteen pounds current money of Virginia, or be by them sold for five years, to the use aforesaid: And if a free christian white woman shall have such bastard child, by a negro, or mulatto, for every such offence, she shall, within one month after her delivery of such bastard child, pay to the church-wardens for the time being, of the parish wherein such child shall be born, for the use of the said parish fifteen pounds current money of Virginia, or be by them sold for five years to the use aforesaid: And

in both the said cases, the church-wardens shall bind the said child to be a servant, until it shall be of thirty one years of age.[65]

Under the guise of providing support to children, the early states also used the poor laws and bastardy acts to target free Black families to take their children from them for forced labor by "binding" them out to "apprenticeships." And after the towns took their children, the Black parents could still be pursued to pay support for the children's costs. A Delaware law of 1852, Of Masters, Apprentices and Servants, made clear that "[s]uch binding shall not in any manner affect the security given by the putative father, or the mother, to indemnify the county."[66] North Carolina enacted legislation in 1777 to require every county to elect "seven Freeholders to serve as Overseers of the Poor."[67] The overseers possessed immense power in interpreting and carrying out the poor laws, including the collection of poor taxes, enforcing payments of support and security by parents of children deemed illegitimate, and collaborating with the county courts "in managing the apprenticeship system for poor children": "Free blacks faced particular problems in southern slave society. Suffering both legal restrictions and limited economic opportunities, free blacks were likely to become objects of attention for local relieving authorities. Free black children were particularly vulnerable to compulsory indentures of apprenticeship. No doubt some free blacks were subject to apprenticeship as orphans, but overseers in York County were zealous in binding out poor black children generally. Indeed, the courts often gave no reason for an order of apprenticeship except that the children were black."[68] Northern states also used the poor laws to carry out inhumane treatment of Black families, again carried out by "Overseers of the Poor." For example, even though Rhode Island enacted emancipation in 1784, the local towns used poor laws to target Black children. An article by Gabriel Loiacono describes how the town councilmen and overseers used the power to "'bind out the children of blacks,'" in order "to take children—as young as three—away from their families and make contracts (or indentures) for those children to live with other families, serve those families . . . until the age of majority."[69] The Providence town council "also used the poor laws to ethnically cleanse the town,'" empowering the "overseer of the poor with walking around town; interviewing black residents, and black residents only; and compiling information the council could use to 'warn out,' or banish, black residents under the poor law."[70]

Historically mirroring the practices described in earlier chapters, in which juvenile courts review their own actions and petitions, Loiacono also describes how an overseer of the poor in Providence "signed a petition to himself" in 1806.[71] According to the article, William Richmond filed a petition to himself as one of the overseers of the poor, seeking to force the Black population out of Providence: "This Town is now infested with swarms of idle, thievish and vagabond blacks, who have no legal settlement therein, nor visible means of getting a livelihood."[72]

While early states used bastardy acts and poor laws to impose financial burdens on impoverished parents to indemnify towns for the costs of their children, the poor laws were simultaneously used to provide poor relief—the earliest form of welfare assistance in America. But the poor relief was only provided to White families. Free Black individuals were required to pay poor taxes to help support the poor relief, but "free blacks in poverty were largely ignored by poor relief officials."[73] An article by James W. Ely Jr. describes how the punishment for failing to pay poor taxes was also racially targeted: "Like whites, free blacks were required by law to pay local poor taxes. The York County Court imposed harsh penalties on blacks who defaulted. In June of 1795 the Sheriff was directed to 'hire out . . . free James, free Stephen, and free Rippon who have failed to pay their county levies and poor rates for the year 1793.' No such punishment was ever imposed on white taxpayers."[74] Other examples of harshly racialized inequality in the application of poor laws, bastardy acts, poor taxes, and laws regarding the enslaved population permeated the early American states, including using the harm of slavery to support the poor White population, as William P. Quigley explains: "[I]n Georgia, authorities imposed importation duties on incoming slaves and used the funds to assist white poor people," and "laws ordered slaveowners to provide their slaves with adequate food and care, and were fined up to twenty pounds for breaches—with the fine going to benefit poor whites within the jurisdiction."[75]

In fact, some southern states—which are now generally more disparaging of public welfare—were initially more generous in the provision of poor relief than states in the North, but it was only provided to White families in an overt effort to support their beliefs in White supremacy. In Professor Tim Lockley's historical account of rural poor relief in South Carolina, he explains that by providing poor relief only to White and not Black families, the "poor relief system was effectively racially exclusive, binding poor whites to the elite with ties of dependency and patronage."[76] According to Lockley, the White "elites" in South Carolina were concerned about poor White families not out of altruism, but because they felt the poor White population made the race look bad and therefore weakened their assertion of White supremacy: "To allow poor whites to subsist on the same meagre rations as slaves ... would have suggested that whites existed on the same basic human level as the enslaved, thereby weakening the racial basis of slavery."[77] Also, the White "elites" were worried the impoverished individuals from both races might align against them: "Anything that divided poor whites from slaves was therefore a good thing. . . . Indeed, there seems to be a direct correlation between the proportion of whites in a society and the level of poor relief offered."[78] By providing generous poor relief only to the White population, a "properly functioning poor relief system had benefits for all segments of white society in colonial South Carolina since it elevated poor whites above the subsistence levels experienced by slaves, while helping to defuse social tensions and reinforce racial hierarchies."[79]

The Bastardy Acts and Poor Laws Continue

America's current child support and welfare policies grew from this starkly racialized and harmful past. The same racist view held by the Providence overseer of the poor against "swarms of idle, thievish and vagabond blacks" tragically adhered to child support and welfare programs as time moved forward. For years to come, as state versions of poor relief continued until they were replaced by federal aid after the New Deal in the 1930s, states continued to find ways to exclude Black families from aid programs while still charging them with taxes to support the programs and pursuing Black fathers for the potential costs of their children. As Professor Dorothy Reports explained in her excellent 1996 review, "Welfare and the Problem of Black Citizenship," "[a]lthough much of the American public now views welfare dependency as a Black cultural trait, the welfare system systematically excluded Black people for most of its history."[80] For example, "in 1931 the first national survey of mothers' pensions broken down by race found that only three percent of recipients were Black."[81] Professor Alma Carten explains how such discrimination also carried over into the federal welfare program, Aid to Dependent Children, that was enacted in 1935 (renamed later Aid to Families with Dependent Children, AFDC): "The ADC was an extension of the state-operated mothers' pension programs, where white widows were the primary beneficiaries. The criteria for eligibility and need were state-determined, so blacks continued to be barred from full participation because the country operated under the "separate but equal" doctrine adopted by the Supreme Court in 1896."[82]

In addition to the other racialized limitations, states and counties mostly refused to provide welfare assistance when both parents lived together with the children. To receive help, the fathers were forced to leave. Several jurisdictions even implemented "man in the house" rules whereby welfare workers would carry out midnight raids—disproportionately targeting poor Black parents—disqualifying households from welfare if a man was found in the home. Black men were often banned from homes but blamed for being absent.

Not until the civil rights activism of the 1960s did Black families gain more access to welfare assistance. However, Professor Roberts describes how "Black welfare activists won a Pyrrhic victory" in finally opening the door to obtain even minimal assistance, as proponents of White supremacy began attacking welfare: "As AFDC became increasingly associated with Black mothers already stereotyped as lazy, irresponsible, and overly fertile, it became increasingly burdened with behavior modification, work requirements, and reduced effective benefit levels. Social Security, on the other hand, effectively transferred income from Blacks to whites because Blacks have a lower life expectancy and pay a disproportionate share of taxes on earnings. Meanwhile, a white backlash had decimated the War on Poverty programs within a decade."[83] As Professor Roberts makes clear, "it was precisely the War on Poverty programs' link to Blacks' civil rights that doomed them: Whites opposed them as an infringement of their economic right to discriminate against Blacks and a threat to white political power."[84] And Professor Tonya Brito explains that "the public became hostile to welfare once welfare became identified with black single mothers."[85]

The labels come, as they always do. The racist labeling and demonization of "welfare queens" grew simultaneously with an increased targeting of impoverished Black fathers, labeled "deadbeat dads" and demonized as both the cause of poverty and the enemy to be pursued—through child support. Professor Ann Cammett describes the racialized trajectory: "The political backlash over expanded access to assistance for Black mothers evolved in tandem with the identification of Deadbeat Dads as the engines of child poverty, even when fathers were poor themselves."[86]

The backlash against Black families gaining access to public assistance led to the creation of the IV-D Child Support Program in 1975, federalizing the same basic structure of the poor laws and bastardy acts.

The primary goal of the IV-D Child Support Program at its creation was to punish poor mothers for receiving aid and ruthlessly pursue poor fathers to reimburse government costs.[87] Senator Russel Long from Louisiana—who openly supported racial segregation and opposed the Civil Rights Act of 1964—led the charge through congressional hearings for the creation of punitive welfare and child support reforms, in his role as the chair of the powerful Senate Committee on Finance. Senator Long titled one of his 1971 hearings "The Welfare Mess: A Scandal of Illegitimacy and Desertion," warning against the increase in Black families accessing welfare benefits, concluding his arguments against illegitimacy and desertion as "the two major causes of the explosive growth of the AFDC rolls" with his "Exhibit 1. Census Data on Blacks—Broken Homes on Increase."[88] In another 1971 hearing, Senator Long argued that in families receiving welfare "[t]he children are taught to lie and deceive from the moment they are able to understand"; that "[w]elfare becomes a way of life, and a welfare subculture is being built upon it"; and that "Uncle Sam will not be the inspiration of the free world while the major cities of America are clogged with trash and pollution and tax-paid welfare loafers wallow in litter and debris."[89] In his statement before the hearing, Long lamented the ending of "man in the house" rules:

> One reason the payments are low in Louisiana is that the Supreme Court has required the State to load the welfare rolls down with people whom the State thought to be ineligible. Because of limited State resources, the result has been to reduce welfare payments to the truly needy in order to accommodate the rolls to large numbers of undeserving persona. . . .
>
> A significant part of today's welfare mess exists because of the conduct of the Supreme Court's outlawing the man-in-the-house rule. . . . A mother could obtain welfare benefits for herself and her children so long as no man were available to support the family. If she demonstrated that her husband had deserted her, or that she was not certain of the identity of the father of her children, she and her children were eligible for welfare. But they would lose welfare payments if the authorities found a man in the house who could support them.[90]

The "man in the house" rules—which Long longed for—had been targeted against Black families until 1968, when the Supreme Court unanimously struck down such a rule in Alabama in *King v. Smith*. An article by Professor Alison Lefkovitz explains that in prior reports, the heads of two county Alabama welfare agencies "admitted that the vast majority if not all of the intimate relationships social workers interfered with were those of black men and women," and "when pressed about her exclusive attention to the boyfriends of black women," one of the county agency directors "sounded a familiar refrain: 'You're from the North and can't really understand our problem.'"[91]

Long's racist views permeated the creation of the IV-D child support system. He employed a combination of coded and openly racialized targeting against low-income Black families, turning gaslighting into national policy. He pointed to the past breakup of many impoverished Black families, caused by the poor laws, bastardy acts, Jim Crow laws, the devastating reverberations of slavery—and existing welfare policies that forced Black fathers from their homes—as a rallying cry to impose yet more punitive policies that would increase the forced breakup of Black families.

The initial AFDC rules that banned fathers from the households receiving benefits, in addition to the "man in the house" rules, slowly eased so that benefits for two-parent families were theoretically available. However, due to much stricter requirements for two-parent families and the flexibility given to states in how to structure their own programs, the vast majority of welfare benefits today are only available when poor fathers are not allowed in the home—and they are instead still demonized and pursued for child support that is owed to the government to reimburse public costs.[92]

Ronald Reagan continued and increasingly popularized the racialized rallying cry against "welfare queens" and "deadbeat dads," first as governor of California and then as a cornerstone of his presidency. President Bill Clinton then signed a conservative welfare reform bill into law in 1996, "ending welfare as we know it" by adding stricter punitive requirements and even further targeting poor fathers as poverty's asserted cause.

This brings us back again to Shelby County, Tennessee. When Nina Bernstein investigated the juvenile court in Memphis in 1994, she described how Judge Kenneth Turner "was years ahead of the curve in cracking down on 'deadbeat dads.'"[93] As Bernstein described, "Turner has used child support enforcement to build a personal empire of patronage and political clout from a juvenile court where critics say poor people have few rights and poverty is often punished by jail."[94] Although the judge was a "former vice squad captain who earned a night-school law degree" and "was never admitted to the bar," he appointed "referees to hear all cases under a system he devised 19 years ago to circumvent a ruling that juvenile judges had to be lawyers."[95] The current juvenile court judge was Judge Turner's chief counsel as of 1995 and became one of his referees in 2001.[96]

The investigation explained that "[c]ollection methods have long made Turner the chief prosecutor, judge and jailer of legally unrepresented men who have fallen behind in support payments, often because of unemployment or adversity in a city where black joblessness is triple the white rate and the gap between black and white household income is the steepest in the nation."[97] During the interview, Bernstein followed the judge through his courthouse, "[b]ypassing a lobby filled with black families," to a "private dining room to share stew and warm cornbread with four of his referees, all white men," and the referees described the judge's accomplishments: "94,000 children 'legitimated' through paternity actions over 30 years, child support collections 80 times higher than when he started."[98]

Bernstein's investigation provided examples of low-income parents being punished through the child support proceedings. For example, a low-income father with "a good payment history fell into arrears when he changed jobs and his new employer failed to honor a wage assignment," and he was "summoned to court, judged guilty of civil contempt—without being given a right to counsel—and sentenced to jail indefinitely unless he made a $200 purge payment." Thus, "[u]nable to pay, he spent sixteen days in jail before a referee ordered his release, and his new employer discharged him for absenteeism."[99] The descriptions are painfully similar to the cases I witnessed day in and day out when I was a legal aid lawyer representing impoverished noncustodial parents in the Baltimore IV-D child support "paternity docket." In 2003 I wrote an article for the *Clearinghouse Review* that described a typical day in the paternity docket:

> The room is packed. Mothers, often with their children, sit on the opposite side of the room from the fathers. . . . The children are despondent. Many parents are in their work clothes reflecting low-paying jobs. Some are in handcuffs. . . .
> The judge criticizes a custodial parent for being on public assistance and states that if she were not on welfare, no one would have to be present that day for a child support proceeding. A noncustodial parent explains that the Social Security Administration just found him disabled and that he should be getting a check for back-benefits. He says that he is "terminal" and has significant prescription drug expenses. He looks skeletal. The agency's attorney pushes him to assign the back-benefits to pay his child support arrearages and quizzes him about how sick he really is.

Ms. W. is before the court now . . . she is working two jobs—one as a part of a drug rehabilitation program and the other in food service at one of the sports arenas, where she makes $6.50 an hour. The court is not satisfied. She was told last time to come in with money or go to jail. She explains that her sister may wire the money, but the court does not want to hear it. She does not have the money, so she is handcuffed and led away crying. The sister does wire the money, and Ms. W. is released from incarceration about a week later. But her job at the arena is gone, and she now is threatened with termination from the rehabilitation program.[100]

I did not fully realize then, as I sat stupefied by the injustices in the crowded courtroom, the connections to the racialized and harmful history that I am trying to accurately write about now.

Today, in IV-D child support courts across the country, the harm continues, disproportionately and devastatingly harming impoverished Black families. And as discussed in prior chapters, the harm is monetized and worsened through the contractual deals of the vast IV-D business operations.

Nationwide, this IV-D system is now processing almost 20 percent of all children in the United States, Black parents are pulled into the system at more than twice the percentage of Black individuals in the overall population, and most of the families in the IV-D system are poor.[101] Over 70 percent of the child support debt is owed by parents with incomes of $10,000 or less.[102] A 2019 Maryland report by Vicki Turetsky explains that "child support policies and practices entangle poor African American men and their families in poverty and have become a destabilizing force."[103] According to data analyzed in the report, over two-thirds of all noncustodial parents statewide who are targeted and pulled into the IV-D child support system are Black parents, and in Baltimore 91 percent are Black parents.[104] Half of these noncustodial parents are unemployed, in significant part due to the harmful child support enforcement practices, and the other half are only able to earn a median income of less than 200 percent of the poverty level.[105] In Baltimore, 42 percent of noncustodial parents in the IV-D system are so poor that they received Supplemental Nutrition Assistance Program (SNAP, or food stamps) benefits.[106] As even further evidence of the racialized impact of the IV-D system, the University of Baltimore School of Law's Legal Data and Design Clinic studied data regarding one of several punitive IV-D child support enforcement mechanisms, driver's license suspensions. In a report provided to the Maryland General Assembly, the clinic found that while Black individuals account for 31 percent of Maryland's population, 71 percent of license suspensions initiated by the IV-D system were against Black parents.[107] It's just a driver's license, right? Pause to consider that question: the reach of your license, the freedom it allows, the identity it protects, the number of times you need it when not driving, and the necessity it carries on the road to self-sufficiency.

The Symbiotic Injustice Enterprise and $hawn

The IV-D child support industry is enormous. But the operations seldom receive significant notice while endlessly churning in the background, in symbiotic relationships that simultaneously power and are powered by the child welfare systems, juvenile justice, mass incarceration, prosecution, probation, and policing. In a vicious, racialized, industrialized, and monetized cycle, harm fuels and feeds on harm.

Michelle Alexander's book *The New Jim Crow* provides starkly disturbing facts about criminal justice and mass incarceration in America: "The racial dimension of mass incarceration is its most striking feature. No other country in the world imprisons so many of its racial or ethnic minorities. The United States imprisons a larger percentage of its black population than South Africa did at the height of apartheid. In Washington, D.C., our nation's capital, it is estimated that three out of four young black men (and nearly all those in the poorest neighborhoods) can expect to serve time in prison."[108]

Interlinked with the devastation of mass incarceration is child support. The IV-D child support system, monetized by courts, prosecutors, probation, and police, both sends impoverished parents to prison and further harms them during and after incarceration. Impoverished parents are often punished by being sent to jail or prison because of child support, from criminal nonsupport charges or civil contempt. Yet again, Black parents are disproportionately targeted. A 2016 report by Noah Zatz found that "African Americans fathers comprise nearly 80% of those incarcerated by the child support enforcement system and are incarcerated at a rate ten times higher than other fathers."[109] According to the report, 15 percent of all Black fathers in US cities have been incarcerated at some point due to child support.[110]

When low-income parents are incarcerated or jailed for any reason, the child support system continues to cause harm. Data from Illinois show that in the one year studied, "[t]here w[ere] 5,589 active orders for currently incarcerated noncustodial parents involved in the IV-D child support program," which means the child support was continuing to accrue while they were incarcerated.[111] Eli Hager completed an excellent investigation for the Marshall Project regarding the interaction between child support and prison: "[M]ostly fathers who are disproportionately black and poor, these parents faced prosecution for not repaying the debt, even after their children were grown," and "what they were not able to pay . . . [t]the state often kept their money as repayment for welfare, child care or Medicaid that had been provided to the family while the dad was locked up."[112] Poor fathers leave prison owing tens of thousands in child support arrearages that accumulated while they were in prison, often owed to the government, and then punitive enforcement practices block the fathers' ability to work, often leading to incarceration again due to the child support owed. In fact, the punitive child support enforcement mechanisms used against poor fathers increase the likelihood of criminal activity as the only way to make ends meet.

Thus, the entanglement between mass incarceration, the juvenile justice system, the child welfare system, and the IV-D system is intensely harmful. As President Reagan spurred the growth of mass incarceration with the war on drugs, which predominantly targeted Black families, he simultaneously spurred a war against "welfare queens" and "deadbeat dads"—also primarily targeting Black families—that would grow this racialized symbiotic disaster between child support, juvenile justice, child welfare, and incarceration.

Imagine $hawn is now twenty. His girlfriend became pregnant, in a state that now criminalizes abortions while providing minimal assistance to impoverished families. Struggling to make ends meet, the young mother applies for the small payments from temporary welfare cash assistance. $hawn wants to help the mother and his child directly, but she tells him he can't move in or the agency will terminate her welfare benefits. The IV-D agency starts pursuing him for government-owed support payments to repay the welfare benefits. $hawn is currently only able to find temporary work, but the IV-D court imputes income, and his monthly child support obligation begins, retroactive several months to when the child support petition was initially filed, thus already over $2,500 in arrears from day one. Due to the arrearage, his driver's license is immediately suspended. If they live in a state like Wyoming, Nebraska, Wisconsin, or Michigan, the child support agency may add thousands more to the arrears to force $hawn to also repay the state Medicaid program for part of the delivery costs.[113]

After a few months, while the arrearage is growing, $hawn luckily finds a new job working full-time, making $12 per hour doing labor at a construction site, but he needs his car to get there. He risks driving. He informs the IV-D agency and court of his new job, as required, and a wage garnishment is issued by the agency and a new court hearing is scheduled to increase his support payments. He receives his paycheck, and 65 percent of his wages has been garnished for the support obligation. On the day of the court hearing, $hawn is worried he will be fired if he leaves work, so he misses the hearing, thinking the court will just increase the ordered support payments whether he is there or not. A warrant for $hawn's arrest is issued for the no-show. The court, agency, and prosecutor's office are all generating revenue through the child support proceedings, and the sheriff's office also has a IV-D contract with the courts to make money by carrying out child support–related arrests. The more enforcement actions, the more IV-D revenue. The more arrests, the more sheriff's revenue.

On his way home from work a couple of days later, a sheriff runs $hawn's plates at a red light and pulls him over. In addition to the warrant for child support, the sheriff discovers his license is suspended—also because of the child support. $hawn is cited and arrested for failure to appear and driving on a suspended license, criminal offenses. Because $hawn is still on probation from a misdemeanor marijuana charge from when he was eighteen, having just left a juvenile residential treatment center (RTC), the new charges are a violation of probation. The probation officer initially recommends revocation, and $hawn is temporarily incarcerated, waiting for a judge to consider his case on the probation revocation while also waiting for another child support hearing. At this point, he is over $5,000 in arrears for the child support, and the new combination of court proceedings results in $2,100 in fines and fees. Then, three months later at the probation revocation hearing, the probation officer recommends, and the judge agrees, that $hawn should be shackled with an electronic ankle monitor. $hawn is charged a $175 setup fee, added to his debt. The private electronic monitoring company has a contract with the city, charging the city courts $5.75 per client per day, and the court in turn charges $hawn a fee for the monitor of $20 per day (about $600 per month), with the extra city revenue providing funds to the court and probation department.[114]

Two weeks after the revocation hearing, the IV-D court orders his monthly order to be increased despite $hawn's plea that he lost his job during incarceration, with the court telling him to just get another construction job. Child support has continued to accrue the whole time, and the charges for the ankle monitor are quickly adding up on top. His increased criminal record makes it harder to find any employer willing to hire him, and the criminal record also bans him from eligibility for public assistance or student loans. The child support and criminal records are reported on his credit, so $hawn also cannot obtain bank loans. His license is still suspended, and he can only get it reinstated if he pays off his full child support arrearage. He could be locked up again for the child support, the debt for the growing court fines and fees, any minor violation of probation, or driving again with his suspended license. He knows if he somehow finds "above ground" work that most of his wages will be garnished, with none of that money going to his son. Meanwhile, the mother is struggling, and his son is at risk of being pulled into foster care. The mother is on a long waitlist for public housing, which will ban $hawn's presence anywhere on the property due to his criminal record.

$hawn knows a couple of people who sell marijuana and other drugs for a large supplier. He is starting to think that may be the only way to get money to help his new son and to try to pay off his debts. The entanglements and financial incentives of the injustice enterprise make it virtually impossible for $hawn to break free, all while his harm—and his family's harm—fuels the factory.

Flash back. When $hawn was only eight years old and in and out of foster care, the child welfare agency plugged him into equations to maximize IV-E foster care revenue. The agency contracted with a private company, traded on the stock exchange, that runs private foster care group homes where $hawn was placed. The agency also hired another private company traded on the stock exchange, a revenue contractor, who helped obtain Social Security disability benefits on $hawn's behalf, without telling him, so the agency could take his money. The school system contracted with another private revenue contractor to use $hawn to maximize school-based Medicaid funds, much of which was redirected to state revenue while $hawn received inadequate education. The agency pursued $hawn's mother for child support to reimburse the cost of foster care, a debt she still owes and that the IV-D court still pursues against her to this day. The court, prosecutors, and sheriff's office have all been contractually incentivized and generating IV-D revenue from the child support proceedings against $hawn's mom. The courts contracted with another private company that makes money by helping to enforce the child support obligations, and with yet another company to collect court-owed fines and fees from his mother. Another large company traded on the stock exchange owns a debt-buying operation that is also aggressively pursuing $hawn's mother, with the courts helping.

When $hawn was thirteen, the juvenile court, child welfare agency, probation department, and prosecutors all used him to generate revenue from their interagency IV-E foster care contracts after prosecuting and adjudicating $hawn as delinquent and placing him in an RTC that has a contract with the court. The RTC, with a history of abuse and seeking to maximize profits by reducing costs, is owned by another large company, also traded on the stock market. While first in foster care and later the RTC, $hawn was prescribed multiple psychotropic medications simultaneously, a tactic used by facilities to sedate children to make them cheaper to warehouse. $hawn's juvenile probation officer, an employee of the juvenile court, sexually abused him, and an RTC staff member repeatedly hit him, but $hawn was fearful and never reported the abuse.

Flash forward. The same IV-D court pursuing his mother for child support is also now pursuing $hawn for child support and generating revenue from both mother and son through the IV-D contracts—the same is being done by the prosecutors and sheriff's office. $hawn is arrested again, brought before the court for a child support contempt proceeding, and ordered to come up with a "purge" amount to avoid incarceration. Out of desperation, $hawn joins his contacts selling marijuana and other drugs to try to pay off his mounting debts, and he is caught up in a police raid. Because of the amount, and because one of the other individuals had a gun, $hawn is charged with multiple felonies. Based on an algorithm developed by a court contract with another private company, he is denied probation because of his algorithmic risk score. He is first in jail until the trial and then in prison, both run by private companies, in turn owned by larger companies, also traded on the stock market. Two other private companies, also traded on the stock market, profit from providing the prison food and health care. Another private company profits through steep charges for phone and video conferencing, the only way $hawn can see his family, through a contract that also provides revenue to the county and court.

Eighteen months later $hawn is released, this time with a parole officer who works for another private company. Again, he is shackled with an ankle monitor, and again he is charged with the fees. His child support arrearage has now grown to over $15,600, and his combined court fines and fees—not including the ankle monitor costs—have risen to $5,900. While $hawn was incarcerated, the court signed a contract with yet another private company that helps to collect court fines and fees, charging another 22 percent fee on top of the amount owed, with interest accruing. His license is still suspended. And the entire injustice enterprise apparatus is readjusting its settings to extract more revenue from $hawn and his mother—and cultivating its revenue plans for his son. $hawn learns that his son was just taken into foster care, and $hawn wishes he could get custody of him. A sheriff generated more revenue by evicting $hawn's mom, so she is staying in a shelter, and $hawn has no home. He stops by to see his mom, and after a long embrace she gives him some mail that was forwarded before she became homeless. In the stack of unpaid bills and notices of legal action, he finds a notice from the juvenile court for a child support hearing scheduled for the following week—and a notice about a foster care review hearing for his son.

Sounds of the factory.

As I write this paragraph, in the shaken shadow of the White nationalist attack on the US Capitol, as voting rights are being subverted across the country, all subsumed within a massive disinformation campaign, the backlash against racial and economic justice continues—as ethicless pundits and politicians pound the drum against any study or discussion of American history that includes an accurate understanding of racial injustice.[115] The absence of ethics is their power. They savage truth, claiming the remains as righteous. And the weak follow. Because the ethical road has always been the harder path.

Conclusion

I do not write this book with hopelessness. There are moments, more than I would like to admit, when I crave the numbing peace of apathy. But when I read numbers, the numbers of children and impoverished adults processed by our justice systems into byzantine contractual revenue schemes, numbers reflecting how the factory-like operations are fueled by over four hundred years of racial and economic inequality, numbers uncovering the extent to which our systems of justice have turned toward unconstitutional and humanly destructive moneyed pursuits, I know that apathy is not an option.

This conclusion is purposefully brief and does not seek to provide step-by-step solutions, because core principles of the solutions are simple—mission and ethics. In each example detailed in this book, the problem arises when institutions of justice try to run like a business, swapping the ethical pursuit of justice with the mission to maximize money. The specific details and process to realign our justice systems toward the ideals of justice will be different state by state, county by county, court by court, department by department, justice official by justice official. However, if we decide to walk a more ethical path toward "Equal Justice Under Law," common themes can guide us.

The most difficult is also the most necessary, honest self-reflection—it is not easy to truly look at yourself in the mirror. I need to pause here, one last time. I started teaching a law school clinic at the University of Baltimore in 2004, in which the students learn while representing impoverished clients. Every semester, until he retired in 2013, Maryland's former chief judge Robert M. Bell would help lead our swearing-in ceremony for student attorneys to impress upon them the honor and ethical obligations of the role of a lawyer in serving justice.[1] His talk would bring me goosebumps mixed with fighting back tears, every time. He always closed with one of his favorite poems, "The Guy in the Glass," about the necessary mirror of honest self-reflection, which Judge Bell connected to being true to the calling to serve justice.[2]

Bell began his justice mission at an early age. At sixteen he joined the effort to push America toward desegregation and racial equality. He became lead plaintiff in a case that went up to the US Supreme Court, *Bell v. Maryland*, in which the court vacated his 1960 conviction for a sit-in protest at a "Whites only" Baltimore restaurant.[3] In a historical twist, Robert C. Murphy was one of the deputy attorneys general who argued in favor of Bell's conviction. Murphy was then named Maryland's top attorney general in 1966, the same year that Bell graduated from Morgan State, a historically Black college and university (HBCU) in Baltimore, and began law school at Harvard.[4] After Murphy was appointed chief judge of the Maryland courts in 1972, Bell became a district court judge a few years later, and he rose to replace Murphy as chief judge in 1996. A Black teenager who had been arrested for protesting segregation became the state's top judge, replacing the person who had argued for his conviction.[5] I still hear his words as he encouraged our students in the process of continuous self-reflection that guided him—toward the unwavering ethical path of equal justice.

Back to the necessary mirror. Each component of our justice system, in every jurisdiction, should heed Judge Bell's call and begin a detailed process of acknowledgment of the ways in which they may be subverting ethics, equality, and justice to moneyed business operations. Such justice audits must be human centered rather than institution centered, improving the provision of justice for individuals the institutions exist to serve—rather than using those individuals to serve the fiscal interests of the institutions. Instead of the Ohio juvenile courts asking the state bureau of fiscal operations for training to maximize revenue from children, they should consider establishing their own independent inspector general's office or ombudsman, who will tell an unvarnished truth when the courts engage in unconstitutional revenue strategies or otherwise deviate from ethics and justice. Instead of the Judicial Council of California issuing an annual report to highlight success in making money from impoverished litigants, the courts should focus on reports that detail needed improvements in providing equal justice to those litigants. Instead of prosecutors, sheriffs, probation departments, and juvenile detention centers issuing reports focused on efficiently generating revenue from the vulnerable, they should engage in audits focused on removing financial conflicts and to better provide justice in serving the vulnerable.

With improved assessments of their failings, our justice systems can better engage in the detailed process of solutions. With opened eyes and trued ethics, our institutions can better demand an appropriate process of state and county funding while ending continued participation in revenue schemes that violate their constitutional and ethical obligations. We the people, as we become more aware, can help push for systems designed to provide equal justice for vulnerable populations and push back against practices that commodify them. Individual justice officials who find themselves surrounded by compromised system structures must take ethical stands, including making formal ethical grievances. Our other branches of government must better respect the importance of an ethical and independent judiciary rather than using the judiciary to make money.

For our institutions and justice officials who do not right their own wrongs, additional investigations and monitoring by state oversight agencies and by the US Department of Justice's Civil Rights Division will be necessary. Also, continued litigation will be necessary to challenge these practices. Ultimately, there is no question that the revenue schemes detailed in this book violate constitutional and ethical requirements. The only question is whether we are ethically true in our analysis and response.

In 1963 Bell was still a teenager, and his case was on its way to the Supreme Court. That same year, Martin Luther King Jr. wrote a letter from a Birmingham jail including these words: "Injustice anywhere is a threat to justice everywhere. We are caught in an inescapable network of mutuality, tied in a single garment of destiny."[6] As long as the factory of injustice keeps churning and our foundational institutions trade away their solemn devotion to justice in order to profit from historically devastating inequality and harm, we are all harmed. And our constitutional democracy is shaking.

Notes

INTRODUCTION

1. See The Supreme Court of Ohio, *Report and Recommendations of the Supreme Court of Ohio: Task Force on the Funding of Ohio's Courts*, November 2015, 14-www.supremecourt.ohio.gov/Boards/courtFunding/Report.pdf (explaining that the "system for funding Ohio courts can best be described as a complex mosaic" and analyzing local courts' struggles with insufficient funding).

2. Patrick Griffin and Gregory Halemba, "Federal Placement Assistance Funding for Delinquency Services," *Children, Families and the Courts Ohio Bulletin*, Winter 2003, www.ncjj.org/PDF/winter2003cfc.pdf, https://perma.cc /UL6B-8PTE (noting that the juvenile courts in Cuyahoga, Guernsey, Holmes and Montgomery Counties first entered such agreements in 1996).

3. "State of Ohio Title IV-E Juvenile Court Contact List," https://jfs.ohio .gov/ocf/JuvenileCourtContactList.stm, https://perma.cc/U6NA-HC55 (listing twenty-seven county "IV-E courts" as of January 3, 2022).

4. Summit County Juvenile Court, *2019 Annual Report*, https://juvenilecourt .summitoh.net/images/AR/annrep19.pdf; Common Pleas Court of Montgomery County, Juvenile Division, *2019 Annual Report*, www.mcjcohio.org/wp-content /uploads/2021/02/2019-Annual-Report.pdf; and Hamilton County Juvenile Court, *2019 Annual Report*, www.juvenile-court.org/juvenilecourt/Annual _Report/2019_Annual_Report.pdf.

5. Common Pleas Court & Clerk of Courts, *2019 Report to the Citizens of Montgomery County*, www.montcourt.oh.gov/wp-content/uploads/2021/04 /2019-Report-to-the-Citizens-of-MC-08-19-20-Ver-16-compressed.pdf (listing the juvenile court with two judges, ten magistrates, two court administrators,

and five hundred court staff); and Montgomery County Juvenile Court, "About the Court: Detention Services," www.mcjcohio.org/about-the-court/court-admin istration/detention-services/, https://perma.cc/TZN3-Y8HC; see also Daniel L. Hatcher, "Juvenile Court Interagency Agreements: Subverting Impartial Justice to Maximize Revenue from Children," NYU *Annual Survey of American Law* 76 (2020): 33, 41–42.

6. Common Pleas Court of Montgomery County, Juvenile Division, *2018 Annual Report*, 74, www.mcjcohio.org/wp-content/uploads/2020/02/2018-JC -Annual-Report.pdf, https://perma.cc/VP3N-VMZ5.

7. Common Pleas Court of Montgomery County, *2018 Annual Report*, 63–75.

8. Montgomery County Juvenile Court, *NRTC* [Nicholas Residential Treatment Center] *Blog*, May 26, 2021, www.mcjcohio.org/about-the-court/court -administration/nicholas-residential-treatment-center/nrtc-blog/, https://perma .cc/SG34-E6F7 (describing the court seeking accreditation of its RTC in order to receive IV-E funding); and Miami County Juvenile Court, *2016 Annual Report*, www.miamicountyohio.gov/ArchiveCenter/ViewFile/Item/1461 (describing a "Youth Center" run by the court as a residential treatment center approved for IV-E).

9. Ohio Rev. Code Sec. 2151.13, https://codes.ohio.gov/ohio-revised-code /section-2151.13; and Montgomery County Common Pleas Court, Juvenile Division, "Notice of Vacancy: Science Teacher," https://perma.cc/TZ74 -TRMH.

10. Chris Stewart, "Hey Watson: Local Judge First to Use IBM Watson's Artificial Intelligence on Juvenile Cases," *Dayton Daily News*, August 3, 2017, www.daytondailynews.com/news/local/county-judge-first-use-ibm-watson -supercomputer-juvenile-cases/InVqz6eeNxvFsMVAe5zrbL/, https://perma .cc/EYP8-RMZB (reporting that "solution [using IBM Watson] beats sifting through anywhere from 30 to 300 pages of paperwork in the five to seven minutes [the judge] may have for each of 30-35 juveniles seen during a typical treatment court docket"); and IBM Watson, "Case Studies, Montgomery County Juvenile Court," www.ibm.com/case-studies/montgomery-county-juvenile-court, https://perma.cc/6R3M-3SLZ.

11. Jefferson County Court of Common Pleas, Probate and Juvenile Division, *2016 Annual Report*, http://jjohio.org/wp-content/uploads/2017/08/Jefferson -County-Juvenile-Court-2016-Report.pdf, https://perma.cc/2S7S-NUSH (listing a juvenile court budget of $1,632,174.88 million, compared to the court's IV-E revenue of over $846,000).

12. Encarnacion Pyle, "Juvenile Courts' Role Debated," *Columbus Dispatch*, September 11, 2006, www.pressreader.com/usa/the-columbus-dispatch /20060911/282033322676879.

13. Although low-income individuals are diverse, and each person faces unique circumstances, this book sometimes refers to the "poor" as a group to describe how they are similarly targeted by commodified injustice practices.

14. For an excellent book and compilation of essays about failings in our safety net programs, see Ezra Rosser, *Holes in the Safety Net: Federalism and Poverty* (New York: Cambridge University Press, 2019).

15. See generally Daniel L. Hatcher, *The Poverty Industry: The Exploitation of America's Most Vulnerable Citizens* (New York: NYU Press, 2016).

16. James Baldwin, *No Name in the Street* (New York: Vintage Books, 1972), 148–49.

17. Baldwin, *No Name in the Street*, 68.

18. See, for example, Dorothy Roberts, *Shattered Bonds: The Color of Child Welfare* (New York: Basic Books, 2002), 27 ("Poverty—not the type or severity of maltreatment—is the single most important predictor of placement in foster care and the amount of time spent there."); Dorothy Roberts, *Torn Apart: How the Child Welfare System Destroys Black Families—and How Abolition Can Build a Safer World* (New York: Basic Books, 2022); Tanya Asim Cooper, "Racial Bias in American Foster Care: The National Debate," *Marquette Law Review* 97 (Winter 2013): 215; Naomi R. Cahn, "Children's Interests in a Familial Context: Poverty, Foster Care, and Adoption," *Ohio State Law Journal* 60 (1999): 1189, 1198; Martin Guggenheim, "The Foster Care Dilemma and What to Do about It: Is the Problem That Too Many Children Are Not Being Adopted out of Foster Care or That Too Many Children Are Entering Foster Care?," *University of Pennsylvania Journal of Constitutional Law* 2 (1999): 141, 145 ("[T]he link between child protection and poverty is staggering."); and Barbara Bennett Woodhouse, "Child Abuse, the Constitution, and the Legacy of Pierce v. Society of Sisters," *University of Detroit Mercy Law Review* 78 (2001): 479, 480 ("Too many children, especially children of color, are being removed from their homes because of poverty and its associated ills.").

19. P. J. Pecora, R. C. Kessler, J. Williams, K. O'Brien, A. C. Downs, D. English, J. White, E. Hiripi, C. Roller White, T. Wiggins, and K. Holmes, *Improving Family Foster Care: Findings from the Northwest Foster Care Alumni Study*, Casey Family Programs, 2005, 1, https://caseyfamilypro-wpengine.netdna-ssl.com/media/AlumniStudies_NW_Report_FR.pdf.

20. US Department of Education, Department of Civil Rights, "Data Snapshot: School Discipline," March 2014, www2.ed.gov/about/offices/list/ocr/docs/crdc-discipline-snapshot.pdf; see also Corey Mitchell, Joe Yerardi, and Susan Ferriss, "When Schools Call Police on Kids," Center for Public Integrity, September 8, 2021, https://publicintegrity.org/education/criminalizing-kids/police-in-schools-disparities/.

21. Iowa Dept. of Human Services, *Out-of-Home Placement Policy and Procedures*, title 17, chapter E, 60–61, www.fostercareandeducation.org/Desktop Modules/Bring2mind/DMX/Download.aspx?EntryId=1689&Command=Core _Download&method=inline&PortalId=0&TabId=124, https://perma.cc/5BUW -Q44Z ("[A]pproach the trustee, seeking to have DHS made payee for the income of the trust. If sufficient funds are not available from the trust to meet the total cost of care, request the trustee to petition the district court to release funds. . . . If the trustee is unwilling to present the petition, request that the child, the child's parent, or representative present a petition [through an attorney]. If the child, parent or responsible person refuses to cooperate, refer the case to the Foster Care Recovery Unit.").

22. Georgia Division of Family and Children's Services, *Child Welfare Policy Manual*, "Applying for Initial Funding," effective December 2018, https://

odis.dhs.ga.gov/ViewDocument.aspx?docId=3005729, https://perma.cc/KT8P -48DC.

23. Md. Regs. Code, 07.02.11.29, Child Support and Other Resources for Reimbursement Towards Cost of Care. ("All of the child's resources, including parental support, the child's own benefits, insurance, cash assets, trust accounts, and, for the child who is preparing for independent living, the child's earnings, are considered, as established in the service agreement, in determining the amount available for reimbursement of the cost of care.").

24. Neb. Admin. Code, 479 NAC 2–001.08 ("1. Cash on hand; 2. Cash in savings or checking accounts; 3. Stocks; 4. Bonds; 5. Certificate of deposit; 6. Investments; 7. Collectable unpaid notes or loans; 8. Promissory notes; 9. Mortgages; 10. Land contracts; 11. Land leases; 12. Revocable burial funds; 13. Trust or guardianship funds; 14. Cash value of insurance policies; 15. Real estate; 16. Trailer houses; 17. Burial spaces; 18. Life estates; 19. Farm and business equipment; 20. Livestock; 21. Poultry and crops; 22. Household goods and other personal effects; and 23. Federal and state tax refunds.").

25. See Hatcher, *Poverty Industry*, 65–110. See also Daniel L. Hatcher, "States Diverting Funds from the Poor," in *Holes in the Safety Net: Federalism and Poverty*, ed. Ezra Rosser (New York: Cambridge University Press, 2019), 151–72.

26. Hatcher, *Poverty Industry*, 4, 82–100.

27. Hatcher, *Poverty Industry*, 83. See also *SSI/SSDI Assessment Report* (Maryland Department of Human Resources, MAXIMUS, Inc., February 22, 2013).

28. Hatcher, *Poverty Industry*, 130–33; and Hatcher, "States Diverting Funds from the Poor," 151–72.

29. Hatcher, *Poverty Industry*, 130–33; Hatcher, "States Diverting Funds from the Poor," 151–72; and New Jersey Department of the Treasury, Office of Management and Budget, *Appropriations Handbook: State of New Jersey, Fiscal Year 2020–2021*, E4, www.nj.gov/treasury/omb/publications/21approp /FY21FullAppropAct.pdf, https://perma.cc/RZM4-HDEF ("Notwithstanding the provisions of any law or regulation to the contrary, each local school district that participates in the Special Education Medicaid Initiative (SEMI) shall receive a percentage of the federal revenue realized for current year claims. The percentage share shall be 17.5 percent of claims approved by the State.").

30. See New Jersey Department of the Treasury, Division of Administration, "Special Education Medicaid Initiative (SEMI) and Medicaid Administrative Claiming (MAC)," www.state.nj.us/treasury/administration/semi-mac/semi .shtml, https://perma.cc/3YWU-H8WT.

31. Hatcher, *Poverty Industry*, 143–82; and Hatcher, "States Diverting Funds from the Poor," 151–72.

32. Ga. Code Ann., § 42-8-103.

33. The injustice enterprise operations also unequally and harmfully impact the Native American population, other populations of color, and the LGBTQ population. However, this book's analysis of commodified inequality primarily focuses on the starkly disproportionate impact on the Black population.

34. United States Census Bureau, "QuickFacts Hamilton County, Ohio," July 1, 2021, www.census.gov/quickfacts/hamiltoncountyohio.

35. Nick Swartsell, "Youth Trauma, Trials, Time: What Drives Disparities in Hamilton County's Juvenile Justice System?," *Cincinnati CityBeat*, September 18, 2019, www.citybeat.com/news/youth-trauma-trials-time-what-is-fueling-disparities-in-hamilton-countys-juvenile-justice-system-12172682.

36. United States Census Bureau, "QuickFacts: Montgomery County, Ohio"; and Common Pleas Court of Montgomery County, Juvenile Division, *2018 Annual Report*, 18–27, 52 (chart listing the court's commitments to its secure Center for Adolescent Services in 2018 of 85 percent Black youth, compared to the state agency's commitments of children from other jurisdictions to the facility of 52 percent Black youth).

37. UN Economic and Social Council (ECOSOC), Resolution 2006/23, Strengthening Basic Principles of Judicial Conduct, E/RES/2006/23 (July 27, 2006), www.refworld.org/docid/46c455abo.html.

CHAPTER 1. CRUMBLING FOUNDATIONS OF JUSTICE

1. *The Federalist*, no. 47 (James Madison), Library of Congress, https://guides.loc.gov/federalist-papers.

2. *Federalist*, no. 51 (James Madison).

3. *Federalist*, no. 51 (James Madison).

4. *Federalist*, no. 78 (Alexander Hamilton).

5. See, for example, Jessie Serfilippi, "'As Odious and Immoral a Thing': Alexander Hamilton's Hidden History as an Enslavor," Schuyler Mansion State Historic Site, 2020, https://parks.ny.gov/documents/historic-sites/Schuyler MansionAlexanderHamiltonsHiddenHistoryasanEnslaver.pdf; Liz Mineo, "Correcting 'Hamilton,'" *Harvard Gazette*, October 7, 2016, https://news.harvard.edu/gazette/story/2016/10/correcting-hamilton/; and Ankeet Ball, "Ambition & Bondage: An Inquiry on Alexander and Slavery," Columbia University and Slavery, https://columbiaandslavery.columbia.edu/content/ambition-bondage-inquiry-alexander-hamilton-and-slavery.

6. Declaration of Independence (1776).

7. Sam J. Ervin Jr., "Separation of Powers: Judicial Independence," *Law & Contemporary Problems* 35 (1970): 108, 121.

8. United States Senate, "Sam Ervin: A Featured Biography," www.senate.gov/senators/FeaturedBios/Featured_Bio_ErvinSam.htm.

9. Paul R. Verkuil, "Separation of Powers, the Rule of Law and the Idea of Independence," *William & Mary Law Review* 30 (1989): 301, 306.

10. Dennis v. United States, 339 U.S. 162 (1950) (concurring opinion).

11. *In re Murchison*, 349 U.S. 133, 136 (1955).

12. *In re Murchison*, 349 U.S. 133, 136 (1955).

13. *In re Murchison*, 349 U.S. 133, 136 (1955) (*quoiting* Offutt v. United States, 348 U.S. 11, 348 U.S. 14 (1954) (Thus, Justice Black concluded that "[f]air trials are too important a part of our free society to let prosecuting judges be trial judges of the charges they prefer.").

14. Kat Eschner, "This Supreme Court Justice Was a KKK Member," *Smithsonian Magazine*, February 27, 2017, www.smithsonianmag.com/smart-news/supreme-court-justice-was-kkk-member-180962254/.

15. Eschner, "This Supreme Court Justice Was a KKK Member."

16. Allison Marston, "Guiding the Profession: The 1887 Code of Ethics of the Alabama State Bar Association," *Alabama Law Review* 49 (1998): 471, www.law.ua.edu/pubs/lrarticles/Volume%2049/Number%202/marston.pdf. See generally David Martin, "The Birth of Jim Crow in Alabama 1865–1896," *National Black Law Journal* 13, no. 1 (1993), https://escholarship.org/content /qt5x65v6ch/qt5x65v6ch.pdf.

17. Allison Marston, "Guiding the Profession," *Alabama Law Review* 49 (1998):479.

18. Marston, "Guiding the Profession."

19. Marston, "Guiding the Profession," 505.

20. See, for example, Albert F. Simpson, "The Political Significance of Slave Representation, 1787–1821," *Journal of Southern History* 7, no. 3 (1941): 315–42, https://doi.org/10.2307/2191525.

21. Kathryn MacKay, "Statistics on Slavery," Weber State University, https:// faculty.weber.edu/kmackay/statistics_on_slavery.htm, https://perma.cc/2Q6L -U57Q; and US Census Bureau, "Heads of Families at the First Census, 1790," www2.census.gov/prod2/decennial/documents/1790m-02.pdf.

22. MacKay, "Statistics on Slavery" ("After the American Revolution, the Southern slave population exploded, reaching about 1.1 million in 1810 and over 3.9 million in 1860."); see also US Census Bureau, "XIV: Statistics of Slaves," table 60, https://www2.census.gov/prod2/decennial/documents/00165 897ch14.pdf.

23. *Federalist*, no. 54 (James Madison), https://founders.archives.gov /documents/Hamilton/01-04-02-0203.

24. *Federalist*, no. 54 (James Madison) ("We have hitherto proceeded on the idea that representation related to persons only, and not at all to property. But is it a just idea? Government is instituted no less for protection of the property, than of the persons of individuals. The one as well as the other, therefore may be considered as represented by those who are charged with the government. . . . The rights of property are committed into the same hands with the personal rights. Some attention ought therefore to be paid to property in the choice of those hands."). See also David Walstreicher, "How the Constitution Was Indeed Pro-Slavery," *Atlantic*, September 19, 2015 (explaining that Madison "actually argued that the three-fifths clause was a good example of how the Constitution would lead to good government—by protecting property").

25. Wilfred U. Codrington III, "The Electoral College's Racist Origins," Brennan Center for Justice, April 1, 2020, www.brennancenter.org/our-work /analysis-opinion/electoral-colleges-racist-origins; and The Avalon Project, "Madison Debates," Yale Law School, July 19, 1787, https://avalon.law.yale .edu/18th_century/debates_719.asp.

26. Codrington, "Electoral College's Racist Origins"; and The Avalon Project, "Madison Debates."

27. See Codrington, "Electoral College's Racist Origins."

28. *Federalist*, no. 68 (Alexander Hamilton), https://avalon.law.yale.edu /18th_century/fed68.asp; see also Garett Epps, "The Electoral College Was Terrible from the Start," *Atlantic*, September 8, 2019.

29. *Federalist,* no 68 (Alexander Hamilton).

30. *See* Donald Ratcliffe, "The Right to Vote and the Rise of Democracy, 1787 to 1828," *Journal of the Early Republic* 221 (Summer 2013): 219, www.jstor.org/stable/24768843.

31. Callie Hopkins, "The Enslaved Household of President Andrew Jackson," The White House Historical Association, www.whitehousehistory.org/slavery-in-the-andrew-jackson-white-house.

32. The American Presidency Project, "Andrew Jackson's 5th Annual Message," December 3, 1833, www.presidency.ucsb.edu/documents/fifth-annual-message-2.

33. Russell Thornton, "Cherokee Population Losses during the Trail of Tears: A New Perspective and a New Estimate," *Ethnohistory* 31, no. 4 (1984): 289–300, https://doi.org/10.2307/482714.

34. "President Jackson's Message to Congress 'On Indian Removal,'" December 6, 1830, Records of the United States Senate, 1789–1990, Record Group 46, National Archives and Records Administration (NARA), www.nps.gov/museum/tmc/manz/handouts/andrew_jackson_annual_message.pdf. For additional description of Jackson's abuse of power regarding Native Americans, see Alfred A. Cave, "Abuse of Power: Andrew Jackson and the Indian Removal Act of 1830," *Historian* 65, no. 6 (2003): 1330–53, http://www.jstor.org/stable/24452618.

35. See, for example, Martin Abbott, "Free Land, Free Labor, and the Freedmen's Bureau," *Agricultural History* 30, no. 4 (1956): 151–52; and Allen Guelzo, "What If Abraham Lincoln Had Lived?," *Washington Post*, April 13, 2015, www.washingtonpost.com/posteverything/wp/2015/04/13/what-if-abraham-lincoln-had-lived/.

36. Mississippi Black Code, 1865, quoted in Senate Executive Documents, *Second Session of the Thirty-Ninth Congress, 1866–67* (Washington, DC: Government Printing Office, 1867), 194–95, https://memory.loc.gov/cgi-bin/query/r?ammem/aaodyssey:@field(NUMBER+@band(llmisc+ody0517)).

37. Mississippi Black Code, 1865, in Senate Executive Documents, *Second Session,* 190.

38. Mississippi Black Code, 1865, in Senate Executive Documents, *Second Session* ("If any apprentice shall leave the employment of his or her master or mistress, without his or her consent, said master or mistress may pursue and recapture said apprentice, and bring him or her before any justice of the peace of the county, whose duty it shall be to remand said apprentice to the service of his or her master or mistress.").

39. See, for example, Michael Kent Curtis, "The Klan, the Congress, and the Court: Congressional Enforcement of the Fourteenth and Fifteenth Amendments and the State Action Syllogism, a Brief Historical Overview," *University of Pennsylvania Journal of Constitutional Law* 11 (2009): 1381; and Kurt T. Lash, "Enforcing the Rights of Due Process: The Original Relationship between the Fourteenth Amendment and the 1866 Civil Rights Act," *Georgetown Law Journal* 106 (2018): 1389.

40. See, for example, Thomas B. Alexander, "Kukluxism in Tennessee, 1865–1869," *Tennessee Historical Quarterly* 8, no. 3 (1949): 195–219, http://www.jstor.org/stable/42621013.

41. During this time, many northern Republicans opposed slavery, and many southern Democrats opposed Reconstruction and either directly enslaved people or supported slavery—until the parties largely flipped ideologies through the complex and painful racialized history after the Civil War through the civil rights movement and the Republican "southern strategy." President Lyndon B. Johnson is reported by his aide to have said after signing the Civil Rights Act of 1964, "I think we just delivered the South to the Republican party for a long time to come." Gordon E. Harvey, Richard D. Starnes, and Glen Feldman, *History and Hope in the Heart of Dixie: Scholarship, Activism and Wayne Flint in the Modern South* (Tuscaloosa: University of Alabama Press, 2006), 28.

42. See Allan Peskin, "Was There a Compromise of 1877," *Journal of American History* 60, no. 1 (1973): 63–75, https://doi.org/10.2307/2936329; and C. Vann Woodward, *Reunion and Reaction: The Compromise of 1877 and the End of Reconstruction* (Boston: Little, Brown, 1951).

43. See, for example, Michael J. Klarman, "Brown, Racial Change, and the Civil Rights Movement," *Virginia Law Review* 80 (1994): 7.

44. See generally Michele Alexander, *The New Jim Crow: Mass Incarceration in the Age of Colorblindness* (New York: The New Press, 2012); and Dorothy Roberts, *Shattered Bonds: The Color of Child Welfare* (New York: Basic Books, 2002).

45. For example, "Promote Fair Courts," Brennan Center, www.brennancenter .org/issues/strengthen-our-courts/promote-fair-courts ("state courts hear 95 percent of all cases"); and Court Statistics Project, *Examining the Work of State Courts*, 2009, www.courtstatistics.org/__data/assets/pdf_file/0024/29805/2009 -EWSC.pdf (past reports providing data that about 95 percent of US cases were filed in state courts).

46. Court Statistics Project, *State Court Caseload Digest, 2017 Data*, www .courtstatistics.org/__data/assets/pdf_file/0021/29820/2017-Digest-print-view .pdf (of state court filings in 2017, 83 million were in state trial courts, compared to 241,000 in state appellate courts); see also Daniel L. Hatcher, "Juvenile Court Interagency Agreements: Subverting Impartial Justice to Maximize Revenue from Children," *NYU Annual Survey of American Law* 76 (2020): 33, 37–39.

47. See Josh Webber et al., *Transforming Juvenile Justice Systems to Improve Public Safety and Youth Outcomes* (Georgetown University Center for Juvenile Justice Reform, 2018), 8; see also Hatcher, "Juvenile Court Interagency Agreements," 37–38.

48. Monrad G. Paulsen, "Juvenile Courts, Family Courts, and the Poor Man," *California Law Review* 54 (1966): 694.

49. Paulsen, "Juvenile Courts, Family Courts, and the Poor Man."

50. Chris Bragg, "Children Died Despite Warnings in New York Family Courts," *Times Union*, March 4, 2020, www.timesunion.com/news/article /When-children-die-what-s-New-York-s-family-court-15104710.php; and Abigail Kramer, "Is Reform Finally Coming to New York City Family Court?," The New School, Center for New York City Affairs, www.centernyc.org/family -court-reform.

51. Lucas County Juvenile Court, *2018 Annual Report*, https://co.lucas.oh
.us/DocumentCenter/View/75032/2018-Annual-Report-LCJC?bidId=, https://
perma.cc/L2W4-N2HQ.

52. Lucas County Juvenile Court, *2018 Annual Report*.

53. Lucas County Juvenile Court, *2018 Annual Report*, 10.

54. Lucas County Juvenile Court, *2018 Annual Report*, A5; and US Census
Bureau, "QuickFacts: Lucas County Ohio," 2021, www.census.gov/quickfacts
/fact/table/lucascountyohio/HCN010212.

55. County Council of Cuyahoga County, Ohio, Resolution no. R2019-0209,
"A Resolution Authorizing an Agreement with Cuyahoga County Prosecutor's Office in the Amount Not-to-Exceed $2,748,203.00," http://council
.cuyahogacounty.us/pdf_council/en-US/Legislation/Resolutions/2019/R2019
-0209.pdf, https://perma.cc/XPC7-VCU5; and County Council of Cuyahoga
County, Ohio, Resolution no. R2019-0074 (authorizing 2019 child support
contract with the prosecutor's office valued over $3.9 million), http://council
.cuyahogacounty.us/pdf_council/en-US/Legislation/Resolutions/2019/R2019
-0074D%20Authorize%20Title%20IV-DAgreements%20with%20Domestic
%20Relations%20and%20Juvenile%20Courts%20and%20Prosecutor
%20for%20child%20support%20services.pdf.

56. Cuyahoga County Prosecutor, "Remarks by Cuyahoga County Prosecutor Timothy J. McGinty Prepared for Delivery to the City Club of Cleveland," January 9, 2015, http://prosecutor.cuyahogacounty.us/pdf_prosecutor/en
-US/2015-01-09-Prosecutor%20McGinty%20City%20Club%20Speech.pdf,
https://perma.cc/TZ75-6VMC.

57. Cuyahoga County Prosecutor, "Remarks."

58. See generally James W. Douglas and Roger E. Hartley, "The Politics
of Court Budgeting in the States: Is Judicial Independence Threatened by the
Budgetary Process?," *Public Administration Review* 63 (2003):441; and Jeffrey
Jackson, "Judicial Independence, Adequate Court Funding, and Inherent Judi-
cial Powers," *Maryland Law Review* 52 (1993): 217; see also Hatcher, "Juvenile
Court Interagency Agreements," 38–39.

59. Ciara McCarthy, "Revenue from Juvenile Detention Center Shows
Growing Trend for Victoria County," *Victoria Advocate*, September 8, 2018,
www.victoriaadvocate.com/news/government/revenue-from-juvenile-detention
-center-shows-growing-trend-for-victoria/article_434d6a6e-b218-11e8-849d
-1f19478df37d.html, https://perma.cc/TB3C-P4A9.

60. McCarthy, "Revenue from Juvenile Detention Center."

61. McCarthy, "Revenue from Juvenile Detention Center."

62. Juvenile Court of Memphis and Shelby County, *Annual Report*, 2019,
https://www.shelbycountytn.gov/DocumentCenter/View/37968/Annual-Report
-2019, https://perma.cc/7TNM-9TNT. See Tenn. Code Ann. § 37-1-107 (2020);
see also Hatcher, "Juvenile Court Interagency Agreements," 43–45 (providing
summary of the Shelby County Juvenile Court).

63. Juvenile Court of Memphis and Shelby County, *Annual Report*.

64. *Ibid.*, 6 ("The Court maintained two special grant agreements with the
Tennessee Department of Human Services that provide funding for four child

support magistrates, six principal court clerks and two management/supervisory personnel.").

65. *Ibid.*, 11.

66. Juvenile Court of Memphis and Shelby County, *Annual Report*, 2012, 2, 7, www.shelbycountytn.gov/DocumentCenter/View/13735/2012-Anual-Report ?bidId=, https://perma.cc/BH4L-WGQL.

67. US Department of Justice, "Investigation of the Shelby County Juvenile Court," 2012, 1, www.justice.gov/sites/default/files/crt/legacy/2012/04/26 /shelbycountyjuv_findingsrpt_4-26-12.pdf.

68. Supreme Court of New Jersey, "Juvenile Referee Program Standards," 2000, www.njcourts.gov/notices/n001207a.pdf, https://perma.cc/XJ9Z-GXLF.

69. N.C.G.S.A § 7A-171.2.

70. N.C.G.S.A. § 7B–1902.

71. AS § 22.15.160, Qualifications of District Judges and Magistrates, State of Alaska, Online Recruitment System, "Magistrate Judge II" (Alaska Court System 41-8401), https://agency.governmentjobs.com/alaska/default.cfm?action= jobbulletin&JobID=692861, https://perma.cc/M4CK-QSDD.

72. 237 Pa. Code § 1182.

73. 49 Pa. Code § 20.11. For additional discussion on family and juvenile courts' reliance on nonlegal staff, *see* Jane C. Murphy and Jana B. Singer, *Divorced from Reality: Rethinking Family Dispute Resolution* (New York: NYU Press, 2015); see also Hatcher, "Juvenile Court Interagency Agreements," 40.

74. IBM Watson, "Case Studies, Montgomery County Juvenile Court," www.ibm.com/case-studies/montgomery-county-juvenile-court, https://perma .cc/6R3M-3SLZ.

75. Chris Stewart, "Hey Watson: Local Judge First to Use IBM Watson's Artificial Intelligence on Juvenile Cases," *Dayton Daily News*, August 3, 2017, www.daytondailynews.com/news/local/county-judge-first-use-ibm-watson -supercomputer-juvenile-cases/InVqz6eeNxvFsMVAe5zrbL/, https://perma.cc /EYP8-RMZB.

76. Stewart, "Hey Watson."

77. National Council of Juvenile and Family Court Judges, "2018 National Conference on Juvenile Justice," presenting Sponsor, IBM Watson, https://perma .cc/GJR4-R9EX; National Council of Juvenile and Family Court Judges, "The Honorable Anthony Capizzi Is NCJFCJ's 73rd President," July 18, 2017, www .ncjfcj.org/news/the-honorable-anthony-tony-capizzi-is-ncjfcjs-73rd-president/, https://perma.cc/Z32R-EL5R,.

78. Partnership on AI, *Report on Algorithmic Risk Assessment Tools in the U.S. Criminal Justice System*, www.partnershiponai.org/report-on-machine -learning-in-risk-assessment-tools-in-the-u-s-criminal-justice-system/.

79. Jeff Larson, "How We Analyzed the COMPAS Recidivism Algorithm," *ProPublica*, May 23, 2016, www.propublica.org/article/how-we-analyzed-the -compas-recidivism-algorithm; see also Tom Simonite, "Algorithms Should've Made Courts More Fair: What Went Wrong?," *Wired*, September 5, 2019, www.wired.com/story/algorithms-shouldve-made-courts-more-fair-what-went -wrong/.

80. Equivant FAQs, www.equivant.com/faq/, https://perma.cc/V5QG-DJ9K.

81. Electronic Privacy Information Center, "AI and Human Rights: Criminal Justice System," www.epic.org/ai/criminal-justice/index.html.

82. See, for example, Michele Gilman, "AI Algorithms Intended to Root out Welfare Fraud Often End Up Punishing the Poor Instead," *The Conversation*, February 14, 2020, https://theconversation.com/ai-algorithms-intended-to-root -out-welfare-fraud-often-end-up-punishing-the-poor-instead-131625; and Virginia Eubanks, *Automating Inequality: How High-Tech Tools Profile, Police, and Punish the Poor* (New York: St. Martin's Press, 2018).

83. See Robert J. Condlin, "Online Dispute Resolution: Stinky, Repugnant, or Drab," *Cardozo Journal of Conflict Resolution* 18 (2017): 717, 717–21.

84. For example, Superior Court of the State of California, for the County of Los Angeles, Standing Order, December 7, 2020, https://my.lacourt.org/odr /assets/ODR-SC_NoticeWithOrder.pdf.

85. Erika Rickard, "Online Dispute Resolution Moves from E-Commerce to the Courts," Pew Charitable Trusts, June 4, 2019, www.pewtrusts.org /en/research-and-analysis/articles/2019/06/04/online-dispute-resolution-moves -from-e-commerce-to-the-courts, https://perma.cc/59FV-9X3V.

86. For example, Jarrett Gorlin, "Online Dispute Resolution Offers Traffic Courts COVID-Safe Justice," GCN, April 8, 2021, https://gcn.com/state -local/2021/04/online-dispute-resolution-offers-traffic-courts-covid-safe-justice /315275/; Matterhorn, "Traffic and Warrant Resolution Results—14A District Court," https://getmatterhorn.com/get-results/traffic-court/traffic-warrant -resolution/, https://perma.cc/6NYH-RGZL ("Online cases close more quickly and close with less staff handling time," and the court "has been able to speed up revenue collection as a result of closing cases sooner.").

87. For example, John D. Bessler, *Private Prosecution in America: Its Origin, History, and Unconstitutionality in the Twenty-First Century* (Durham, NC: Carolina Academic Press, 2022); and, National Union of Special Police Officers, "About SPO's," www.nuspo.org/about-spos, https://perma.cc/V48Y -BR47 (describing privatized police in multiple states with full state police powers).

88. See generally Anna VanCleave, Brian Highsmith, Judith Resnik, Jeffrey Selbin, and Lisa Foster, "Money and Punishment, Circa 2020," Yale Center for Public Interest Law, Fines & Fees Justice Center, and UC Berkley Policy Advocacy Clinic, 2020, https://law.yale.edu/sites/default/files/area/center/liman /document/money_and_punishment_circa_2020.pdf.

89. Judicial Council of California, *Report on Statewide Collection of Court-Ordered Debt for 2019–20*, www.courts.ca.gov/documents/lr-2020-JC -statewide-court-ordered-debt-2019-20-pc1463_010c.pdf.

90. Judicial Council of California, *Report on Statewide Collection*.

91. Paulina Maqueda Escamilla, "Unholy Alliance: California Courts' Use of Private Debt Collectors," California Reinvestment Coalition, May 2018, http:// ebclc.org/wp-content/uploads/2018/05/Unholy-Alliance-California-Courts-Use -of-Private-Debt-Collectors.pdf.

92. Clackamas County, Oregon, Justice Court 2020–2021 Budget Presentation, https://dochub.clackamas.us/documents/drupal/2988bc3b-8a3d-4605 -9064-36388d131c8b, https://perma.cc/TXQ7-FNBF.

93. Clackamas County, Oregon, Justice Court 2020–2021 Budget Presentation.

94. US Federal Trade Commission, *The Structure and Practices of the Debt Buying Industry*, January 2013, www.ftc.gov/sites/default/files/documents /reports/structure-and-practices-debt-buying-industry/debtbuyingreport.pdf.

95. US FTC, *Structure and Practices of the Debt Buying Industry*.

96. US Consumer Financial Protection Bureau, "Market Snapshot: Third-Party Debt Collections Tradeline Reporting," July 2019, www.consumerfinance .gov/data-research/research-reports/market-snapshot-third-party-debt -collections-tradeline-reporting/.

97. Midland Credit Management, "Who Is Midland Credit Management?," www.midlandcredit.com/who-is-mcm/, https://perma.cc/83J5-MPFB.

98. Encore Capital Group, *2020 Annual Report*, https://encorecapital.gcs -web.com/static-files/01f2272e-2aaa-4fbc-b59c-4b34c762ac25, https://perma .cc/ENV6-Y8NF.

99. Illinois Attorney General, "Madigan Announces $6 Million Settlement with Encore Capital to Reform Debt Buying and Collection Practices," press release, December. 4, 2018, https://illinoisattorneygeneral.gov/pressroom/2018 _12/2018124b.html.

100. "How Debt Collectors Are Transforming the Business of State Courts," Pew Charitable Trusts, May 2020, www.pewtrusts.org/-/media/assets/2020/06 /debt-collectors-to-consumers.pdf.

101. Bill Smith, "Debt Collectors Flex Muscle in People's Court, System Not Much Help to People Who Owe," *News-Press*, August 4, 2017, www.news -press.com/story/news/2017/08/04/sxdx/484768001/.

102. Human Rights Watch, *U.S. Courts, Debt Buying Corporations, and the Poor*, 2016, www.hrw.org/report/2016/01/20/rubber-stamp-justice/us-courts -debt-buying-corporations-and-poor.

103. For example, Mariele McGlazer, *Default Justice: Debt Buyer Lawsuits in Philadelphia Municipal Court*, Fells Institute of Government, July 31, 2020, https:// fels.upenn.edu/sites/default/files/Default%20Justice_McGlazer%20Capstone _FINAL.pdf ("In the rare cases where defendants were represented, they were more likely to win: 57% in these cases resulted in judgements for the defendant, compared to just 1% of cases where the defendant was unrepresented.").

104. Yamil Berard, "Debt Cases Clog Courts, Leave Consumers Feeling Exploited," *Atlanta Journal-Constitution*, April 26, 2019, www.ajc.com/news /crime--law/consumers-face-long-odds-battling-debt-collectors-local-courts /SoL4ouXk7naRVFi6MFYwlI/.

105. Berard, "Debt Cases Clog Courts."

106. Berard, "Debt Cases Clog Courts."

CHAPTER 2. JUVENILE COURTS MONETIZING CHILD REMOVALS

1. See Cedric J. Robinson, *Black Marxism: The Making of the Black Radical Tradition* (Chapel Hill, NC: UNC Press, 1983) (Robinson developed the concept of "racial capitalism").

2. *See* Daniel L. Hatcher, *The Poverty Industry: The Exploitation of America's Most Vulnerable Citizens* (New York: NYU Press, 2016), 15.

3. See Daniel L. Hatcher, "Juvenile Court Interagency Agreements: Subverting Impartial Justice to Maximize Revenue from Children," *NYU Annual Survey of American Law* 76 (2020): 33, 45–53 (summarizing the Ohio juvenile court IV-E contractual strategies).

4. Patrick Griffin and Gregory Halemba, "Federal Placement Assistance Funding for Delinquency Services," *Children, Families and the Courts Ohio Bulletin* (Winter 2003), www.ncjj.org/PDF/winter2003cfc.pdf, [https://perma.cc/3U7N-ZGHH].

5. See Ohio Department of Job and Family Services, Subgrant Agreement, https://lcapps.co.lucas.oh.us/carts/resos/23039.pdf, https://perma.cc/WME9-DTSN; see also Daniel L. Hatcher, "States Diverting Funds from the Poor," in *Holes in the Safety Net: Federalism and Poverty*, ed. Ezra Rosser, 151–72 (providing a summary of the Ohio juvenile court subgrant agreement practices, along with several other state revenue strategies that use vulnerable populations as a source of revenue).

6. Ohio Department of Job and Family Services, Subgrant Agreement, Article I, Section B.

7. Jefferson County Court of Common Pleas, Probate and Juvenile Division, *2016 Annual Report*, http://jjohio.org/wp-content/uploads/2017/08/Jefferson-County-Juvenile-Court-2016-Report.pdf, https://perma.cc/2S7S-NUSH (listing juvenile court budget of approximately $1.6 million, compared to the court's IV-E revenue of over $845,000).

8. Muskingum County Juvenile Court, *2015 Annual Report*, www.muskingumcountyoh.gov/Media/Muskingum-County-Juvenile-Court-Detention-Center-2015-Annual-Report.pdf, https://perma.cc/7LYS-PKU3.

9. County of Cuyahoga, *2017 Results of Operations*, 25, https://fiscalofficer.cuyahogacounty.us/pdf_fiscalofficer/en-US/obm/2017ResultsOfOperations.pdf, https://perma.cc/VF98-NN9Q; and County of Cuyahoga, "2018–2019 Biennial Budget," 168, https://fiscalofficer.cuyahogacounty.us/pdf_fiscalofficer/en-US/obm/2018-2019BudgetPlan.pdf, https://perma.cc/T7XY-KTHG.

10. Montgomery County, Ohio, Office of Management and Budget, "2020 Adopted Budget and Plan," 363, www.mcohio.org/FINAL%20PRINTED%20BUDGET%20DOCUMENT%207.23.2020%20193614_complete.pdf.

11. "State of Ohio Title IV-E Juvenile Court Contact List," https://jfs.ohio.gov/ocf/JuvenileCourtContactList.stm, https://perma.cc/U6NA-HC55 (listing 27 county "IV-E courts" as of January 3, 2022).

12. Denise Navarre Cubbon and Steve Hanson, "Permanency–A Forever Home for Children in Foster Care: What Courts Can Do," *Children, Family and the Courts Ohio Bulletin* (Fall 2012): 8, http://ohiofamilyrights.com/Reports/Special-Reports-Page-3/Permanency---A-Forever-Home-for-Children-in-Foster-Care-What-Courts-Can-Do.pdf, https://perma.cc/54J5-EQP4 ("The Bureau of Fiscal Administration and Fiscal Accountability, located within the Ohio Department of Job and Family Services' Office of Families and Children is offering a two-day 'Guidance Training' for courts interested in understanding ways to increase funding through the Title IV-E program.").

13. Ohio Department of Job and Family Services, Bureau of Fiscal Accountability, "How to Allocate Costs (Develop the Allowable Cost Pool) and Complete the Quarterly Billing Form (JFS 01797) for Title IV-E," http://jfs.ohio.gov/ocf/JVCIV_ECostAllocation_QBillTrain020613Final1.stm, https://perma.cc/4AN4-7ZHE. See also Hatcher, "States Diverting Funds from the Poor," 162; and Hatcher, "Juvenile Court Interagency Agreements," 47–48.

14. The last name of the cartoon character Betty Rubble from the *Flintstones* is apparently misspelled, unless the error was purposeful to refer to Betty having money, since "ruble" is the form of currency used in Russia. Ohio Department of Job and Family Services, "How to Allocate Costs," 58.

15. Ohio Department of Job and Family Services, Office of Families and Children, "Title IV-E Reimbursement Ceilings for April 1, 2021 through March 21, 2022," https://jfs.ohio.gov/ocf/IVECeilings2122.stm, https://perma.cc/P6JH-KK5H. See also Hatcher, "Juvenile Court Interagency Agreements," 47.

16. Social Security Act § 472(c)(2).

17. National Council of Juvenile and Family Court Judges, Juvenile Sanctions Center, "Using Federal Title IV-E Money to Expand Sanctions and Services for Juvenile Offenders," *Training and Technical Assistance Program Bulletin* 2, no. 2 (2004): 4, http://docplayer.net/18586465-Using-federal-title-iv-e-mony-to-expand-sanctions-and-services-for-juvenile-offenders.html, https://perma.cc/36W9-4ACV.

18. Aram Roston, "Fostering Profits: Abuse and Neglect at America's Biggest For-Profit Foster Care Company," *Buzzfeed*, February 20, 2015, www.buzzfeednews.com/article/aramroston/fostering-profits.

19. Roston, "Fostering Profits"; and Aram Roston, "Senate Finds 86 Children Died in Care of Giant For-Profit Foster Care Firm," *Buzzfeed*, October 18, 2017, www.buzzfeednews.com/article/aramroston/senate-finds-86-children-died-in-care-of-giant-for-profit.

20. Ohio Mentor, "Ohio MENTOR Executive Director Appointed to Statewide Foster Care Advisory Council," November 12, 2019, www.oh-mentor.com/about/success-stories/ohio-mentor-executive-director-appointed-to-statewide-foster-care-advisory-council, https://perma.cc/G8YW-U2UY.

21. US Securities and Exchange Commission, "Centerbridge Partners Completes Acquisition of Civitas Solutions, Inc.," March 18, 2019, www.sec.gov/Archives/edgar/data/1608638/000119312519069320/d713806dex992.htm, https://perma.cc/DSP9-G28V; and Patrick Thomas, "Centerbridge Partners Buying Civitas for $1.4 Billion," *Wall Street Journal*, December 18, 2018.

22. Hamilton County Juvenile Court, *2013 Annual Report*, 1,4, www.juvenile-court.org/juvenilecourt/Annual_Report/2013_Annual_Report.pdf, https://perma.cc/XH5U-SKFX.

23. Hamilton County Juvenile Court, *2013 Annual Report*.

24. Hamilton County Juvenile Court, *2013 Annual Report*.

25. Hamilton County Juvenile Court, *2013 Annual Report*, 30.

26. Ohio Department of Job and Family Services, Bureau of Fiscal Accountability, "How to Develop the Allowable Cost Pool and Complete the Quarterly Billing Form (JFS 01797) for Title IV-E," http://jfs.ohio.gov/ocf/JVCIV_ECostAllocation_QBillTrain020613Final1.stm, https://perma.cc/UU7F

-CNT5; Lucas County Juvenile Court, Subgrant Agreement, Attachment B, https://lcapps.co.lucas.oh.us/carts/resos/19244.pdf, https://perma.cc/2EG8-BZNJ. See also Hatcher, "Juvenile Court Interagency Agreements," 48–49.

27. Ohio Department of Job and Family Services, Bureau of Fiscal Account-ability, "How to Develop the Allowable Cost Pool." See also Hatcher, "Juvenile Court Interagency Agreements," 49.

28. Lucas County Juvenile Court, 2016 Annual Report, 35, www.co.lucas.oh .us/DocumentCenter/View/70170/2016-Annual-Report-LCJC, https://perma.cc /HTW9-6G4J.

29. Justice Benefits, Inc., "Web Based System for the Ohio Juvenile Courts," http://jfs.ohio.gov/ocf/WebBasedRMSinformation.pdf, https://perma.cc/C7SD -A453. See also Miami County, Ohio, "Commissioners, Meeting Minutes Sum-mary," July 19, 2018, www.co.miami.oh.us/ArchiveCenter/ViewFile/Item/1469, https://perma.cc/6M38-DK5D.

30. Miami County, Ohio, Commissioners Meeting Minutes Summary, December 30, 2014, www.co.miami.oh.us/Archive/ViewFile/Item/379, https:// perma.cc/FCP7-L8GP.; see also Hatcher, "States Diverting Funds from the Poor," 163; and Hatcher, "Juvenile Court Interagency Agreements," 49.

31. Justice Benefits, Inc., "Web Based System for the Ohio Juvenile Courts"; Ohio Department of Job and Family Services, Office of Families and Children, "Title IV-E Foster Care Candidacy and RMS Overview," video, June 20, 2018, www.youtube.com/watch?v=mxtFccp5XGw&feature=youtu.be, https://perma .cc/VKG7-6827 (training provided by Justice Benefits, Inc. and state agency staff); and State of Ohio, SACWIS Knowledge Base, "Candidacy for Foster Care Webinars," https://jfskb.com/sacwis/index.php/ofc-policy/862-candidacy -for-foster-care-webinar-qa.

32. Juvenile Court of the Parish of Jefferson, State of Louisiana, "Finan-cial Statements, . . . Year Ended December 31, 2005," https://app.lla.state .la.us/PublicReports.nsf/AC395D55385EFD5D862571CB00533F01/$FILE /00000544.pdf, https://perma.cc/M8CE-LE2G. See also Hatcher, "Juvenile Court Interagency Agreements," 50.

33. Juvenile Court of the Parish of Jefferson, State of Louisiana, "Financial Statements, . . . Year Ended December 31, 2005." See also Hatcher, "Juvenile Court Interagency Agreements," 50.

34. Juvenile Court of the Parish of Jefferson, Harvey, Louisiana, "Financial Statements, December 31, 2017," https://app.lla.state.la.us/PublicReports.nsf /06DBEDF6B7F7A7F8862582D500627D06/$FILE/0001A193.pdf, https:// perma.cc/2SNQ-CUVK. See also Orleans Parish Juvenile Court, "2018 Pro-posed Annual Budget," template 4, http://cityofno.granicus.com/MetaViewer .php?view_id=3&clip_id=2782&meta_id=387149, https://perma.cc/LRQ6-3VSG (noting $250,000 in IV-E revenue in 2018).

35. Jefferson Parish Council, Minutes of April 8, 2020 meeting, "Jefferson Parrish Legals," www.nola.com/content/tncms/assets/v3/editorial/f/41/f414f60e -7f27-11ea-a04b-e7d2da102968/5e971ea5ccd33.pdf.pdf, https://perma.cc/NLK9 -38HU]

36. For example, in Muskegon County, Michigan, the Circuit Court-Family Division entered a contract with JBI to "capture new Title IV-E federal

reimbursement dollars." Muskegon County Board of Commissioners, Minutes, January 9, 2001, 202, www.co.muskegon.mi.us/DocumentCenter/View/5514 /2001-Board-Minutes-PDF, https://perma.cc/N978-A8Y8; see also Muskegon County Board of Commissioners, Agenda, December 6, 2011, www.co.muskegon .mi.us/AgendaCenter/ViewFile/Agenda/_12062011-653, https://perma.cc/8CTY -UNT4 ("The IV-E Funding Coordinator, under the general direction of the Deputy Circuit Court Administrator is responsible for management of the funding streams used by the court when placing children removed from their homes pursuant to Michigan law and to ensure that the available IV-E funding streams are maximized when appropriate and possible."); and Nebraska Department of Health and Human Services, "Nebraska's Five-Year Title IV-E Prevention Program Plan," 2020, 10, https://dhhs.ne.gov/Documents/NE%20FFPSA%205 %20Year%20Plan.pdf, https://perma.cc/SS5V-9LUK (encouraging interagency agreements with juvenile probation departments, which are run by the juvenile courts in Nebraska, so the courts' probation officers can claim IV-E funds from children, referencing Nebraska Revised Statute §29-2260.02).

37. Missouri Department of Social Services, Children's Division, "IV-E Authority—Juvenile Courts," FY 2021, https://oa.mo.gov/sites/default/files /dss_iv-e_courts.pdf, https://perma.cc/2N2K-QE98; see also Jeffrey M. Barlow, "Title IV-E Administrative Claiming in Juvenile Courts," Institute for Court Management, April 9, 2000, https://ncsc.contentdm.oclc.org/digital/api /collection/financial/id/58/download, https://perma.cc/BED8-KZMH; and Missouri Department of Social Services v. Leavitt, 448 F.3d 997 (8th Cir. 2006) (holding that under previous interagency contract, the Missouri courts' attempts to seek IV-E funds were not allowable).

38. Iowa Department of Human Services, *Employee's Manual*, 6, https:// dhs.iowa.gov/sites/default/files/13-B.pdf, https://perma.cc/5KSS-RN7C; see also Iowa Judicial Branch, Juvenile Court Services, "Request for Quotation, Random Moment Sampling System and Title IV-E Administrative Claim Support," October 6, 2020, www.iowacourts.gov/static/media/cms/RFQ_RMS_JB100620 _C50A8FDEFE85E.pdf, https://perma.cc/F6SU-2JB6.

39. Pima County, Arizona, "FY 2019/2020 Budget," 5–161, https://webcms .pima.gov/UserFiles/Servers/Server_6/File/Government/Finance%20and %20Risk%20Management/Reports/budget%20reports/2019-2020/2019 -2020%20Recommended%20Budget%20Book.pdf. See also Hatcher, "Juvenile Court Interagency Agreements," 51–53 (summarizing state juvenile court IV-E strategies, in addition to Ohio).

40. Almost half of the juvenile probation departments across the country are run by the juvenile courts, increasing the potential for the court systems to generate IV-E funds from children. See National Center for State Courts, "Branch Responsibility for Probation," www.ncsc.org/__data/assets/pdf_file /0022/25672/branch-responsible-for-probation.pdf.

41. 705 ILCS 405, Art. VI.

42. Cook County Government Office of the Chief Judge Juvenile Probation and Court Services, Professional Services Agreement with Justice Benefits, Inc., Contract no. 1490-13306, http://opendocs.cookcountyil.gov/procurement

/contracts/1490-13306.pdf, https://perma.cc/2RWS-B268. See also McLean County, Illinois, Minutes of the Justice Committee, April 1, 2008, www .mcleancountyil.gov/Archive/ViewFile/Item/1861, https://perma.cc/N92J-Y8XN ("Motion by Nuckolls/Harding to Recommend Approval of an Addendum to the Justice Benefits Contract to seek Title IV-E Administrative Claims Funds for McLean County Court Services, Juvenile Division").

43. State of Texas, Interagency Cooperation Contract, contract no. 530-12-0224-00001, "Title IV-E Services—Foster Care Maintenance Administrative and Training," www2.tjjd.texas.gov/procurementfiles//Interagency /DFPS%20-%20Title%20IV-E/CON0000206-Amend_3-Executed.PDF, https://perma.cc/Y5LU-RN46.

44. Bexar County Juvenile Probation Department, *2017 Annual Report*, http://home.bexar.org/JPDAnnualReport/2017/BCJPD_annualreport_2017 _web.pdf, https://perma.cc/A7TB-FN27. See also State of Texas, County of Bexar, 436th Juvenile District Court, biography of Judge Lisa A. Barrett, www .bexar.org/1801/436th-Juvenile-District-Court, www.bexar.org/1801/436th -Juvenile-District-Court; and Texas Code, Human Resources, § 152.0032 (Composition of Juvenile Board).

45. Nueces County Commissioners Court, Meeting December 12, 2014, AI-5835, Agreement between Justice Benefits, Inc. and Nueces County Juvenile Board, https://destinyhosted.com/agenda_publish.cfm?id=68323&mt=ALL&fp =swagit&get_month=6&get_year=2021&dsp=agm&seq=5835&rev=0&ag= 283&ln=11432&nseq=5851&nrev=0&pseq=5832&prev=0#ReturnTo11432, https://perma.cc/DH2S-TBAG; Mauricio Julian Cuellar, and "Juvenile Board Members Review Next Year's Probation Dept. Budget," *Alice Echo-News Journal*, December 19, 2008, www.alicetx.com/article/20081219/News/312199996. Similarly, in Harris County, Texas, the judges of the Juvenile Board approved a contract with Justice Benefits, Inc. to claim IV-E funds, outside of the normal competitive bid process. Harris County Juvenile Board, Meeting, Feb. 24, 2010, https://hcjpd.harriscountytx.gov/Board%20Agendas/Board%20Agenda%20 -%20February%2024,%202010.pdf, https://perma.cc/D592-NDY5 (approval of exemption from competitive bid process and renewal of contract with Justice Benefits, Inc.).

46. G. Alan Tarr, "Interpreting the Separation of Powers in State Constitutions," *NYU Annual Survey of American Law* 59 (2003): 329. Further, states still recognize the separation of powers doctrine when not explicitly stated in their state constitution. See Curtis Rodebush, "Separation of Powers in Ohio: A Critical Analysis," *Cleveland State Law Review* 51 (2004): 505.

47. Paul R. Verkuil, "Separation of Powers, the Rule of Law and the Idea of Independence," *William & Mary Law Review* 30 (1989): 301, 306.

48. Verkuil, "Separation of Powers."

49. See Hatcher, "Juvenile Court Interagency Agreements," 64–82 (summarizing separation of powers concerns with juvenile court foster care and child support interagency revenue contracts); see generally Josh Gupta-Kagan, "Where the Judiciary Prosecutes in Front of Itself: Missouri's Unconstitutional Juvenile Court Structure," *Missouri Law Review* 78 (2013): 1245 (excellent

article discussing separation of powers concerns where juvenile court officials carry out agency functions in abuse, neglect, and delinquency cases).

50. Encarnacion Pyle, "Juvenile Courts' Role Debated," *Columbus Dispatch*, September 11, 2006, www.pressreader.com/usa/the-columbus-dispatch /20060911/282033322676879.

51. Pyle, "Juvenile Courts' Role Debated"; and Ohio Updates, "Title IV-E Courts Receive Support of Ohio Judicial Conference," *Children, Families and the Courts Ohio Bulletin* (Fall 2006): 17, www.supremecourt.ohio.gov/JCS /CFC/resources/bulletin/fall2006.pdf, https://perma.cc/9LAJ-2RVX. See also Hatcher, "Juvenile Court Interagency Agreements," 68–69.

52. Ohio Judicial Conference, Juvenile Law and Procedure Committee, "Resolution to Support Optional Juvenile Court Participation as a Title IV-E placing Agency," November 17, 2006, www.ohiojudges.org/Document.ashx?DocGuid =400faab0-352d-474a-bcb9-d85a82f81bd7, https://perma.cc/G88S-9JQX. See also Hatcher, "States Diverting Funds from the Poor," 163.

53. Ohio Judicial Conference, Juvenile Law and Procedure Committee, "Resolution to Support Optional Juvenile Court Participation."

54. Ohio Code 5101:9-7-08 ("The county juvenile court and the board of county commissioners may enter into a subgrant agreement with ODJFS to administer Title IV-E of the Social Security Act, which allows the juvenile court to assume full responsibility for the placement and care of adjudicated unruly and delinquent children. The subgrant agreement enables these courts to receive Title IV-E reimbursement for allowable foster care maintenance (FCM), administration, and training costs as outlined in this rule.").

55. US Department of Health and Human Services, Administration for Children and Families, *Child Welfare Manual*, 8.3A.12 TITLE IV-E, Foster Care Maintenance Payments Program, Eligibility, Responsibility for placement and care, question 4, www.acf.hhs.gov/cwpm/public_html/programs/cb /laws_policies/laws/cwpm/policy_dsp.jsp?citID=31; see also Ohio Code 5101: 2-42-04.

56. See Hatcher, "Juvenile Court Interagency Agreements," 71–72; and Ohio Code 5101:2-47. In addition to the agency responsibilities of ensuring proper administration of funds, determining eligibility, maintaining case records, and even overseeing the provision of adequate education services, the

Title IV-E agency having responsibility for the placement and care of the child shall:

(5) Facilitate service planning and provision of services under the FCM program. Service planning and provision of services shall include but are not limited to:

(a) Placement prevention efforts.
(b) Determining the appropriateness of placement.
(c) Ensuring all procedural safeguards are provided.
(d) Case management.
(e) Family reunification efforts.
(f) Providing support to the child's caregivers.
(g) Discharge planning.
(h) Independent living.
(i) Referral to other programs as required or necessary.

57. See *Federal Placement Assistance Funding for Delinquency Services* (citing 45 CFR 1356.21(E), 45 CFR 1356.21(b)(1), Sec. 471(a)(15), Social Security Act [42 U.S.C. 671(a)(15)], 65 FR 4053, 45 CFR 1356.21(b)).

58. Ohio Rules of Juvenile Procedure, Rule 19 (Motions) and Rule 35 (Continuing Jurisdiction).

59. Ohio Code Sec. 2151.61.

60. *Federalist*, no. 10 (James Madison). See also Verkuil, "Separation of Powers," 305.

61. See Ohio Department of Job and Family Services, Subgrant Agreement. See also Hatcher, "Juvenile Court Interagency Agreements," 74–75.

62. US Department of Justice, Civil Rights Division, *Investigation of the St. Louis County Family Court*, July 31, 2015, https://sites.ed.gov/underservedyouth/files/2017/01/Report-Investigation-of-the-St-Louis-County-Family-Court.pdf. See also Hatcher, "Juvenile Court Interagency Agreements," 75.

63. See Hatcher, "Juvenile Court Interagency Agreements," 83–90 (summarizing due process concerns with juvenile court IV-E and IV-D interagency contracts).

64. Caperton v. A.T. Massey Coal Co., Inc., 556 U.S. 868, 877–78 (2009) (discussing and quoting *Tumey v. Ohio*, 273 U.S. 510, 520–35 (1927)). See also, Hatcher, "States Diverting Funds from the Poor," 165; and Hatcher, "Juvenile Court Interagency Agreements," 83–85.

65. Ward v. Village of Monroeville, 409 U.S. 57 (1972).

66. Caliste v. Cantrell, 937 F.3d. 525 (5th Cir. 2019).

67. Cain v. White, 937 F.3d. 446 (5th Cir. 2019).

68. In fact, contract language reveals the juvenile courts are aware that the conflict undermines impartiality. Due to the financial incentives, the contract includes a line that warns each juvenile court to "not deliberately adjudicate a child unruly or delinquent for the sole purpose of receiving Federal Financial Participation (FFP) [federal IV-E funds]." Ohio Department of Job and Family Services, Subgrant Agreement.

69. County Council of Cuyahoga County, Ohio, Resolution no. R2017-0142, http://council.cuyahogacounty.us/pdf_council/en-US/Legislation/Resolutions/2017/R2017-0142C%20OBM%20Fiscal%20Items%20for%208-8-2017%20and%20amending%20R2017-0098.pdf, https://perma.cc/JH3A-HQVH (The budget maneuver illustrates that the salary increases were to be paid out of the county general fund, but the juvenile court simultaneously transferred money from its IV-E revenue to pay the full amount back to the county general fund.). See also Hatcher, "Juvenile Court Interagency Agreements," 85–86.

70. Pyle, "Juvenile Courts' Role Debated." See also Hatcher, "States Diverting Funds from the Poor," 164–65.

71. Ohio Department of Youth Services, RECLAIM Ohio, https://dys.ohio.gov/courts-and-community/reclaim#RECLAIMOhio.

72. Ohio Revised Code § 5139.41. See also National Conference of State Legislatures (NCSL), "Juvenile Justice Incentive Funding Overview," www.ncsl.org/documents/nalfo/JuvenileJusticeWilliams.pdf, https://perma.cc/T5RT-SPQ5 ("Under the formula, each court is given a number of 'credits' based on the court's four-year average of youth adjudicated for felony offenses. Those

credits are reduced by one credit for each chargeable DYS bed day used during the previous year and 2/3 credit for each chargeable community corrections facility bed day used during the previous year. Each court's percentage of the remaining credits statewide translates into that court's percentage of the total RECLAIM funds allocated to the courts.").

73. Matter of Dependency of A.E.T.H., 446 P.3d 667 (Wash. Ct. App., 2019), www.courts.wa.gov/opinions/pdf/769642.pdf.

74. *Matter of Dependency of A.E.T.H.*

75. *Matter of Dependency of A.E.T.H.* ("Here, Judge Farris displayed no personal bias and attempted to conduct an unbiased proceeding. But the sticky wicket is that the tribunal in which A.H.'s dependency and termination proceedings took place was biased because of the involvement of superior court employees working against the parents in this case. . . . In short, based on the above findings, Judge Farris correctly concluded that '[t]he Superior Court, its direct agents, and its own attorneys, all under the supervision of the judges repeatedly aligned with and literally became a party litigating this case against the parents . . . throughout the case.' These circumstances, which existed before, during, and after the termination trial, resulted in a tribunal that was biased and violated both parents' right to due process and the appearance of fairness doctrine."). See also Hatcher, "Juvenile Court Interagency Agreements," 90–91 (summarizing ethical concerns of interagency contracts).

76. Supreme Court of Ohio, Code of Judicial Conduct, Canon 4.

CHAPTER 3. JUDICIAL CHILD SUPPORT FACTORY

1. William P. Quigley, "Backwards into the Future: How Welfare Changes in the Millennium Resemble English Poor Law of the Middle Ages," *Stanford Law & Policy Review* 9 (1998): 101, 103–9 (internal quotation marks omitted), quoting 27 Hen. 8, c. 25 (1535) (Eng.), reprinted in Danby Pickering, ed., *Statutes at Large* (1762), 4:387–88.

2. Virginia v. Autry, 441 A.2d 1056, 1060 (Md. 1982) (citing 1781 Md. Laws, ch. 13, § 1) ("[A]ny justice of the peace . . . informed of any female person having an illegitimate child . . . shall call on her for security to indemnify the county from any charge that may accrue by means of such child, and, upon neglect or refusal, to commit her . . . until she shall give such security; but in case she shall on oath discover the father, then the said justice is hereby required to discharge her . . . and directed to call such father . . . to indemnify the county from all charges that may arise for the maintenance of such child.").

3. See Daniel L. Hatcher, "Child Support Harming Children: Subordinating the Best Interests of Children to the Fiscal Interests of the State," *Wake Forest Law Review* 42 (2007): 1029, 1035–41.

4. Hatcher, "Child Support Harming Children"; see also Jacobus tenBroek, "California's Dual System of Family Law: Its Origin, Development, and Present Status," Part I, *Stanford Law Review* 16 (1964): 257, 283–84.

5. 42 U.S.C. § 602(a)(11) (repealed 1996); see also Office of Child Support Enforcement, US Department of Health & Human Services, "Essentials for Attorneys in Child Support Enforcement," A-1 app. A (2002), www.acf.hhs.gov

/sites/default/files/documents/ocse/essentials_for_attorneys_appendix_a.pdf (noting the legislative history of child support enforcement).

6. See, for example, Daniel L. Hatcher, "Don't Forget Dad: Addressing Women's Poverty by Rethinking Forced and Outdated Child Support Policies," *Journal of Gender, Social Policy & the Law* 20 (2012): 775, 793; and Lee A. Harris, "From Vermont to Mississippi: Race and Cash Welfare," *Columbia Human Rights Law Review* 38 (2006): 1, 40–41.

7. Lucy A. Williams, "The Ideology of Division: Behavior Modification Welfare Reform Proposals," *Yale Law Journal* 102 (1992): 719, 737 (describing the false racialized view against parents receiving welfare).

8. See Hatcher, "Child Support Harming Children," 1041–42; and Daniel L. Hatcher, *The Poverty Industry: The Exploitation of America's Most Vulnerable Citizens* (New York: NYU Press, 2016), 143–51.

9. Hatcher, *Poverty Industry*, 143–51; see also S. Rep. No. 1356 (1974), reprinted in 1974 U.S.C.C.A.N. 8133, 8158.

10. See US Department of Health & Human Services, Office of Child Support Enforcement, *FY 2019 Preliminary Data Report*, June 23, 2020, www.acf .hhs.gov/css/policy-guidance/fy-2019-preliminary-data-report; and Children's Defense Fund, "The State of America's Children 2021," www.childrensdefense .org/state-of-americas-children/soac-2021-child-population/ (listing population of children in the U.S. at approximately 73 million).

11. US Department of Health & Human Services, Office of Child Support Enforcement, "Characteristics of Families Served by the Child Support (IV-D) Program," November 19, 2018, www.acf.hhs.gov/archive/css /report/characteristics-families-served-child-support-iv-d-program-2016-census -survey. The federal agency data shows that 27 percent of custodial parents in the IV-D system are Black parents, while the Census Bureau estimates that Black individuals account for 13.4 percent of the US population. US Census Bureau, "QuickFacts: United States, Population Estimates, July 1, 2021," www.census .gov/quickfacts/fact/table/US/PST045219.

12. US Department of Health & Human Services, Office of Child Support Enforcement, "Who Owes the Child Support Debt?," September 15, 2017, www .acf.hhs.gov/css/ocsedatablog/2017/09/who-owes-the-child-support-debt.

13. Vicki Turetsky, "Reforming Child Support to Improve Outcomes for Children and Families," *Abell Report* 32, no. 5 (June 2019), https://abell.org /sites/default/files/files/Abell%20Child%20Support%20Reform%20-%20Full %20Report%202_20_2020%20edits%20v1_3.pdf. For additional excellent analysis regarding the harm and flawed IV-D policies, including the impact on low-income fathers and families, see Jane C. Murphy, "Legal Images of Fatherhood: Welfare Reform, Child Support Enforcement, and Fatherless Children," *Notre Dame Law Review* 81 (2005): 325; see also Stacy L. Brustin and Lisa Vollendorf Martin, "Bridging the Justice Gap in Family Law: Repurposing Federal IV-D Funding to Expand Community-Based Legal and Social Services for Parents," *Hastings Law Journal* 67 (2016): 1265; and Tonya L. Brito, "The Child Support Debt Bubble," *University of California Irvine Law Review* 9 (2019): 953.

14. See US Department of Health & Human Services, *FY 2019 Preliminary Data Report*.

15. Heather Hahn, "Relief from Government-Owed Child Support Debt and Its Effects on Parents and Children," Urban Institute, August 2019, www.urban .org/sites/default/files/publication/100812/relief_from_government-owed_child _support_debt_and_its_effects_on_parents_and_children_4.pdf.

16. For example, Attorney General of Texas, "Child Support and Public Assistance: How Can TANF and Medicaid Affect My Child Support?," www .texasattorneygeneral.gov/child-support/get-started/child-support-and-public -assistance, https://perma.cc/QMW4-H55K.

17. For simplicity, I sometimes refer to custodial parents as mothers and noncustodial parents as fathers, although certainly recognizing that the situation is often reversed.

18. See Hatcher, *Poverty Industry*, 144–45.

19. See Daniel L. Hatcher, "Collateral Children: Consequence and Illegality at the Intersection of Foster Care and Child Support," *Brooklyn Law Review* 74 (2009): 1333. After several years of advocacy and increased awareness and attention to the harm from child support enforcement in child welfare cases, the US Department of Health and Human Services' Children's Bureau issued an important modified policy guidance that encourages states to adopt new policies to reduce the limitation of child support against families pulled into the foster care system. Although this is an important change, the policy unfortunately does not prohibit the harmful actions—but rather clarifies that states have the option to stop the harm. See US Department of Health and Human Services, Office of the Administration for Children & Families, Children's Bureau, *Child Welfare Policy Manual*, 8.4C, question 5, June 8, 2022, www.acf.hhs.gov/cwpm /public_html/programs/cb/laws_policies/laws/cwpm/policy_dsp.jsp?citID=170 &utm_medium=email&utm_source=cwpmqaCB060322.

20. Orange County Department of Child Support Services, "Child Support and Foster Care," August 2019, www.css.ocgov.com/sites/css/files/import/data /files/100280.pdf.

21. Hatcher, "Collateral Children."

22. See Hatcher, "Child Support Harming Children," 1070–74.

23. Orange County Department of Child Support Services, "Child Support and Foster Care."

24. See Daniel L. Hatcher, "Juvenile Court Interagency Agreements: Subverting Impartial Justice to Maximize Revenue from Children," *NYU Annual Survey of American Law* 76 (2020): 33, 54–60 (summarizing juvenile court interagency IV-D contracts).

25. 45 CFR § 304.21 ("Federal financial participation is not available in . . . (2) Costs of compensation (salary and fringe benefits) of judges.").

26. The First Judicial District of Pennsylvania, The Philadelphia Courts, *2017 Annual Report*, 86, www.courts.phila.gov/pdf/report/2017-First-Judicial -District-Annual-Report.pdf, https://perma.cc/E2NZ-U9MH.

27. First Judicial District of Pennsylvania, *2017 Annual Report* (Exceptions to actual judges only occurred in 1,183 out of 31,181 cases.)

28. Philadelphia Family Court, *2012: Year in Review*, 2012, 49, https://courts .phila.gov/pdf/report/2012/FC-2012-Annual-Report.pdf, https://perma.cc /L358-AS9M ("Philadelphia Domestic Relations serves as the county Title IV-D

child support agency."); see also PA Child Support Program, Pennsylvania Department of Human Services, Bureau of Child Enforcement, September 17, 2016, www.humanservices.state.pa.us/CSWS/csws_controller.aspx?PageId=CSWS%2Fbcse_about.ascx&Preference=Desktop&Owner=Client, https://perma.cc/WES5-JMA8 ("The Department of Human Services, Bureau of Child Support Enforcement (BCSE), administers Pennsylvania's Child Support Enforcement Program through Cooperative Agreements with the 67 counties and county Courts of Common Pleas. The Domestic Relations Sections (DRSs) of the Courts of Common Pleas provide child support services in the counties."); Hatcher, "Juvenile Court Interagency Agreements," 59–60.

29. Pennsylvania Department of Human Services, 2015–2020 IV-D Cooperative Agreement with Domestic Relations Section of the Court of Common Pleas, Summerset County, https://contracts.patreasury.gov/Admin/Upload/331135_4100070496_201510201057.pdf, https://perma.cc/8JZR-F3MT; see also PA Child Support Program, Pennsylvania Department of Human Services, Bureau of Child Enforcement, September 17, 2016.

30. Pennsylvania Department of Human Services, 2015–2020 IV-D Cooperative Agreement, § 1.1.

31. Pennsylvania Department of Human Services, 2015–2020 IV-D Cooperative Agreement, § 2.2(i).

32. *In re Murchison*, 349 U.S. 133, 136 (1955).

33. *In re Murchison*, 349 U.S. 133, 137 (1955).

34. Pennsylvania Department of Human Services, 2015–2020 IV-D Cooperative Agreement, § 2.2(a).

35. Pennsylvania Department of Human Services, 2015–2020 IV-D Cooperative Agreement, § 3.12.

36. Pennsylvania Department of Human Services, 2015–2020 IV-D Cooperative Agreement, § 3.8.

37. Pennsylvania Department of Human Services, 2015–2020 IV-D Cooperative Agreement, § 4.4(p).

38. Pennsylvania Department of Human Services, 2015–2020 IV-D Cooperative Agreement, § 6.1.

39. Pennsylvania Department of Human Services, 2015–2020 IV-D Cooperative Agreement, 25.

40. Pennsylvania Department of Human Services, 2015–2020 IV-D Cooperative Agreement, 26 (explaining that "[t]he current support payment performance level for a DRS for a FFY is determined by dividing the current amount of total support collected during the FFY by the total amount of current support owed for the FFY").

41. Pennsylvania Department of Human Services, 2015–2020 IV-D Cooperative Agreement, 31.

42. Pennsylvania Department of Human Services, 2015–2020 IV-D Cooperative Agreement, § 7.

43. Pennsylvania Department of Human Services, 2015–2020 IV-D Cooperative Agreement, 30.

44. Pennsylvania Department of Human Services, 2015–2020 IV-D Cooperative Agreement, 30–31.

45. Pennsylvania Department of Human Services, 2015–2020 IV-D Cooperative Agreement, § 1.2.

46. See, for example, *Friend of the Court Model Handbook*, prepared by the Friend of the Court Bureau, State Court Administrative Office, Michigan Supreme Court, 2018, https://courts.michigan.gov/Administration/SCAO/Resources/Documents/Publications/Manuals/focb_hbk.pdf [https://perma.cc/JFP2-SUHU]; and Third Judicial Circuit Court of Michigan, 2017 *Annual Report* (2017), 29–30, www.3rdcc.org/Documents/Administration/General/Annual Reports/2017%5EAnnual%20Report%20for%202017%5E%5E.pdf, https://perma.cc/82UU-6V4Q ("The FOC is an administrative arm of the Court."); see also Hatcher, "Juvenile Court Interagency Agreements," 58–59.

47. Friend of the Court Act 294 of 1982, Mich. Comp. L. §§ 552.503, 552.507.

48. Board of Commissioners of the Court of Allegan, Friend of the Court Title IV-D Cooperative Reimbursement Agreement 2017/2021, State of Michigan, September 8, 2016, http://cms.allegancounty.org/sites/pages/Calendar/Lists/Board%20of%20Commissioners/Attachments/737/D1_147-607_FOC_approve5YRCRPAgreement.pdf, https://perma.cc/B966-WGC5.

49. Board of Commissioners of the Court of Allegan, Friend of the Court Title IV-D Cooperative Reimbursement Agreement.

50. John Schneider, "Tough Stance Is Paying Off," *Lansing State Journal*, October 10, 2004.

51. Schneider, "Tough Stance Is Paying Off."

52. Michigan State Court Administrative Office, Michigan Trial Court Administration, *Reference Guide*, 253, https://courts.michigan.gov/Administration/SCAO/Resources/Documents/Publications/Manuals/carg/carg.pdf, https://perma.cc/YWZ6-YN27.

53. See Ingham County, Friend of the Court, Attorney Referee, Posting #17-119, http://pe.ingham.org/Portals/PE/Job%20Posting/Attorney%20Referee%20FOC%206-24-17.pdf, https://perma.cc/5KPT-CQ7M (In the FOC's job announcement to hire a "referee," one of the duties listed is conducting enforcement hearings "at the County jail on lodged persons who have been arrested on bench warrants.").

54. "Incentive Payments: How to Maintain & Increase Funding," *Pundit* 24 (November 2011): 5, 8, https://courts.michigan.gov/Administration/SCAO/OfficesPrograms/FOC/Documents/Pundits/2011%2011%20Pundit.pdf, https://perma.cc/NV25-EV7A.

55. "Incentive Payments."

56. See Michigan Trial Court Administration, 254; and MCL § 400.18a.

57. Michigan Supreme Court, "Michigan Department of Health and Human Services 15 Percent Medical Support Incentive," memorandum, August 16, 2015, https://courts.michigan.gov/Administration/SCAO/OfficesPrograms/FOC/Documents/Memoranda/IncentivePayments.pdf, https://perma.cc/5A4R-LG6G.

58. See Michigan Trial Court Administration, 247; and MCL § 712A.18.

59. Michigan Trial Court Administration, 247 ("Title IV-E Money collected by the court for youth funded through Title IV-E may be retained and reported in the same manner as described under State Ward Board and Care. A 25 percent

administration fee is retained and the remaining 75 percent is either retained and reported or submitted to the state in the same ratio as costs are shared.").

60. Ohio Department of Job and Family Services, IV-D Contract, Warren County Child Support Enforcement Administration and Warren County Juvenile Court, https://www.co.warren.oh.us/Commissioners/Resolutions/2019/031919.pdf, https://perma.cc/7PGJ-AYPE; see also Hatcher, "Juvenile Court Interagency Agreements," 56–57.

61. Franklin County, Ohio, Resolution 0134-19, February 26, 2019, https://commissioners.franklincountyohio.gov/COMM-website/media/Documents/General%20Session/Agendas/(15)Feb-26-19.pdf?ext=.pdf, https://perma.cc/CSD6-MEFA; Lucas County Juvenile Court, 2013 Annual Report, 25, www.co.lucas.oh.us/DocumentCenter/View/70173/2013-Annual-Report-LCJC, https://perma.cc/KDJ5-D2ZK; and County Council of Cuyahoga County, Minutes, March 12, 2019 (describing the value of the 2019 IV-D contract with the County Domestic Relations Court of over $3.5 million and with the Juvenile Court of over $3.8 million); see also County Council of Cuyahoga County, Ohio, Resolution R2011-0104 (2011), http://council.cuyahogacounty.us/pdf_council/en-US/Legislation/Resolutions/2011/R2011-0104s.pdf, https://perma.cc/ZY42-QQX7.

62. U.S. v. Will, 449 U.S. 200, 218 (1980).

63. U.S. v. Will (emphasis was in the original Federalist, no. 79).

64. U.S. v. Will.

65. Lucas County, Ohio, Resolution no. 16-289, "Approval of Amendment to the Title IV-D Service Contract Between Lucas County Job & Family Services and Lucas County Common Pleas Court Juvenile Division for Magistrate Services," November 12, 2019, https://lcapps.co.lucas.oh.us/carts/resos/17713.pdf, https://perma.cc/7SVZ-7YNM; see also Holmes County Commissioners, minutes, Resolution no. 05-11-20-1, "Resolution Approving Title IV-D Contract," May 11, 2020, https://holmescountycommissioners.com/wp-content/uploads/2020/05/May-11-2020-Meeting-Minutes.pdf, https://perma.cc/D8ZF-AKKC.

66. County Council of Cuyahoga County, Meeting Agenda with Attachments, March 12, 2019, 138–39.

67. County Council of Cuyahoga County, Meeting Agenda with Attachments, 138.

68. Holmes County Commissioners, Minutes, May 11, 2020, Juvenile Court, IV-D Contract, https://holmescountycommissioners.com/wp-content/uploads/2020/05/May-11-2020-Meeting-Minutes.pdf, https://perma.cc/NQ8M-U6RU.

69. ABA Model Code of Judicial Conduct, Canon 1.

70. The facts of his case are in the public court documents and appellate opinions. See Hatcher, Poverty Industry, 154–57 (providing a more detailed description of Mr. Harvey's case, and the legal and policy analysis).

71. Hatcher, Poverty Industry, 155; and Harvey v. Marshall, 389 Md. 243 (2005).

72. Harvey v. Marshall, 158 Md. App. 355, 385 (2005); see also, Hatcher, Poverty Industry, 154–57.

73. Harvey v. Marshall, 158 Md. App. 355, 385 (2005); see also Hatcher, Poverty Industry, 154–57.

74. See MAXIMUS, Inc., and Brian Shea, Vice President, Program Modernization Consulting, https://maximus.com/making-impact-brian-shea, https://perma.cc/9875-QN58.

75. Maryland Judiciary, *Managing the Judiciary's Cooperative Reimbursement Agreement*, October 2015, 3, www.mdcourts.gov/sites/default/files/import/family/grants/cra/managingjudiciaryscramanualforadminjudgesmagistratesct administrators.pdf, https://perma.cc/R6HU-RU63; and *Managing the Judiciary's Title IV-D Child Support Cooperative Reimbursement Agreement (CRA)*, September 2018, https://mdcourts.gov/sites/default/files/import/procurement /grants/family/2019/cramanualmagistratesffy192012.pdf, https://perma.cc/6S2R -EHW9; see also Hatcher, "Juvenile Court Interagency Agreements," 58.

76. State of Maryland, Department of Human Services, Child Support Administration, Cooperative Reimbursement Agreement Terms and Conditions, Administrative Office of the Courts, October 1, 2018–September 30, 2021 (on file with author).

77. State of Maryland, Department of Human Services, Cooperative Reimbursement Agreement Terms and Conditions.

78. State of Maryland, Department of Human Services, Cooperative Reimbursement Agreement Terms and Conditions.

79. State of Maryland, Department of Human Services, Cooperative Reimbursement Agreement Terms and Conditions.

80. State of Maryland, Department of Human Services, Cooperative Reimbursement Agreement Terms and Conditions.

81. State of Maryland, Department of Human Services, Cooperative Reimbursement Agreement Terms and Conditions.

82. In addition to the other constitutional and ethical concerns, the contracts also require that the courts must agree to "collaboration" meetings with the child support agency for the purpose of resolving cases. These contractually required collaborations between the courts and the agency apparently do not include the parents who are also parties in the proceedings, raising the potential of violations of ethical rules prohibiting ex parte communications. MD Rules Judges, Rule 18-202.9, Ex Parte Communications; and State of Maryland, Department of Human Services, Child Support Administration, Cooperative Reimbursement Agreement Terms and Conditions, Circuit Court for Prince George's County, October 1, 2019–September 30, 2020, addendum A and attachment 1 (on file with author).

83. For example, the Judicial Council of California contracts to generate millions in IV-D child support revenue. In the resulting California IV-D courts, most of the families are poor, and 40 percent of the payments are owed to the government rather than to children. Laurence Du Sault and Jackie Botts, "California Keeps Millions in Child Support While Parents Drown in Debt," *CalMatters*, May 3, 2021, https://calmatters.org/projects/california-keeps -millions-in-child-support-while-parents-drown-in-debt/. The Judicial Council first enters a contract with the executive branch Department of Child Support Services (DCSS), and then contracts with the superior courts to pass through the money—providing over $55 million annually to the courts. Judicial Council of California, Audits and Financial Accountability Committee, Meeting Agenda,

October 3, 2018, www.courts.ca.gov/documents/audit-20181003-materials.pdf, https://perma.cc/E9KT-M9NY. The contract requires the courts to submit to audits and control by the executive branch. The state child support agency funds court "commissioners" and "facilitators" to adjudicate and mediate the child support cases, and each local court is required to enter a plan of coopera- tion (POC) with each respective local child support office. County of Kings, Board of Supervisors, Department of Child Support Services, Plan of Coopera- tion (POC) with the Kings County Superior Court, September 12, 2017, www .countyofkings.com/Home/ShowDocument?id=16518, https://perma.cc/BW4E -UXYP. As an example of the moneyed incentives, an audit report highlights how the Alameda County Superior Court inaccurately reported more hours than the court staff actually worked for the child support agency—adding up to over $440,000 inappropriately claimed by the court: "As a result, overall grant hours were recorded based on a methodology that maximizes grant funding, not in accordance with the JCC policy and procedures or federal regulations that require salary to be allocated based in the actual direct labor hours worked in the program." California Department of Child Support Services, *Judicial Council of California Contract Review Audit Report*, 2017, 3, www.courts.ca .gov/documents/Audit-Report-dcss-Alameda-20170901.pdf, https://perma.cc /4LTT-NCPS.

Other states have also used similar contracts. The New Jersey child support agency "has a cooperative agreement with the state's Administrative Office of the Courts (AOC) for assistance in the establishment and enforcement of child support orders." New Jersey Department of Treasury, "Appendix E, Project Management Structure," www.state.nj.us/treasury/purchase/bid/attachments /37829-e.pdf, https://perma.cc/E6QQ-84CN. In Hamilton County, Tennessee, the juvenile court contracted with the executive branch agency to create the Juvenile Court IV-D Child Support Division, in a contract worth up to $1.8 million. Hamilton County Board of County Commissioners, Resolution no. 521-6, May 5, 2021, www.hamiltontn.gov/PDF/Agenda/5-5-21%20Passed %20Agenda.pdf, https://perma.cc/4CPT-U5WP. Also, the annual report for the juvenile court in Shelby County explains that "[t]he Court maintained two spe- cial grant agreements with the Tennessee Department of Human Services that provide funding for four child support magistrates, six principal court clerks and two management/supervisory personnel." Juvenile Court of Memphis and Shelby County, *Annual Report*, 2016, 3, https://dashboard.shelbycountytn .gov/sites/default/files/file/pdfs/Annual%20Report%202016%20v3%2010 -11-17%20.pdf, https://perma.cc/DXT9-CFMC. And similar contracts exist in numerous other states. See, for example, "Appendix 5, State of Minnesota Interagency Agreement between the Department of Human Services and the Supreme Court," https://www.srln.org/system/files/attachments/SRLN%20IV -D%20Resource%20Guide%20Appendix%205%20%20MN%20project %20cooperative%20agreement%202011_0.pdf; N.M. Stat. § 40-4B-4 ("The child support hearing officers shall be paid pursuant to a cooperative agree- ment between the human services department and the judicial districts."); Dunn County Child Support Agency, *2020 Annual Report*, www.co.dunn.wi .us/vertical/Sites/%7BD750D8EC-F485-41AF-8057-2CE69E2B175A%7D

/uploads/Child_Support(1).pdf (discussing the child support agency's service agreement with the family court commissioner); North Dakota Department of Human Services, Cost Allocation Plan (discussing an interagency agreement with the North Dakota Supreme Court to operate a IV-D program); New Hampshire Department of Health and Human Services, Requested Action, May 26, 2020, https://sos.nh.gov/media/zsueh1kf/019-gc-agenda-062420.pdf (seeking authorization for the agency to "enter a sole source agreement with the Supreme Court of the State of New Hampshire"); Rhode Island Department of Children, Youth and Families, "Department Operating Procedure, Child Support Enforcement for Children in DCYF Care," February 5, 2020, https://datadcyf.ri.gov /policyregs/child_support_enforcement_for_children_in_dcyf_care_policy.htm ("[R]esponsibilities of the respective Departments and the Rhode Island Family Court are outlined in an Interagency Cooperative Agreement executed by and between the Family Court, the Department of Human Services, and the Department of Children, Youth and Families."); and US Department of Health & Human Services, Office of Inspector General, "Vermont's Office of Child Support Needs Better Oversight," A-01-18-02501, www.oversight.gov/sites/default /files/oig-reports/11802501.pdf (discussing a cooperative agreement between the Vermont child support agency and the state's supreme court and finding the court's claims for IV-D revenue were unsupported).

CHAPTER 4. PROSECUTING THE POOR FOR PROFIT

1. American Bar Association, *Model Rules of Professional Conduct*, Rule 3.8, Comment.

2. Robert H. Jackson, "The Federal Prosecutor" (address presented at Second Annual Conference of United States Attorneys, April 1, 1940), www.justice .gov/sites/default/files/ag/legacy/2011/09/16/04-01-1940.pdf.

3. See Daniel L. Hatcher, "Juvenile Court Interagency Agreements: Subverting Impartial Justice to Maximize Revenue from Children," *NYU Annual Survey of American Law* 76 (2020): 33, 60–64 (summarizing interagency contracts entered by prosecutors' offices).

4. Michigan Department of Human Services, Federal Compliance Division, *Fiscal Year 2010*, www.michigan.gov/documents/dhs/571_Federal-Compliance -July10_329307_7.pdf, https://perma.cc/H9SV-VWP2.

5. Oakland County Board of Commissioners, Misc. Resolution no. 15061, March 18, 2015, https://openoakland2.oakgov.com/WebLink/ElectronicFile.aspx ?docid=21752&dbid=0&repo=Open-Oakland, https://perma.cc/B9FX-PVBZ.

6. Michigan Department of Human Services, Agreement no. PROFC14- 61001, www.co.muskegon.mi.us/DocumentCenter/View/221/DHS-Contract -PDF, https://perma.cc/FTL4-25PT; see also Wasco County Board of Commissioners, minutes, June 3, 2015, http://cms5.revize.com/revize/wascocounty /BOCC%20Archives/2015/(15)%206-3-2015%20BOCC%20Regular %20Session%20Minutes.pdf, https://perma.cc/6ATE-A9EM.

7. Wisconsin Department of Health and Human Services, "Title IV-E Reimbursement for Legal Services," August 27, 2005, https://dcf.wisconsin.gov/files /cwportal/policy/pdf/memos/2005-13.pdf, https://perma.cc/S3WV-G3GL.

8. Wisconsin Department of Children and Families, "Application Instructions: Title IV-E Legal Services Applications for Calendar Year 2021," https://dcf.wisconsin.gov/files/cwportal/funding/pdf/title4e/legalinstructions.pdf, https://perma.cc/3J6L-VY37.

9. Milwaukee County District Attorney's Office, "Budget Summary," 2021, https://county.milwaukee.gov/files/county/administrative-services/PSB/BudgetsCopy-1/2021-Budget/2021-Requested-Budget/4500-DistrictAttorney1.pdf, https://perma.cc/3VEX-WE4M.

10. Milwaukee County District Attorney's Office, "Budget Summary."

11. Milwaukee County District Attorney's Office, "Budget Summary."

12. Mark J. Perry, "The General Public Thinks the Average Company Makes a 36% Profit margin, Which Is about 5X Too High," AEI, www.aei.org/carpe-diem/the-public-thinks-the-average-company-makes-a-36-profit-margin-which-is-about-5x-too-high-part-ii/; see also, NYU Stern, "Margins by Sector", http://pages.stern.nyu.edu/~adamodar/New_Home_Page/datafile/margin.html.

13. Board of Commissioners of Green County, Ohio, minutes, January 18, 2018, 12, www.co.greene.oh.us/AgendaCenter/ViewFile/Minutes/_01182018-582, https://perma.cc/K6WU-FSQB; see also Athens County Children's Services Board, Agreement with Athens County Prosecuting Attorney, January 29, 2019, www.co.athensoh.org/document_center/Commissioners%20Office/2019%20Commissioners/Jan.29.19.M.signed.pdf, https://perma.cc/N3QK-XUZP; and Texas Department of Family and Protective Services, Contract for Title IV-E County Legal Services, August 29, 2018, https://co.jefferson.tx.us/agenda/agendas_pl/20180910_471/Attachments/cc091018%20-TITLE%20IV-E%20LEGALSERV.CONTRACT.pdf, https://perma.cc/9RBS-RZDL.

14. Potters County Commissioners Court, Agenda, August 24, 2015, www.co.potter.tx.us/upload/page/7425/docs/Commissions/CourtMinutes/2015/8.24.15%20Agenda.pdf, https://perma.cc/2MDH-WWSS.

15. Wasco County Board of Commissioners, Agenda, 39, State of Oregon Intergovernmental Agreement, June 3, 2015, http://cms5.revize.com/revize/wascocounty/BOCC%20Archives/2015/(15)%206-3-2015%20BOCC%20Regular%20Session%20Minutes.pdf, https://perma.cc/C8TZ-EWNW.

16. Ingham County Board of Commissioners, Resolution no. 09-212, "Resolution Authorizing Contract with MAXIMUS, Inc., for the Preparation and Billing for Title IV-D and IV-E Grants," June 23, 2009.

17. See, for example, Dunn County Child Support Agency, 2020 Annual Report, www.co.dunn.wi.us/vertical/Sites/%7BD750D8EC-F485-41AF-8057-2CE69E2B175A%7D/uploads/Child_Support(1).pdf, https://perma.cc/K7B3-5BYX (describing IV-D cooperative reimbursement contracts with the Family Court and with the Corporation Counsel's Office); and National Child Support Enforcement Association, 2016 NCSEA Leadership Symposium, July 31–August 3, 2016, www.ncsea.org/documents/2016-CLE-Workshops7.7.16-1.pdf, https://perma.cc/JT6A-G9TJ (describing a IV-D cooperative reimbursement agreement with the Milwaukee District Attorney's Office).

18. Missouri Department of Social Services, "Rules of Department of Social Services: Division 30—Child Support Enforcement," www.sos.mo.gov

/CMSImages/AdRules/csr/previous/13csr/13csr0417/13c30-1.pdf, https://perma
.cc/5AAK-DSXZ.

19. Jackson County, Missouri, Resolution no. 20370, "A Resolution
Authorizing the County Executive and Prosecuting Attorney to Execute a
Child Support Enforcement Cooperative Agreement," February 10, 2020,
https://jacksonco.legistar.com/LegislationDetail.aspx?ID=4325903&GUID=
44217972-7836-42DC-A503-3FA48F8C4D69&Options=ID|Text|&Search=co
operative+agreement, https://perma.cc/6MKH-Y9Y5; see also Mo. Rev. Stat. §
568.040 ("Beginning January 1, 1991, every prosecuting attorney in any county
which has entered into a cooperative agreement with the division of child support enforcement shall report to the division on a quarterly basis the number of
charges filed and the number of convictions obtained under this section by the
prosecuting attorney's office on all IV-D cases. The division shall consolidate
the reported information into a statewide report by county and make the report
available to the general public.").

20. See Jackson, "Federal Prosecutor."

21. Lucas County, Ohio, "Approval of Title IV-D Service Contract between
Lucas County Department of Job & Family Services and Lucas County Prosecutor's Office for Criminal Non-support Prosecution Services," January 8, 2019,
https://lcapps.co.lucas.oh.us/carts/resos/22144.pdf, https://perma.cc/4CBZ
-HQTK.

22. Katie Moore, "Missouri Sends Hundreds to Jail for Not Paying Child
Support," *Kansas City Star*, January 26, 2020, www.kansascity.com/news/state
/missouri/article239046268.html.

23. Moore, "Missouri Sends Hundreds to Jail."

24. Moore, "Missouri Sends Hundreds to Jail."

25. See generally Josh Gupta-Kagan, "Rethinking Family-Court Prosecutors: Elected and Agency Prosecutors and Prosecutorial Discretion in Juvenile
Delinquency and Child Protection Cases," *University of Chicago Law Review*
85 (2018): 743, 757; and Bruce A. Green and Rebecca Roiphe, "Rethinking
Prosecutors' Conflicts of Interest," *Boston College Law Review* 58 (2017): 463.

26. Marshall v. Jerrico, Inc., 446 U.S. 238, 250 (1980).

27. Marshall v. Jerrico.

28. Marshall v. Jerrico.

29. Portage County Prosecutor's Office, home page, http://portageprosecutor
.com/, https://perma.cc/8RCJ-2F3A; see also Hatcher, "Juvenile Court Interagency Agreements," 93.

30. Lane County Department of District Attorney, "FY 17–18 Proposed
Budget," www.lanecounty.org/UserFiles/Servers/Server_3585797/File/Budget
/FY%2017-18%20Proposed/District%20Attorney.pdf, https://perma.cc/28D3
-EFHL; see also Oregon Department of Justice, "Agency Budget Request 2019–21:
Division of Child Support," August 19, 2018, 8 ("District Attorney Participation:
The statewide Oregon Child Support Program represents the combined efforts
of the DOJ Division of Child Support and the 23 Oregon county DA offices that
contract with DOJ to provide child support services. These 22 counties receive
the same federal matching funds as the Division of Child Support and share in
the Program's federal incentive payments based on the county's performance.").

31. Susan K. Mladenoff, prosecuting attorney, to Calhoun County Board of Commissioners, "Request for Appropriation and Signatures on 2009/2010 Title IV-D Cooperative Reimbursement Contract," September 3, 2009, https://cms5.revize.com/revize/calhouncountymi/Agendas%20&%20Minutes/2009/090903_BOC_Agenda.pdf, https://perma.cc/CZW3-WUXQ; and Calhoun County, "2011 General Funds—2011 Adopted Budget: Prosecuting Attorney," 38, https://cms5.revize.com/revize/calhouncountymi/Finance/Budget%20Information/2011%20General%20Funds%20-%202011%20Adopted%20Budget.pdf, https://perma.cc/S7R2-ZPE5 ($550,000 is over 20 percent of 2009 total operating expenditures of $2,524, 620).

32. Ken Paxton and John Montgomery, "Office of the Attorney General, Summary of Recommendations–Senate," State of Texas Budget, January 17, 2019 ($382.6 million in federal child support funding is over 30 percent of the AG's office total listed funding of $1.24 billion).

33. For an example of performance requirements imposed on prosecutors who have entered IV-D child support contracts, see Missouri Rules of Department of Social Services, Child Support Enforcement, "Performance Measures," 13 CSR 30-2.010, www.sos.mo.gov/cmsimages/adrules/csr/previous/13csr/13csr0311/13c30-2.pdf, https://perma.cc/33R7-DCRC.

34. Minnesota Department of Human Services, "Child Support Financial Training," September 27, 2016, slide 47, www.dhs.state.mn.us/main/groups/county_access/documents/pub/dhs-290378.pdf, https://perma.cc/9YPC-6PG3.

35. Office of the Attorney General of the State of Texas, "Agency Strategic Plan: Fiscal Years 2017–2021," 19, June 21, 2016, www.texasattorneygeneral.gov/sites/default/files/files/divisions/general-oag/AgencyStrategicPlan2017-2021.pdf, https://perma.cc/N4NQ-PL2P.

36. Susan Brown, "Proper Use of Child-Support Bonuses in Question," *Lake City News*, March 8, 2010, www.nwitimes.com/news/local/lake/proper-use-of-child-support-bonuses-in; see also Hatcher, "Juvenile Court Interagency Agreements," 94.

37. Steve Sonnega, "Prosecutor's Budgets," 41, PowerPoint presentation, https://www.docslides.com/pamella-moone/prosecutor-s-budgets, https://slidetodoc.com/prosecutors-budgets-by-steve-sonnega-morgan-county-prosecutor/, https://web.archive.org/web/20200414145925/https://www.docslides.com/pamella-moone/prosecutor-s-budgets, https://perma.cc/HF6Q-64LR]; see also Hatcher, "Juvenile Court Interagency Agreements," 94.

38. Sonnega, "Prosecutor's Budgets."

39. Sonnega, "Prosecutor's Budgets."

40. Sonnega, "Prosecutor's Budgets."

41. See, for example, Arizona Department of Economic Security and the Navajo County Board of Supervisors, Office of the County Attorney, Intergovernmental Agreement, www.navajocountyaz.gov/Portals/0/Departments/Board%20of%20Supervisors/Documents/Agendas/2015/120815/7.pdf?timestamp=1449254293430&timestamp=1449254293430, https://perma.cc/8S45-VLCR; District Attorney of Amite Louisiana, "Annual Financial Statements for 2014," https://app.lla.state.la.us/PublicReports.nsf/01EF760E7E434AD586257E820069192A/$FILE/00008EDD.pdf, https://perma.cc/YUC6

-3KYJ; Department of Justice, Washington County, and the District Attorney for Washington County, Department of Justice Cooperative Agreement: Child Support Services, www.co.washington.or.us/BOC/Meetings/Agendas/2015/upload/CD-DA-CSE-Cooperative-IGA.pdf, https://perma.cc/R6P9-UBAK; and Hardin County Fiscal Court, Commonwealth of Kentucky, Resolution no. 2014-23, March 11, 2014, http://hcky.org/wp-content/uploads/2017/08/2014-023.pdf, https://perma.cc/PC7L-LKY8; see also District Attorney of the Twenty-First Judicial District, Amite, Louisiana, "Annual Financial Statements," December 31, 2014, https://app.lla.state.la.us/PublicReports.nsf/01EF760E7E434AD586257E820069192A/$FILE/00008EDD.pdf, https://perma.cc/2H5F-34B9 ("There are no restrictions on how incentive payments may be expended, except as may be required by state law for any other funds of the District Attorney.").

42. Association of Indiana Counties, "Incentive Bonuses and Salary Supplements," MAXIMUS, www.indianacounties.org/egov/documents/1476976202_30477.pdf, https://perma.cc/36PG-FVKU.

43. Association of Indiana Counties, "Incentive Bonuses and Salary Supplements."; see also Association of Indiana Counties Annual Conference 2012, "Title IV-D Compliance and Revenue Opportunities" (prepared by John. M. Mallers MAXIMUS, Inc.), www.indianacounties.org/egov/apps/document/center.egov?view=item;id=1113, https://perma.cc/EM6F-XJAA (providing additional details for using child incentive funds for bonuses). Also, a 2020 story in the *Chicago Tribune* reports that prosecutors in Porter County, Indiana, asked for an appropriation of the incentive fund payments, which "would be used to increase salaries for three deputy prosecutors in that division." Amy Lavalley, "Porter County Council Votes in Favor of Raise Requests by Department Heads," *Chicago Tribune*, February 28, 2020, www.chicagotribune.com/suburbs/post-tribune/ct-ptb-porter-council-meet-st-0302-20200228-ww3rlcpejnfwth2sfkilzud7l4-story.html; see also Plummer v. Hegel, 535 N.E.2d 568, 570 (1989) (An Indiana court previously addressed the pursuit of the federal child support incentive payments and ruled that the prosecutor "could be paid the incentive payments as additional salary."); Kenton County Fiscal Court v. Elfers, 981 S.W.2d 553, 55 (Ky. Ct. App. 1998) (A Kentucky court recognized that "[i]n order to entice county attorneys" to participate in child support contracts, the state agency "encouraged and assisted county attorneys in getting their local fiscal courts to pass resolutions allowing the incentive payments received from the federal government to be paid directly to the county attorneys."); see also Hatcher, "Juvenile Court Interagency Agreements," 95.

44. County of Muskegon Friend of the Court, "Title IV-D Cooperative Reimbursement," 2013, 1, www.co.muskegon.mi.us/DocumentCenter/View/160/Cooperative-Reimbursement-PDF, https://web.archive.org/web/20200403132441/https://www.co.muskegon.mi.us/DocumentCenter/View/160/Cooperative-Reimbursement-PDF, https://perma.cc/8B46-HEZD, www.co.muskegon.mi.us/AgendaCenter/ViewFile/Agenda/_08172010-794, https://perma.cc/FK7L-4NC4.

45. Jane Hess, "Muskegon County's Holistic Approach to Child Support Is Becoming a National Model," *Pundit* 31 (2017): 1, https://courts.michigan

.gov/Administration/SCAO/OfficesPrograms/FOC/Documents/Pundits/Pundit
-March2017.pdf, https://perma.cc/H6CT-X3WB.

46. Muskegon County Prosecutors, Child Support Division, www.co
.muskegon.mi.us/581/Child-Support-Division, https://perma.cc/876C-GPN7;
see also Hatcher, "Juvenile Court Interagency Agreements," 77–78.

47. See Hess, "Muskegon County's Holistic Approach to Child Support."

48. See Tex. Fam. Code Ann. § 231.001 (West 1995). Similarly, the Washington, D.C., child support courts work "collaboratively" with the Attorney General's
office, which is the D.C. child support agency. District of Columbia Courts, Par-
entage and Child Support Branch, www.dccourts.gov/superior-court/family-court
-operations/parentage-and-child-support-branch, https://perma.cc/X77C-VUR6.
In its role as the IV-D agency, the D.C. Attorney General's office receives federal
child support incentive payments, so the agency is financially incentivized in how
it prosecutes and enforces cases. D.C. Code Ann. § 46-226.01 (West, 2001). See
also Hatcher, "Juvenile Court Interagency Agreements," 62–64.

49. Cooperative Agreement between the Office of the Attorney General of
Texas and the Office of Court Administration (hereafter Texas OAG Cooperative Agreement), Agreement no. 20-C0018, effective September 1, 2019 to
August 31, 2024 (on file with author); see also Title IV-D Child Support Court,
Midland County Tex., www.co.midland.tx.us/315/Title-IV-D-Child-Support
-Court, https://perma.cc/H8RE-997H ("The child support courts program is
funded with federal and state funds. The Office of Court Administration receives
the funds through a cooperative agreement with the Child Support Division of
the Office of the Attorney General.").

50. Texas OAG Cooperative Agreement, § 3.1.2.

51. Texas OAG Cooperative Agreement, § 3.1.2.

52. Texas OAG Cooperative Agreement, § 3.1.2.

53. Texas OAG Cooperative Agreement, § 4.

54. Texas OAG Cooperative Agreement, § 4.2.2.

55. Texas OAG Cooperative Agreement, § 4.2.2.

56. Tex. Fam. Code Ann. § 201.107; and Texas OAG Cooperative Agreement, § 4.2.1

57. Tex. Fam. Code Ann. § 231.001.

58. Haw. Rev. Stat. § 576D-2 (2013); see also Hatcher, "Juvenile Court Interagency Agreements," 77.

59. Haw. Rev. Stat. § 576E-2 (2013).

60. Haw. Rev. Stat. § 576E-2 (2013).

61. Haw. Rev. Stat. §§ 576E-10, 12 (2013).

62. Hawaii Department of Attorney General, "Operating Budget, FY 2022–
2023," https://budget.hawaii.gov/wp-content/uploads/2020/12/10.-Department
-of-the-Attorney-General-FB21-23-PFP.8ag.pdf (estimated federal revenue from
child support listed at about $15.8 million, compared to $103.6 million total
AG budget).

63. Haw. Rev. Stat. § 576D-9 (2013).

64. Homberg v. Holmberg, 588 N.W.2d 720 (Minn. 1999); Seubert v. Seubert,
301 Mont. 382 (2000). In *Hansen v. State Dept. of Social Services*, 226 S.W.3d
137 (MO. 2007), the Supreme Court of Missouri reached a different conclusion,

finding a child support administrative process did not violate the separation of powers doctrine, but only because the structure allowed the agency to seek court orders rather than issue court orders—and the court opinion did not consider due process concerns. By comparison, the Hawaii AG's office usurped the full power to issue orders and is financially incentivized to do so.

65. Brian Lyman, "As Covid-19 Closes Courts, Alabama Prosecutors Face Collapse in Revenues," *Montgomery Advertiser*, April 30, 2020, www .montgomeryadvertiser.com/story/news/2020/04/30/covid-19-closes-courts -alabama-prosecutors-face-collapse-revenues/3052219001/.

66. Lyman, "As Covid-19 Closes Courts."

67. Lyman, "As Covid-19 Closes Courts."

68. Lyman, "As Covid-19 Closes Courts."

69. Lyman, "As Covid-19 Closes Courts."

70. Ala. Code § 45-20-82.65.

71. See Iowa Legislative Services Agency, Fiscal Services Division, "Court Debt Collection," January 3, 2018, 2, www.legis.iowa.gov/docs/publications/IR /916685.pdf, https://perma.cc/GM7E-FN6R.

72. See, for example, Ben Sutherly, "Ohio Fees for Debt Collection Questioned," *Columbus Dispatch*, September 27, 2015, www.dispatch.com/article/20150927 /NEWS/309279827; Christine L. Pratt, "Homes Court Turns to Ohio AG for Collections," *Daily Record*, November 19, 2016, www.the-daily-record.com/news /20161119/holmes-court-turns-to-ohio-ag-for-collections; and Denise G. Callahan, "Butler County Governments and Courts Owed Millions," *Journal-News*, September 8, 2019, www.journal-news.com/news/butler-county-cities-and-courts -are-owed-millions-here-how-they-collect/tPhLqQUa1wChhENLLq9VRM/.

CHAPTER 5. THE PROBATION BUSINESS

1. US Department of Justice, Office of Justice Programs, Bureau of Justice Statistics, "Probation and Parole in the United States, 2019," https://bjs.ojp.gov /content/pub/pdf/ppus19.pdf; and National Center for Juvenile Justice, Juvenile Court Statistics, 2018, https://ojjdp.ojp.gov/sites/g/files/xyckuh176/files/media /document/juvenile-court-statistics-2018.pdf.

2. County of Los Angeles, Probation Department, "Probation," https://lacounty .gov/residents/public-safety/probation/, https://perma.cc/VHK6-MHPM.

3. James Baldwin, *No Name in the Street* (New York: Vintage Books, 1972), 148–49.

4. Michele S. Phelps, "Ending Mass Probation: Sentencing, Supervision, and Revocation," *Future of Children* 28, no. 1 (Spring 2018), https://files.eric.ed.gov /fulltext/EJ1179164.pdf.

5. Patricia Torbet Kurlychek and Melanie Bozynski, "Focus on Accountability: Best Practices for Juvenile Court and Probation," *JAIBG Bulletin*, August 1999, www.ncjrs.gov/pdffiles1/177611.pdf.

6. Stephen Handelman, "How Juvenile Probation Lands More Youths in Jail," *Crime Report*, August 26, 2020, https://thecrimereport.org/2020/10/26 /how-juvenile-probation-lands-more-young-people-in-jail/.

7. Holmes County Juvenile Court, Probation Officer Position Description, April 9, 2019, https://ocpoa.org/forms/2019-04-Holmes-Co-Juv-Probation-Officer.pdf, https://perma.cc/R3L2-48AQ (The employment listing by the Holmes County Juvenile Court in Ohio provides a long, nonexhaustive list of juvenile probation officer duties, with no college degree required, providing an example of the power of probation officers.); see also Fayette County Common Pleas Court Juvenile Division, Juvenile Probation Officer Job Posting, revised May 20, 2019, https://ocpoa.org/forms/2019-06-Juvenile-Probation-Officer.pdf, https://perma.cc/735U-9LSE; Wayne County Court of Common Pleas Probate and Juvenile Divisions, Probation Officer 1 Job Posting, 2019, https://ocpoa.org/forms/2019-04-Probation-Officer-Wayne-County-Juvenile-Court.pdf, https://perma.cc/8K9Z-ZGTJ; and Clark County Department of Human Resources, Juvenile Probation Officer I/II Job Posting, Exam Number JPO-2014, https://agency.governmentjobs.com/clarkcounty/job_bulletin.cfm?JobID=846464, https://perma.cc/8A5W-FERX.

8. For example, Peggy McGarry, "Probation and Parole as Punishment, Brennan Center for Justice," June 28, 2021 ("Without time and resources, with scant encouragement from their agencies, officers have little reason to work patiently with supervisees to help them stabilize and be successful. Officers are not given raises or promotions based on the successes achieved by people on their caseloads, and the decision to revoke someone back to jail or prison at the first sign of trouble is affirmed by how often their revocation recommendations are approved."); and Amanda Claire Curcio and Ginny Monk, "Probation in Arkansas Often Hurts Kids Instead of Helping Them," *Arkansas Democrat Gazette*, March 4, 2018.

9. Stanton v. State, 130 P.3d 486 (Wyo. 2006).

10. See US Department of Justice, Civil Rights Division, Letter to Los Angeles County Board of Supervisors, Investigation of the Los Angeles County Probation Department Camps, October 31, 2008, www.justice.gov/sites/default/files/crt/legacy/2010/12/15/lacamps_findings_10-31-08.pdf.

11. Los Angeles County Probation Department, Office of Independent Review, *Second Annual Report*, March 2013, http://shq.lasdnews.net/shq/LASD_Oversight/OIR%20Second%20Annual%20Report%202013%20Final.pdf.

12. Los Angeles County Probation Department, *Second Annual Report*.

13. Los Angeles County Probation Department, *Second Annual Report*.

14. Bacerra v. Los Angeles County County, Complaint, Case No. 21STCV01309, January 13, 2020, https://oag.ca.gov/sites/default/files/LACPD%20-%20Complaint%20-%20file-stamped.pdf ("including by: (a) relying on excessive and inappropriate physical and chemical use of force; (b) failing to sustain sufficient staffing at the Juvenile Halls; (c) failing to train staff on de-escalation methods; (d) failing to ensure accurate reporting of use of force incidents; and (e) failing to implement functional data collection systems for effective oversight and accountability, resulting in youth being more susceptible to harm from staff and other youth").

15. California Department of Justice, Office of Attorney General, "Attorney General Becerra, Los Angeles County Enter into Groundbreaking Settlements to

Protect the Rights of Youth in the Juvenile Justice System," press release, January 13, 2021, https://oag.ca.gov/news/press-releases/attorney-general-becerra-los -angeles-county-enter-groundbreaking-settlements.

16. For example, "Former NorCo Probation Officer Charged with Official Oppression," *Lehigh Valley Ramblings* (blog), June 30, 2015, https://lehighvalley ramblings.blogspot.com/2015/06/former-norco-probation-officer-charged.html; and Terry Van Lewis, "Juvenile Probation Officer Accused of Rape, Sexual Abuse," *Greenville Advocate*, March 15, 2019, www.greenvilleadvocate.com/2019/03/15 /juvenile-probation-officer-accused-of-rape-sexual-abuse/.

17. The Associated Press, "Ex-probation Officer Gets Prison for Texas Sex Trafficking," *Denver Post*, June 30, 2015, www.denverpost.com/2015/06/30/ex -probation-officer-gets-prison-for-texas-sex-trafficking/; and Aaron Martinez, "Gangs Increasingly Force Teens, Women into Prostitution," *El Paso Times*, April 2, 2014, www.elpasotimes.com/story/archives/2014/04/02/gangs-turn-sex -trade-boost-profits/73897590/.

18. Orange County Board of Supervisors, Internal Audit Department, Internal Control Audit: Probation Department Title IV-E Foster Care Program Claims Process, Audit no. 822, September 16, 2009, https://acdcweb01.ocgov .com/wp-content/uploads/2017/08/2822-Probation-091609.pdf, https://perma .cc/V8YZ-DECD.

19. Orange County Board of Supervisors, Internal Audit Department, Audit no. 822.

20. Orange County Board of Supervisors, Internal Audit Department, Audit no. 822.

21. Chief Probation Officers of California, Title IV-E Probation Claiming, https://player.slideplayer.com/8/2373009/, https://www.slideserve.com/lecea /title-iv-e-probation-claiming.

22. Chief Probation Officers of California, Title IV-E Probation Claiming.

23. Orange County Board of Supervisors, Internal Audit Department, Audit no. 822.

24. Orange County Board of Supervisors, Internal Audit Department, Audit no. 822.

25. Orange County Board of Supervisors, Internal Audit Department, Audit no. 822.

26. The contract summary from Orange County explains that the purpose is to "maximize funding for Probation," and it describes giving the company both a fixed fee and a contingency fee cut of the revenue. Orange County Board of Supervisors, Agenda Item, Contract with Justice Benefits, Inc. for Title IV-E Administrative Claims, June 25, 2019, http://cams.ocgov.com/Web_Publisher _Sam/Agenda06_25_2019_files/images/A19-000384.HTM, https://perma.cc /HBP5-8DX6. Also, the contract with the Los Angeles Probation Department describes how the company provides "Candidates for Foster Care" training to ensure the most money possible is claimed. County of Los Angeles Probation Department, "Approval of Sole Source Contract with Justice Benefits, Incorporated," May 31, 2016, http://file.lacounty.gov/SDSInter/bos/supdocs/104084 .pdf, https://perma.cc/5HRK-WRHB.

27. State of Texas, Interagency Cooperation Contract, Contract no. 530-12-0224-00001, Title IV-E Services—Foster Care Maintenance Administrative and Training, www2.tjjd.texas.gov/procurementfiles//Interagency/DFPS%20 -%20Title%20IV-E/CON0000206-Amend_3-Executed.PDF, https://perma.cc /95BK-5S9G.

28. Hidalgo County, Texas, Programs and Units within the Juvenile Probation Department, www.hidalgocounty.us/1072/Programs-Units, https://perma .cc/ETN2-FXU2.

29. Hidalgo County, Texas, Programs and Units ("TJPC aimed at accessing these federal funds in order to increase the amount of placement funds available to juvenile probation departments," and "Hidalgo County Juvenile Probation entered into a contracted [sic] with TJPC sequentially to benefit from the provisions of residential care for more youth.").

30. The Nueces County Juvenile Board entered such a contract under a contingency fee arrangement paid to the company of "fifteen percent (15%) of all revenue paid to the Board.". Nueces County Juvenile Board Texas, Professional Services Agreement with Justice Benefits, Inc., November 20. 2014, https://destinyhosted.com/nuecedocs/2014/CC-REG/20141203_271/5835_JBI %20Agreement%20executed%2011-20-14.pdf, https://perma.cc/YR3C-P5F8.

31. The Illinois juvenile probation departments report directly to chief judges of each county. 705 Ill. Comp. Stat. 405/Art. VI (1987). And the Cook County Office of the Chief Judge Juvenile Probation and Court Services contracted with Justice Benefits, Inc., to help maximize IV-E funds from children, through a contingency fee structure in which the company would get 10 percent of the first $15 million in IV-E funds and 15 percent of all claims over $15 million. Cook County Government Office of the Chief Judge, Juvenile Probation and Court Services, Professional Services Agreement with Justice Benefits, Inc., Contract no. 1490-13306 (2014), 2, http://opendocs.cookcountyil.gov/procurement /contracts/1490-13306.pdf, https://web.archive.org/web/20200611192513 /http://opendocs.cookcountyil.gov/procurement/contracts/1490-13306.pdf, https://perma.cc/D8AQ-8QZ5; see also McLean County, Illinois, Minutes of the Justice Committee, April 1, 2008, 4, www.mcleancountyil.gov/Archive/ViewFile /Item/1861, https://perma.cc/Y3YA-9EHU ("Motion by Nuckolls/Harding to Recommend Approval of an Addendum to the Justice Benefits Contract to Seek Title IV-E Administrative Claims Funds for McLean County Court Services, Juvenile Division").

32. Michigan Supreme Court, Judicial Institute, *Judicial Probation Officer and Caseworker Self-Instruction Manual*, https://mjieducation.mi.gov/documents /resources-for-trial-court-staff/180-juv-po-manual/file, https://perma.cc/TMM3 -BWJ7.

33. Indiana Department of Children's Services, Interagency Agreement, Effective Date July 1, 2006, www.in.gov/dcs/files/11-Tool-Interagency-Agreement -Archived.pdf, https://perma.cc/TG8E-553L.

34. California Rules of Court, Rule 5.820.

35. Christie Renick, "Bigger in Texas: Number of Adoptions, and Parents Who Lose Their Rights," *Imprint*, May 24, 2018, https://imprintnews.org

/featured/bigger-in-texas-adoptions-and-parents-who-lose-their-rights/30990 ("Texas has terminated parental rights for 91,589 children, according to federal data. The next highest total is 79,918 for California.").

36. See, for example, New Jersey, Department of Treasury, Contract Document, Current State Organization, www.state.nj.us/treasury/purchase/bid /attachments/37829-e.pdf, https://perma.cc/HG68-NCRY.

37. New Jersey Courts, Office of Probation Services, Frequently Asked Questions, https://njcourts.gov/forms/12232_probation_services_faq.pdf, https://perma.cc/NDX3-KFLX.

38. New Jersey Legislature, Office of Legislative Services, "Analysis of the New Jersey Budget: The Judiciary, FY 2019–2020," www.njleg.state.nj.us /legislativepub/budget_2020/JUD_analysis_2020.pdf.

39. See United States Commission on Civil Rights, "Targeted Fines and Fees against Communities of Color," September 2017, www.usccr.gov/pubs/2017 /Statutory_Enforcement_Report2017.pdf.

40. See Lancaster County, Court of Common Pleas, Probation Collections Enforcement Unit, www.court.co.lancaster.pa.us/125/Collections-Enforcement -Unit, https://perma.cc/6494-PCUW; and 42 Pa. CSA § 9728.

41. Ga. Code § 42-8-103 (2015).

42. See Sharon Brett, Neda Khoshkhoo, and Mitali Nagrecha, *Paying on Probation: How Financial Sanctions Intersect with Probation to Target, Trap and Punish People Who Cannot Pay*, Harvard Law School Criminal Justice Policy Program, June 2020, https://mcusercontent.com/f65678cd73457docbde864do5/files/f05e951e -60a9-404e-b5cc-13c065b2a630/Paying_on_Probation_report_FINAL.pdf.

43. Brett, Khoshkhoo, and Nagrecha, *Paying on Probation*, 12.

44. Brett, Khoshkhoo, and Nagrecha, *Paying on Probation*.

45. Michigan State Court Administrative Office, *Manual for District Court Probation Officers*, revised February 2021, https://courts.michigan.gov /administration/SCAO/Resources/Documents/Publications/Manuals/prbofc/prb .pdf, https://perma.cc/94YM-633Q.

46. Brett, Khoshkhoo, and Nagrecha, *Paying on Probation*, 25.

47. Brett, Khoshkhoo, and Nagrecha, *Paying on Probation*, 34.

48. Brett, Khoshkhoo, and Nagrecha, *Paying on Probation*, 38.

49. E.g., Tumey v. Ohio, 273 U.S. 510 (1927); *In re* Murchison, 349 U.S. 133 (1955); Ward v. Vill. of Monroeville, 409 U.S. 57 (1972); and Marshall v. Jerrico, Inc., 446 U.S. 238 (1980).

50. *Tumey*, 273 U.S. at 522; and *Marshall*, 446 U.S. at 248.

51. Harper v. Professional Probation Services, Inc., 976 F.3d 1236, 1238-39 (11th Cir. 2020).

52. Harper v. Professional Probation Services.

53. *Marshall*, 446 U.S. at 249-250.

54. McNeil v. Community Probation Services, LLC, 2021 WL 365844 (M.D., Tennessee, February 3, 2021).

55. Bearden v. Georgia, 461 U.S. 660, 674 (1983).

56. Kern County Probation, Juvenile Work Program, www.kernprobation .com/juvenile/supervision/juvenile-court-work-program-home-supervision/, https://perma.cc/762D-FYWW.

57. Missouri Department of Corrections, Community Service, https://doc .mo.gov/programs/community-service, https://perma.cc/EH8T-YXKH.

58. Jackson County, Oregon, Community Service Program, https://jackson countyor.org/community-justice/Adult-Services/Community-Service, https:// perma.cc/BWH2-BKL9.

59. 18th District Court of Westland, Michigan, Probation Department, Work Program, https://18thdistrictcourt.com/?page_id=43, https://perma.cc/Z9RT -2TUR.

60. Lucero Herrera, Tia Koonse, Menanie Sonsteng-Person, and Noah Zatz, "Work, Pay or Go to Jail: Court-Ordered Community Service in Los Angeles," UCLA Labor Center and UCLA School of Law, October 2019, www.labor.ucla .edu/wp-content/uploads/2019/10/UCLA_CommunityServiceReport_Final _1016.pdf.

61. Herrera et al., "Work, Pay or Go to Jail."

62. Herrera et al., "Work, Pay or Go to Jail."

63. Fulton County Board of Commissioners, Agenda Item Summary, BOC Meeting Date January 7, 2015, https://fulton.legistar.com/View.ashx?M=A& ID=861613&GUID=65957874-EC21-443E-AF7A-48B9FC61915A, https:// perma.cc/JKF6-TNUE.

64. Fulton County, Contract Documents for 14RFP65898A-CJC, Misde-meanor Probation Services for State and Magistrate Court (on file with author).

65. Fulton County, Contract Documents for 14RFP65898A-CJC, exhibit E.

66. Professional Probation Services, Management, https://ppsfamily.com /management/, https://perma.cc/D7EL-YF4E.

67. The Council on State Governments, Justice Center, July 2017, https:// csgjusticecenter.org/wp-content/uploads/2020/02/JR-in-GA_Strengthening -Probation-and-Increasing-Public-Safety.pdf, https://perma.cc/9VMV-UNRB; and Carrie Teegardin, "Georgia Leads Nation in Probation," *Atlanta-Journal Constitution*, August 28, 2016, www.ajc.com/news/crime--law/georgia-leads -nation-probation/4DgAXu3UHx5716BmSfYLVP/.

68. Human Rights Watch, *Profiting from Probation: America's 'Offender-Funded' Probation Industry*, February 5, 2014, www.hrw.org/report/2014/02/05 /profiting-probation/americas-offender-funded-probation-industry#_ftnref12.

69. Southern Poverty Law Center, Gina Harper, et al. v. Professional Pro-bation Services, Inc., et al., www.splcenter.org/seeking-justice/case-docket/gina -harper-et-al-v-professional-probation-services-inc-et-al.

70. For example, American Civil Liberties Union, Thompson v. Dekalb County, www.aclu.org/cases/thompson-v-dekalb-county; Equal Justice Under Law, Rodriquez v. Providence Community Corrections, https://equaljusticeunderlaw .org/case-pcc-probation; and Civil Rights Corps, "Giles County, TN: Private Probation," https://www.civilrightscorps.org/work/criminalization-of-poverty /giles-county-tn-private-probation.

71. McNeil v. Cmty. Prob. Servs., No. 1:18-cv-00033, Corrected First Amended Complaint (M.D. Tenn. July 13, 2018), https://cdn.buttercms.com /OfrTteU4S8eTEQDPYBDr.

72. Anita Wadhwani, "In Giles County, Private Probation Companies Profited from Probationers," *Tennessee Lookout*, June 1, 2021, https://tennesseelookout

.com/2021/06/01/in-giles-county-private-probation-company-fees-profits-from-probationers/.

73. Wadhwani, "In Giles County, Private Probation Companies."

CHAPTER 6. POLICING AND PROFITING FROM THE POOR

1. Arlington, Virginia, Sheriff, "History of Sheriff's Office," www.arlingtonva.us/Government/Departments/Sheriffs-Office/About/History, https://perma.cc/SGP2-JQGP.

2. Also, the demographics of law enforcement departments continue to be strikingly unequal: as of 2020, 90 percent of elected sheriffs were White men, and 67 percent of all police officers were White. See *Reflective Democracy: Confronting the Demographics of Power*, 2020, https://wholeads.us/wp-content/uploads/2020/06/reflectivedemocracy-americassheriffs-06.04.2020.pdf; and Data USA, "Police Officers" (data from 2019 Census Bureau American Community Survey), https://datausa.io/profile/soc/police-officers, https://perma.cc/H6UD-7K3N.

3. Berks County, Ordinance no. 04-2020, September 24, 2020, www.co.berks.pa.us/Dept/Commissioners/County%20Ordinances/Ordinance%20No%2004%202020.pdf, https://perma.cc/A5TG-EQA7.

4. Samantha Melamed, "Sheriffs Target 'Deadbeat Dads' with Midnight Raids, Debtors Prison: But Does It Help Kids?," *Philadelphia Inquirer*, September 11, 2018, www.inquirer.com/philly/news/child-support-arrests-deadbeat-dads-pennsylvania-20180911.html.

5. Melamed, "Sheriffs Target 'Deadbeat Dads.'"

6. Melamed, "Sheriffs Target 'Deadbeat Dads.'"

7. Melamed, "Sheriffs Target 'Deadbeat Dads.'"

8. See. for example, Worchester County Commissioners, Cooperative Reimbursement Agreement 2017–2019, www.co.worcester.md.us/sites/default/files/meetings/Commissioner%20Meeting/packet/2016/07-05-16.pdf, https://perma.cc/5QZY-XA3M; Wadena County Office of Human Services, IV-D Child Support Cooperative Agreement, www.co.wadena.mn.us/AgendaCenter/ViewFile/Item/979?fileID=1784, https://perma.cc/ESK7-NHKT; DC Code Sec. 13-302.01 (IV-D agreement); Cook County, Illinois, Board of Commissioners, Proposed Intergovernmental Agreement, May 21, 2020, https://cook-county.legistar.com/LegislationDetail.aspx?ID=4537397&GUID=AFD111BF-5DBE-4CAE-9484-899875CBD71B&Options=&Search=, https://perma.cc/M7LM-SNGS; "Part 3: Child Support Violators Difficult to Track Even If They're Government Employees," WRCBtv, August 15, 2015, www.local3news.com/local-news/local-3-investigates/part-3-child-support-violators-difficult-to-track-even-if-theyre-government-employees/article_ebc7e334-a25b-5c8c-81e2-fd59202f89b0.html; and Hamilton County Sheriff's Office, *2019 Annual Report*, www.hcsheriff.gov/support/annual_reports/hcso_2019_annual_report.pdf, https://perma.cc/DGZ6-LURR (The state agency funds a "Department of Human Services (Child Support)" division within the sheriff's office: "In 2019, the Department of Human Service (DHS) made 440 arrests, 1,764 attempts and served 750 official documents. DHS also supports the efforts of the fugitive division

for nonpayment of child support. The Department of Human Service Juvenile Grant ensures court papers are served or an attempt is made related to Child Support servicing Circuit Court, Juvenile Court and Maximus Court Systems in Hamilton County, Tennessee.").

9. Prince George's County, Office of the Sheriff, "FY 2019 Budget Summary," 271, https://princegeorgescountymd.gov/DocumentCenter/View/21407/Office-of-the-SheriffPDF, https://perma.cc/PX9U-UVX5.

10. Michigan State Court Administrative Office, Michigan Trial Court Administration, *Reference Guide*, 253, https://courts.michigan.gov/Administration/SCAO/Resources/Documents/Publications/Manuals/carg/carg.pdf, https://perma.cc/YWZ6-YN27.

11. The Florida Senate, "Bill Analysis and Fiscal Impact Statement," SB 1092, March 20, 2017, www.flsenate.gov/Session/Bill/2017/1092/Analyses/2017s01092.pre.cf.PDF, https://perma.cc/H349-NUML; see also, Fla. Stat. § 39.3065.

12. Florida Department of Law Enforcement, "Professional Standards and Criteria to Hold the Office of Sheriff in the State of Florida," www.fdle.state.fl.us/FCJEI/Programs/SLP/Documents/Full-Text/Hall_MH.aspx, https://perma.cc/EH64-B56S.

13. Florida Senate, "Bill Analysis and Fiscal Impact Statement," SB 1092.

14. For example, Christopher O'Donnell and Kathryn Varn, "Pinellas Sheriff Blasts Foster Agency, but His Office Removed Children at Florida's Highest Rate," *Tampa Bay Times*, December 21, 2021, www.tampabay.com/news/pinellas/2021/12/21/while-sheriff-blasted-foster-agency-his-investigators-removed-children-at-a-higher-rate-than-any-other-county/.

15. O'Donnell and Varn, "Pinellas Sheriff Blasts Foster Agency."

16. O'Donnell and Varn, "Pinellas Sheriff Blasts Foster Agency."

17. O'Donnell and Varn, "Pinellas Sheriff Blasts Foster Agency."

18. Florida Senate, "Bill Analysis and Fiscal Impact Statement," SB 1092.

19. Sandra McDaniel, "Where the City's Marshals Get Their Power," Retro Report, November 11, 2020, https://www.retroreport.org/articles/where-the-city-s-marshals-get-their-power/.

20. The Laws of New York, New York City Civil Courts Act, Article 16, Marshals, www.nysenate.gov/legislation/laws/CCA/A16; and NY CPLR § 8012 (2012).

21. New York City, Independent Budget Office, *Revenue Options: Make City Marshals City Employees*, February 2019, https://ibo.nyc.ny.us/iboreports/revenue-options-fares-tolls-and-other-revenue-generators-2019.pdf, https://perma.cc/HU9K-XMRL.

22. New York City, Independent Budget Office, *Revenue Options*.

23. Duncan Bryer, "More Than Ever: Abolish the City Marshal," *Gotham Gazette,* www.gothamgazette.com/open-government/130-opinion/9323-abolish-the-new-york-city-marshal-coronavirus-evictions-debt.

24. Zachary Mider and Zeke Faux, "The $1.7 Million Man," *Bloomberg*, November 27, 2018, www.bloomberg.com/graphics/2018-confessions-of-judgment-millionaire-marshal/

25. Mider and Faux, "The $1.7 Million Man."

26. "Who Are the New York City Marshals?," *deBanked*, November 28, 2018, https://debanked.com/2018/11/who-are-the-new-york-city-marshals/.

27. Edward A. Gargan, "Koch Nominates 9 City Marshals to 5-Year Terms," *New York Times*, March 10, 1981, www.nytimes.com/1981/03/10/nyregion /koch-nominates-9-city-marshals-to-5-year-terms.html.

28. La. Rev. Stat. § 13:5807 (2018).

29. Miranda Klein, "Here's How Much Alexandria's City Marshal Gets Paid," *Town Talk*, September 14, 2017, www.thetowntalk.com/story/news/local /alexandria/2017/09/14/heres-how-much-alexandrias-city-marshal-gets-paid /659762001/, https://perma.cc/L4B7-MA4Q.

30. Matthew Reid, "Police Say It's 'Outrageous' That Untrained, Unchecked Constables Are Making Criminal Arrests," *MetroWest Daily News*, August 20, 2019, www.metrowestdailynews.com/news/20190820/police-say-its-outrageous -that-untrained-unchecked-constables-are-making-criminal-arrests; and MGL c. 262, sec. 8, Sheriffs, deputy sheriffs and constables; enumeration of fees.

31. Texas Comptroller, *2014 Sheriffs' and Constables' Fees Manual*, www .co.walker.tx.us/egov/documents/1388695166_730651.pdf, https://perma.cc /9X2N-JP8L.

32. P. J. Green, "13th Annual Great Texas Warrant Roundup Begins," Texoma's Homepage, Feb. 4, 2020, www.texomashomepage.com/news/local-news/13th -annual-great-texas-warrant-roundup-begins/, https://perma.cc/MU7X-X87U.

33. Ind. Code Title 6. Taxation § 6-8.1-8-3; Indiana State Board of Accounts, *Audit of County Sheriff, Elkhart County*, Indiana, January 1, 2005, www.in.gov /sboa/WebReports/B27686.pdf; see also, for example, N.J. Rev. Stat. § 22A:4-8 (2013); N.C. Gen. Stat. § 7A-311; S.D. Codified Laws § 7-12-18; La. Rev. Stat. § 13:5530; Comal County, Texas, "2022 Sheriff's Office Fees," www.co.comal .tx.us/SO/SO_Fees.pdf; Boulder County Sherriff, "Civil Fee for Service," www .bouldercounty.org/safety/sheriff/civil/fees-for-service/.

34. David Cruz, "Pandemic Puts NYC's Obscure Law Enforcement Agency in the Spotlight: The Sheriff's Office Explained," Gothamist, December 9, 2020, https://gothamist.com/news/pandemic-sheriff-office-explained-nyc-enforcement

35. Harford County Sheriff's Office, "Personnel Policy: Code of Ethics," https://harfordsheriff.org/wp-content/uploads/2018/05/PER-0104-Code-of -Ethics.pdf, https://perma.cc/Q5RE-N77W.

36. Lauren M. Peace, "Behind the Badge," *Bronx Ink*, October 22, 2019, http://bronxink.org/2019/10/22/28790-behind-the-badge/, https://perma.cc /PKJ9-GCAY.

37. Sara Foss, "Schenectady Deputy Commended for How He Handles the Tough Task of Evictions," *Daily Gazette*, February 5, 2012, https://dailygazette .com/2012/02/05/0205_officer/, https://perma.cc/9P5E-7HW3.

38. Foss, "Schenectady Deputy Commended."

39. Foss, "Schenectady Deputy Commended."

40. 85 FR 55292 (Temporary Halt in Residential Evictions to Prevent the Further Spread of COVID-19).

41. Putnam County Sheriff's Department, *2020 Annual Report*, https:// putnamsheriff.com/sites/default/files/2021/docs/2020annualrep.pdf, https:// perma.cc/TV3A-VBU5.

42. See CNN Politics, search results for PPP Business Loans, www.cnn.com /projects/ppp-business-loans/search?industry=922120, https://perma.cc/R7HG -EJNE; Federalpay.org, "PPP Loan Data—New York City Marshal Henry Daley," www.federalpay.org/paycheck-protection-program/new-york-city-marshal-henry -daley-rosedale-ny, https://perma.cc/YZ63-ED2Y; CNN Politics, [PPP Business Loans for] New York, www.cnn.com/projects/ppp-business-loans/states/ny?page =644&limit=50, https://perma.cc/7ZAJ-QCST; Pro Publica, Tracking PPP: City Marshal Ronald Moses, https://projects.propublica.org/coronavirus/bailouts /loans/city-marshal-ronald-moses-1176537706, https://perma.cc/4UKS-AZ8C.

43. § 8.01-499 (officer receiving money to make return thereof and pay net proceeds; commission, etc.); and New York Correction History Society, "The History of the Office of Sheriff: Chapter 8," www.correctionhistory.org/html /chronicl/sheriff/ch8.htm, https://perma.cc/5VJZ-U6DQ.

44. La. Rev. Stat. § 13:5530.

45. N.J. Stat. Title 22A. Fees and Costs 22A § 4-8.

46. The *Natchez Weekly Courier and Journal*, Natchez Mississippi, June 3, 1840, archived at www.newspapers.com/image/248855080/.

47. Phillip Ludwell, *An Abridgment of the Laws of Virginia: Compiled in 1694*, https://babel.hathitrust.org/cgi/pt?id=mdp.35112202571685&view=1up &seq=41.

48. Marvin L. Michael Kay and Lorin Lee Cary, "The Planters Suffer Little or Nothing: North Carolina Compensations for Executed Slaves, 1748–1772," *Science & Society* 40, no. 3 (Fall 1976): 288–306.

49. Thomas D. Russell, "South Carolina's Largest Slave Auctioneering Firm—Symposium on the Law of Slavery: Criminal and Civil Law of Slavery," *Chicago-Kent Law Review* 68 (1992); 1241, 1273.

50. S.C. Code § 15-39-610 (2013); and S.C. Code § 23-19-10 (2012).

51. Christine A. Budasoff, "Modern Civil Forfeiture Is Unconstitutional," *Texas Review of Law & Politics* 23 (2019): 467, 468.

52. For example, Eric Blumenson and Eva S. Nilsen, "Policing for Profit: The Drug War's Hidden Economic Agenda," *University of Chicago Law Review* 65 (1998): 35.

53. For example, Sarah Stillman, "Taken," *New Yorker*, August 5, 2013, www.newyorker.com/magazine/2013/08/12/taken.

54. K.S.A. 60-4113; see also Congressional Research Service, *Asset Forfeiture, Selected Legal Issues and Reforms*, February 2, 2015, www.everycrsreport.com /files/20150202_R43890_aa33f2c331a60c609f70b596ec9a891d8fccb623.pdf.

55. Stacy St. Clair, "Illinois Law Enforcement Takes in More Than $319 Million in Forfeited Property," *Chicago Tribune*, November 28, 2016, www.chicagotribune .com/news/ct-police-forfeiture-seizure-illinois-20161128-story.html.

56. Buda, Texas, Interlocal Agreement Regarding Asset Forfeitures within Hays County, http://tx-buda.civicplus.com/AgendaCenter/ViewFile/Item/315 ?fileID=765, https://perma.cc/MLF8-W2GK.

57. Tyler Arnold, "Wayne County Doubling Down On Forfeiture as Leg-islature Moves to Reform It," *Capital Confidential*, March 28, 2019, www .michigancapitolconfidential.com/wayne-county-doubling-down-on-forfeiture -as-legislature-moves-to-reform-it, https://perma.cc/98TL-N53F.

58. Institute for Justice, *Policing for Profit: The Abuse of Civil Asset Forfeiture*, December 2020, https://ij.org/report/policing-for-profit-3/pfp3content/executive-summary/.

59. Institute for Justice, *Policing for Profit*; see also, for example, Louis S. Rulli, "Prosecuting Civil Asset Forfeiture on Contingency Fees: Looking for Profit in All the Wrong Places," *Alabama Law Review* 72 (2021): 531; Dawn Fritz, "Timbs v. Indiana: Civil Forfeiture, Racism, and the War on Drugs," Denver Law Forum, 2021, www.denverlawreview.org/dlr-online-article/timbs; and Stillman, "Taken."

60. Timbs v. Indiana, 586 U.S. ___(2019).

61. Emma Anderson, "The Supreme Court Didn't Put the Nail in Civil Asset Forfeiture's Coffin," *ACLU* (blog), March 15, 2019, www.aclu.org/blog/criminal-law-reform/reforming-police/supreme-court-didnt-put-nail-civil-asset-forfeitures.

62. Anderson, "The Supreme Court Didn't Put the Nail."

63. Marshall v. Jerrico, Inc., 446 U.S. 238 (1980).

64. US Department of Justice, "Equitable Sharing Payments Grand Total of Cash and Sale Proceeds: FY 2019," www.justice.gov/afp/page/file/1250751/download; Department of Criminal Justice Services, *Forfeited Asset Sharing Program Manual*, April 2019, www.dcjs.virginia.gov/sites/dcjs.virginia.gov/files/publications/dcjs/forfeited-asset-sharing-program-manual.pdf, https://perma.cc/K7BC-8TSU; Ella Fisher, "Equitable Sharing Aids Circumventing State Civil Asset Forfeiture," in *Economic Crime Forensics Capstones* (2018), https://digitalcommons.lasalle.edu/cgi/viewcontent.cgi?article=1024&context=ecf_capstones.

65. William H. Freivogel, "'For Phelps County, Seizing Suspects' Assets Is Like 'Pennies from Heaven,'" St. Louis Public Radio, February 21, 2019, https://news.stlpublicradio.org/government-politics-issues/2019-02-21/for-phelps-county-seizing-suspects-assets-is-like-pennies-from-heaven.

66. Freivogel, "'For Phelps County, Seizing Suspects' Assets."

67. The Associated Press, "South Carolina Police Are Collecting Millions off Civil Forfeitures, Blacks Targeted Most," WJCL, February 4, 2019, www.wjcl.com/article/south-carolina-police-are-collecting-millions-off-civil-forfeitures-blacks-targeted-most/26129025.

68. Isaac Safier, "We Need to Talk about Civil Asset Forfeiture," *New America*, Sept. 10, 2020, www.newamerica.org/weekly/we-need-talk-about-civil-asset-forfeiture/, https://perma.cc/QL3F-PGQR.

69. Joseph Shapiro, "In Ferguson, Court Fines and Fees Fuel Anger," NPR, Aug. 15, 2014, www.npr.org/2014/08/25/343143937/in-ferguson-court-fines-and-fees-fuel-anger.

70. US Dept. of Justice, Civil Rights Division, *Investigation of the Ferguson Police Department*, March 4, 2015, www.justice.gov/sites/default/files/opa/press-releases/attachments/2015/03/04/ferguson_police_department_report.pdf.

71. Lauren Williams, "Ferguson, MO, Is 67 Percent Black, but Just 3 out of Its 53 Police Officers Are," *Vox*, August 12, 2014, www.vox.com/xpress/2014/8/12/5994181/ferguson-is-67-percent-black-and-its-police-force-is-94-percent-white.

72. US Dept. of Justice, Civil Rights Division, *Investigation of the Ferguson Police Department*.

73. US Dept. of Justice, Civil Rights Division, *Investigation of the Ferguson Police Department.*

74. U.S. vs. The City of Ferguson, Complaint, Case:4:16-cv-00180, Feb. 10, 2016, www.justice.gov/crt/file/832451/download (the complaint led to a wide-ranging consent decree).

75. John Archibald, "Police in This Tiny Alabama Town Suck Drivers into Legal 'Black Hole," AL.com, January 20, 2022, www.al.com/news/2022/01 /police-in-this-tiny-alabama-town-suck-drivers-into-legal-black-hole.html.

76. Archibald, "Police in This Tiny Alabama Town."

77. Archibald, "Police in This Tiny Alabama Town." Illustrating the power of good journalism, the news story quickly led to the resignation of the police chief and calls for formal investigations and restitution. See John Archibald, "Drivers Tell Brookside Horror Stories; Call for Restitution, Dissolution," AL.com, February 2, 2022, www.al.com/news/2022/01/police-in-this-tiny-alabama-town -suck-drivers-into-legal-black-hole.html.

78. Jeremy Redmon, "Company Helps Ga. Counties Get Funding Tied to Illegal Immigrants," *Atlanta Journal-Constitution*, August 10, 2012, www.ajc .com/news/local-govt--politics/company-helps-counties-get-funding-tied-illegal -immigrants/Lf6ZocVOOQDZGpQeRxnEvM/.

79. Lucas County, Resolution, "Approval of Renewal Contract with Justice Benefits, Inc. for Federal Financial Participation Funding Opportunity Research for a Period of 1 Year for the Lucas County Sheriff's Office," July 26, 2016, https://lcapps.co.lucas.oh.us/carts/resos/18108.pdf, https://perma.cc/CL85 -2HF7; and Alameda County Sheriff's Office, Letter to Board of Supervisors, Authorize a First Contract Modification with Justice Benefits, Inc., April 21, 2020, www.acgov.org/board/bos_calendar/documents/DocsAgendaReg_04_28 _20/PUBLIC%20PROTECTION/Regular%20Calendar/Sheriff_294091.pdf, https://perma.cc/4GDD-P4QG.

80. Scott Smith, "Sheriffs Moving toward Straight Salaries," *Kokomo Tribune*, July 15, 2006, www.kokomotribune.com/news/local_news/sheriffs-moving-toward -straight-salaries/article_5edf4446-957c-5b84-99fc-aeaee5ad008f.html.

81. Smith, "Sheriffs Moving toward Straight Salaries."

82. Connor Sheets, "Etowah Sheriff Pockets $750k in Jail Food Funds, Buys $740k Beach House," *Birmingham Real Time News*, March 13, 2018, www.al .com/news/birmingham/2018/03/etowah_sheriff_pocketed_over_7.html.

83. Ala. Code § 14-6-47.

84. Lauren Gill, "On Tuesday, Two Alabama Sheriffs Regained Power to Divert Jail Food Funds," *Appeal*, March 5, 2020, https://theappeal.org/politicalreport /two-alabama-sheriffs-jail-food-funds/, https://perma.cc/5QG3-PD5F.

85. National Union of Special Police Officers, About SPO's, www.nuspo.org /about-spos, https://perma.cc/VB7W-UCZ8.

86. National Union of Special Police Officers, About SPO's; and Code of D.C. § 23–582.

87. CIS Resources, LLC, BlackFalls, www.uspdsecurity.com/, https://perma .cc/8HMA-ML9T; and OpenCorporates, CIS Resources LLC, https://open corporates.com/companies/us_dc/EXTUID_4252330.

88. Moorehead vs. District of Columbia, 747 A.2d 138 (2000).

89. Moorehead vs. District of Columbia.

90. For lowered accountability, see, for example, Amelia Pollard, "The Rise of Private Police," *American Prospect*, March 3, 2021, https://prospect.org/justice/rise-of-the-private-police/; and Jamal Rich, "Private Police Harass Residents at Brookland Manor Community Event in D.C.," *People's World*, March 25, 2021, www.peoplesworld.org/article/private-police-harass-residents-at-brookland-manor-community-event-in-d-c/. For less transparency, see, for example, Jodie Fleischer, "DC Residents Say MPD Ignored Complaints against Special Police Officer," NBC4 Washington, April 1, 2019, www.nbcwashington.com/news/local/dc-residents-say-mpd-ignored-complaints-against-special-police-officer/138304/. For less training, see, for example, Justin Jouvenal, "Private Police Carry Guns and Make Arrests, and Their Ranks Are Swelling," *Washington Post*, February 28, 2015, www.washingtonpost.com/local/crime/private-police-carry-guns-and-make-arrests-and-their-ranks-are-swelling/2015/02/28/29f6e02e-8f79-11e4-a900-9960214d4cd7_story.html. For fewer constitutional protections, see, for example, Elizabeth E. Joh, "The Paradox of Private Policing," *Journal of Criminal Law & Criminology* 95 (2004): 49, 115–16; and Karena Rahall, "The Siren Is Calling: Economic and Ideological Trends Toward Privatization of Public Police Forces," *Miami Law Review* 68 (2014): 633.

91. Marshall v. Jerrico, Inc., 446 U.S. 238, 250 (1980).

92. See, for example, Harjo v. City of Albuquerque, 326 F. Supp. 3d 1145 (D.N.M. 2018); Flora v. Sw. Iowa Narcotics Enf't Task Force, 292 F. Supp. 3d 875, 903-04 (S.D.Iowa 2018); Brucker v. City of Doraville, 391 F. Supp. 3d 1207, 1217 (N.D. Ga. 2019); and McNeil v. Community Probation Services, LLC, 2021 WL 365844 (M.D., Tennessee, Feb. 3, 2021).

93. Flora v. Sw. Iowa Narcotics Enf't Task Force, 292 F. Supp. 3d 875, 903-04 (S.D.Iowa 2018).

94. A Georgia federal court judge recognized the weight of this concern in his 2020 order in the case of *Brucker v. City of Doraville,* explaining that if such a shift toward revenue over justice were allowed to continue, it "might in fact distort the system of justice itself, creating faulty incentives for those charged with administering it," because "[s]uch a shift turns the justice system on its head." However, despite the concern, the judge found that constitutional violations did not occur (although recognizing that due process impartiality applies to law enforcement). At the time of this writing, the decision is on appeal to the 11th Circuit. Brucker v. City of Doraville, No. 1:18-cv-02375-RWS, 2020 WL 8173291 (N.D. Georgia 2020), https://ij.org/wp-content/uploads/2018/05/Doraville-MSJ-decision.pdf.

CHAPTER 7. BODIES IN THE BEDS: THE BUSINESS OF JAILING CHILDREN AND THE POOR

1. "Transcript: White House Chief Of Staff John Kelly's Interview with NPR," *NPR*, May 11, 2018, www.npr.org/2018/05/11/610116389/transcript-white-house-chief-of-staff-john-kellys-interview-with-npr.

2. Deniz Cam, "One in Six Migrant Children in the U.S. Are Staying at a Shelter Operated by a Private Equity Tycoon," *Forbes*, April 10, 2019, www.forbes

.com/sites/denizcam/2019/04/10/one-in-six-migrant-children-in-the-us-are
-staying-at-a-shelter-operated-by-a-private-equity-tycoon/?sh=2b91fcc2687e.

3. Graham Kates, "Some Detention Facilities for Migrant Children Not Subject to State Inspections," *CBS News*, July 5, 2018, www.cbsnews.com/news
/some-detention-centers-for-immigrant-children-wont-be-subject-to-traditional
-inspections/.

4. Flores vs. Barr, Case CV 85-4544 DMG-AGRx, Exhibits in Support of
Plaintiff's Motion to Enforce the Settlement Agreement, vol. 1 OF 5, May 31,
2019, www.courtlistener.com/recap/gov.uscourts.cacd.45170/gov.uscourts.cacd
.45170.547.3_27.pdf.

5. Monique Madan, "Homestead Migrant shelter Operator Gets Big No-
Bid Deal," *Miami Herald*, May 1, 2019, www.miamiherald.com/news/local
/immigration/article229744049.html; US Department of Health and Human
Services, Office of Inspector General, "The Office of Refugee Resettlement Did
Not Award and Manage the Homestead Influx Care Facility Contracts in Accor-
dance with Federal Requirements," A-12-20-20001, December 2020, https://oig
.hhs.gov/oas/reports/region12/122020001.pdf.

6. In 2021, Caliburn International announced it was separating into two
companies, Acuity International and Valiance Humanitarian. "Caliburn International Announces Intention to Split into Two Companies: Acuity International and Valiance Humanitarian," *Business Wire*, April 7, 2021.

7. Salvador Rizzo, "John F. Kelley Joins Board of Contractor Running Shelters
for Migrants," *Washington Post*, May 4, 2019, www.washingtonpost.com/politics
/john-kelly-joins-board-joins-board-of-contractor-running-shelter-for-migrant
-teens/2019/05/04/e28000fc-6e87-11e9-a66d-a82d3f3d96d5_story.html.

8. Rizzo, "John F. Kelley Joins Board."

9. Alisson Money, "Shriveling Economy Brings Tough Times to Siler City,"
News and Record, June 19, 2008, https://greensboro.com/editorial/columnists
/shriveling-economy-brings-tough-times-to-siler-city/article_a82106bd-a103
-5fce-ac26-0c267500b593.html, https://perma.cc/S62T-PSL2.

10. Money, "Shriveling Economy."

11. "Jeff Davis Parish Competing for Juvenile Detention Center," *KPLC
News*, May 25, 2011, www.kplctv.com/story/14716270/jeff-davis-parish-could
-be-home-to-new-juvenile-justice-facility/.

12. "Jeff Davis Parish."

13. City of Chesapeake/Commonwealth of Virginia Partnership, "Joint Juvenile
Justice Center," www.cityofchesapeake.net/Assets/documents/departments/public
_works/active_projects_spotlights/JJJC+Paper.pdf, [https://perma.cc/Q7K8-5BPK].

14. Department of Juvenile Services and Department of General Services,
*Report on the Site Selection Process for a New Regional Juvenile Detention Cen-
ter in Southern Maryland*, July 13, 2012, https://djs.maryland.gov/Documents
/publications/SRCC_Report.pdf, https://perma.cc/M45V-Z7RF.

15. Department of Juvenile Services and Department of General Services,
Report on the Site Selection Process.

16. "Richland Juvenile Detention Facility Helps Serve Morrow County,"
Morrow County Sentinel, September 8, 2020, www.morrowcountysentinel.com
/news/33645/richland-juvenile-detention-facility-helps-serve-morrow-county.

17. Ciara McCarthy, "Revenue from Juvenile Detention Center Shows Growing Trend for Victoria," *Victoria Advocate*, September 8, 2018, www .victoriaadvocate.com/news/government/revenue-from-juvenile-detention -center-shows-growing-trend-for-victoria-county/article_434d6a6e-b218-11e8 -849d-1f19478df37d.html, https://perma.cc/NZW5-PCWD.

18. McCarthy, "Revenue from Juvenile Detention Center."

19. Sally Ousley, "Martin Hall Revenue Said on Stable Ground," *Whitman County Gazette*, July 10, 2014, www.wcgazette.com/story/2014/07/10/news /martin-hall-revenue-said-on-stable-ground/15352.html, https://perma.cc/6KKR -J6A8.

20. Ousley, "Martin Hall Revenue Said on Stable Ground."

21. Union County, New Jersey, "Union County Considers Contract to Provide Beds at Detention Center for Hudson County Juvenile Detainees," press release, December 12, 2014, https://ucnj.org/press-releases/public-info/2014/12 /12/union-county-considers-contract-to-provide-beds-at-detention-center-for -hudson-county-juvenile-detainees/, [https://perma.cc/6Z7N-F7P3].

22. Union County, New Jersey, "Union County Considers Contract."

23. Union County, New Jersey, "Union County Considers Contract."

24. McCarthy, "Revenue from Juvenile Detention Center."

25. McCarthy, "Revenue from Juvenile Detention Center."

26. US Department of Justice, Office of Juvenile Justice and Delinquency Prevention, "Juvenile Residential Programs Literature Review," March 2019, https://ojjdp.ojp.gov/mpg/literature-review/juvenile-residential-programs.pdf

27. US Department of Justice, OJJDP, "Juvenile Residential Programs Literature Review."

28. US Department of Justice, OJJDP, "Juvenile Residential Programs Literature Review."

29. US Department of Justice, OJJDP, "Juvenile Residential Programs Literature Review."

30. Alice Hines, "Dangerous Restraints Were Routine at This Youth Home: Then a Black Teen Died," *Vice News*, July 24, 2020, www.vice.com/en/article /n7w4pk/dangerous-restraints-were-routine-at-youth-home-where-7-staffers -fatally-held-down-a-black-teen; and Fredericks vs. Lakeside for Children, Complaint and Jury Request, https://s3-us-west-2.amazonaws.com/maven -user-documents/pinacnews/eye-on-government/LhlGTxQVnU-jb5b_cF6-uA /2hq4-scY4Uuryzf2wSyBbQ/466546286-Cornelius-Fredericks-Civil-Rights -Complaint.pdf, https://perma.cc/ZVK8-Z9ZR.

31. Tyler Kingkade and Hannah Rappleye, "The Brief Life of Cornelius Frederick: Warning Signs Missed before a Teen's Fatal Restraint," *NBC News*, July 23, 2020, www.nbcnews.com/news/us-news/brief-life-cornelius-frederick -warning-signs-missed-teen-s-fatal-n1234660.

32. Rose White, "Released Video Shows Fatal Restraint of 16-Year-Old at Kalamazoo Youth Home," *Fox 61*, July 7, 2020, www.fox61.com/article /news/local/video-fatal-restraint-16-year-old-kalamazoo-youth-home-cornelius -fredericks/69-bda959ab-85fb-4338-ab9d-9a54b41c7a3d.

33. Justin Carissimo and Li Cohen, "Three Charged in Death of Black Teen Who Died after Being Restrained at Youth Facility," *CBS News*, June 27, 2020,

www.cbsnews.com/news/cornelius-fredericks-death-lakeside-academy-staffers
-charged-kalamazoo-michigan/.

34. "Mass Escape at Michigan Youth Facility after Staff Restrain Teen to
Death," *Perilous Chronicle*, May 1, 2020, https://perilouschronicle.com/2020
/05/01/disturbance-and-mass-escape-at-michigan-youth-facility-after-staff
-restrain-teen-to-death/, https://perma.cc/D98M-N2KJ.

35. "Mass Escape at Michigan Youth Facility."

36. Justin Dwyer, "State Says It Will Ban Restraints That Led to Death of
16-Year-Old," *Michigan Radio*, July 16, 2020, www.michiganradio.org/post
/state-says-it-will-ban-restraints-led-death-16-year-old.

37. White, "Released Video Shows Fatal Restraint of 16-Year-Old."

38. "The Bad Place," *Reveal News*, November 21, 2020, https://revealnews
.org/podcast/the-bad-place/, https://perma.cc/3BPQ-FSCX.

39. "Bad Place."

40. Hannah Rappleye, Tyler Kingkade, and Kate Snow, "A Profitable 'Death-
trap': Sequel Youth Facilities Raked in Millions, While Accused of Abusing Children,"
NBC News, December 16, 2020, www.nbcnews.com/news/us-news/profitable
-death-trap-sequel-youth-facilities-raked-millions-while-accused-n1251319.

41. Bennett Haeberle, "More States Sever Ties with For-Profit Sequel
Youth and Family Services after Reports of Abuse," 10 WBNS, December 17,
2020, www.10tv.com/article/news/investigations/10-investigates/more-states
-sever-ties-with-sequel-youth-and-family-services-after-reports-of-abuse/530
-b6f995b7-13c3-40a5-8893-5326af948a19 [https://perma.cc/45NH-V5MN].

42. "Bad Place."

43. US Securities and Exchange Commission, Sequel Youth and Family Services, Global Partner Acquisition Corp., Investor Presentation, May 2017, www
.sec.gov/Archives/edgar/data/1643953/000121390017004915/ex99_1.htm,
https://perma.cc/8DJH-AWWM.

44. US SEC, Sequel Youth and Family Services, Investor Presentation.

45. Haeberle, "More States Sever Ties with For-Profit Sequel Youth."

46. US SEC, Sequel Youth and Family Services, Investor Presentation.

47. Clarinda Youth Corporation d/b/a Clarinda Academy, 2018 Financial
Statements, www.legis.iowa.gov/docs/publications/DF/1045597.pdf, https://
perma.cc/T9AS-C98Z.

48. Clarinda Youth Corporation, 2018 Financial Statements.

49. Andrea May Sahouri, "Clarinda Academy Closing after Years of Alleged
Abuse, Sexual Assault of Teens in Iowa," *Des Moines Register*, February 5,
2021, www.desmoinesregister.com/story/news/2021/02/05/clarinda-academy
-iowa-closing-after-years-alleged-abuse-sexual-assault-teens/4414216001/

50. Sahouri, "Clarinda Academy Closing."

51. Savannah Tryens-Fernandes, "Alabama Advocacy Groups Claim Illegal
Restraints, Strangulation at Sequel Youth Facility," AL.com, December 30, 2021,
www.al.com/news/2021/12/alabama-advocacy-groups-claim-illegal-restraints
-strangulation-at-sequel-youth-facility.html.

52. Tryens-Fernandes, "Alabama Advocacy Groups Claim Illegal Restraints."

53. U.S. Department of Justice, *The False Claims Act: A Primer*, www.justice
.gov/sites/default/files/civil/legacy/2011/04/22/C-FRAUDS_FCA_Primer.pdf.

54. U.S. Department of Justice, "Extendicare Health Services Inc. Agrees to Pay $38 Million to Settle False Claims Act Allegations," press release, October 10, 2014, www.justice.gov/opa/pr/extendicare-health-services-inc-agrees-pay-38-million-settle-false-claims-act-allegations.

55. Universal Health Services, Inc., 2020 *Annual Report,* https://ir.uhsinc.com/static-files/c60693a6-ee46-48b1-8220-48fddobod293.

56. US Securities and Exchange Commission, Universal Health Services, Inc., Form 8K, July 6, 2020, https://seekingalpha.com/filings/pdf/14268115.pdf, https://perma.cc/G34E-ZKKJ.

57. US SEC, Universal Health Services, Inc., Form 8K.

58. U.S. Department of Justice, "Residential Youth Treatment Facility for Medicaid Recipients in Marion, Virginia Agrees to Resolve False Claims Act Allegations," press release, March 28, 2012, www.justice.gov/opa/pr/residential-youth-treatment-facility-medicaid-recipients-marion-virginia-agrees-resolve-false.

59. Walter F. Roche Jr., "New Life Lodge Whistleblower Acted after Death of Patient," *Tennessean,* April 22, 2014, www.tennessean.com/story/news/health/2014/04/21/woman-whose-complaints-led-state-federal-investigation-new-life-lodge-says-death-patient-led-act/7982135/, https://perma.cc/F32U-YJUC.

60. Roche, "New Life Lodge Whistleblower."

61. Roche, "New Life Lodge Whistleblower."

62. Nate Rau and Walter F. Roche Jr., "$14.5M Suit Filed in Another Former New Life Patient Death," *Tennessean,* December 5, 2012.

63. Nate Rau, "Arcadia to Buy CRC Health, Owner of New Life Lodge," *Tennessean,* October 29, 2014, www.tennessean.com/story/money/industries/health-care/2014/10/29/acadia-buy-crc-health-owner-new-life-lodge/18146249/.

64. Timothy J. Mullaney, "Youth Services Firm Loses Another Executive, Ripley," *Baltimore Sun,* June 29, 1995, www.baltimoresun.com/news/bs-xpm-1995-06-29-1995180054-story.html.

65. Margie Menzel, "Florida Ends Contract with Juvenile Detention Provider," *CJCT News,* March 21, 2016, https://news.wjct.org/post/florida-ends-contract-juvenile-detention-provider.

66. Carol Marbin Miller, "At This Juvenile Justice Program, Staffers Set Up Fights—and Then Bet on Them," *Miami Herald,* October 10, 2017, www.miamiherald.com/news/special-reports/florida-prisons/article177946531.html.

67. U.S. Department of Justice, OJJDP, "Juvenile Residential Programs Literature Review."

68. U.S. Department of Justice, Office of Juvenile Justice and Delinquency Prevention, "Census of Juveniles in Residential Placement," https://ojjdp.ojp.gov/research-and-statistics/research-projects/Census-of-Juveniles-in-Residential-Placement/overview.

69. Miss. Code § 43-15-111 (2019).

70. Caleb Bedillion, "As Litigation Mounts, Daily Journal Investigation Probes Boarding School for Troubled Youth," *Daily Journal,* April 9, 2020, www.djournal.com/news/local/as-litigation-mounts-daily-journal-investigation-probes-boarding-school-for-troubled-youth/article_f479344d-29ea-5470-b157-a891f0706536.html.

71. Alissa Zhu, "Runaways, Claims of 'Aggression, Abuse': Mississippi Boys Ranch Operates with Little Oversight," *Clarion Ledger*, June 14, 2020, www.clarionledger.com/story/news/2020/06/14/abuse-claims-arise-mississippi -troubled-youth-camp/3122938001/.

72. Caleb Bedillion, "As Litigation Mounts."

73. Zhu, "Runaways, Claims of 'Aggression, Abuse.'"

74. Tyler Kingkade, Liz Brown, and Keith Morrison, "Legal Loopholes Allow Abuse to Go Undetected at Religious Boarding Schools, Advocates Say," *NBC News*, February 12, 2021, www.nbcnews.com/news/us-news/legal-loopholes -allow-abuse-go-undetected-religious-boarding-schools-advocates-n1257203.

75. Kingkade, Brown, and Morrison, "Legal Loopholes Allow Abuse."

76. Church of the Lukumi Babalu Aye, Inc. v. Hialeah, 508 U.S. 520 (1993).

77. Roman Catholic Diocese of Brooklyn v. Cuomo, 592 U. S. ____ (2020), https://www.supremecourt.gov/opinions/20pdf/20a87_4g15.pdf

78. Torcaso v. Watkins, 367 U.S. 488 (1961).

79. Epperson v. Arkansas, 393 U.S. 97 (1968).

80. "Nonprofit Explorer, Lakeside for Children," *ProPublica,* 2019 Form 990, https://projects.propublica.org/nonprofits/organizations/381360532/2020 31079349300328/IRS990, https://perma.cc/HLV6-JXQB.

81. "Nonprofit Explorer, Lakeside for Children."

82. Curtis Gilbert, "How Sequel Wins Business from California," *APM Reports*, September 18, 2020, www.apmreports.org/story/2020/09/28/how -sequel-wins-california-business.

83. Juaquin Palomino, Sara Tiano, and Cynthia Dizikes, "California Uses Out-of-State Youth Facilities Marred by Rampant Abuse," *Imprint*, December 11, 2020, https://imprintnews.org/child-welfare-2/california-ends-out-of -state-placements/50095, [https://perma.cc/9RPN-9LG2].

84. Palomino, Tiano, and Dizikes, "California Uses Out-of-State Youth Facilities."

85. See, for example, Deborah L. Rhode and Amanda K. Packel, "Ethics and Nonprofits," *Stanford Social Innovation Review*, Summer 2009, https:// ssir.org/articles/entry/ethics_and_nonprofits#; Terri L. Helge, "Joint Ventures of Nonprofits and For-Profits," *Texas Tax Lawyer* 41 (2014): 1; Jean Wright and Jay H. Rotz, "Illegality and Public Policy Considerations," Internal Revenue Service, 1994 EO CPE Text, www.irs.gov/pub/irs-tege/eotopicl94.pdf; Internal Revenue Service, "Activities That Are Illegal or Contrary to Public Policy," 1985 EO CPE Text, www.irs.gov/pub/irs-tege/eotopicj85.pdf; Internal Revenue Service, "Overview of Inurement/Private Benefit Issues in IRC 501(c)(3)," 1990 EO CPE Text, www.irs.gov/pub/irs-tege/eotopicc90.pdf; and Internal Revenue Service, "Health Care Organizations under IRC 501(c)(3)," 1981 EO CPE Text, www.irs.gov/pub/irs-tege/eotopica81.pdf.

86. Pennsylvania Department of Human Services, Decision Revoking License, October 24, 2016, http://media.philly.com/documents/WordsworthReport.pdf, https://perma.cc/ZMT5-K3ZE.

87. Pennsylvania Department of Human Services, Decision Revoking License.

88. Nancy Phillips and Chris Palmer, "Death, Rapes and Broken Bones at Philly's Only Residential Treatment Center for Troubled Youth," *Philadelphia*

Inquirer, April 22, 2017, www.inquirer.com/philly/news/pennsylvania/philadelphia
/Death-rape-Philadelphia-Wordsworth-residential-treatment-center-troubled
-youth.html.

89. Phillips and Palmer, "Death, Rapes and Broken Bones."

90. Phillips and Palmer, "Death, Rapes and Broken Bones."

91. Phillips and Palmer, "Death, Rapes and Broken Bones."

92. Public Health Management Corporation, www.phmc.org/site/, https://
perma.cc/8TKG-MVQG.

93. Public Health Management Corporation, "Public Health Management Corporation to Acquire Wordsworth," press release, www.phmc.org/site
/newsroom/press/102-press-releases/2017-1/1229-public-health-management
-corporation-to-acquire-wordsworth, https://perma.cc/H75H-LBQB.

94. Harold Brubaker, "Wordsworth Academy Files for Bankruptcy, Will
Be Acquired," *Philadelphia Inquirer*, June 30, 2017, www.inquirer.com/philly
/business/wordsworth-academy-files-for-bankruptcy-will-be-acquired-2017
0630.html.

95. Brubaker, "Wordsworth Academy Files for Bankruptcy."

96. City of Philadelphia, "Community Behavioral Health Names Dr. Faith
Dyson-Washington as New CEO," press release, September 28, 2020, www
.phila.gov/2020-09-28-community-behavioral-health-names-dr-faith-dyson
-washingtonas-new-ceo/, https://perma.cc/4CH8-F3UG ("Prior to accepting
the CEO position at CBH, Washington served as senior director of behavioral
health integration at Public Health Management Corp., where she oversaw
behavioral health services across integrated health services.").

97. "Nonprofit Explorer, Public Health Management Corporation," *Pro-
Publica*, 2019 Form 990, https://projects.propublica.org/nonprofits/organizations
/237221025/202011539349300021/full, https://perma.cc/DVX7-2NUQ.

98. Devereux Advanced Behavior Health, www.devereux.org/site/SPage
Server/.

99. Melissa Jacobs, "Looking Back on Robert Kreider's 23-Year Legacy at
Devereux," *Main Line Today*, December 12, 2017, https://mainlinetoday.com
/life-style/looking-back-on-robert-kreiders-23-year-legacy-at-devereux/, https://
perma.cc/D7PK-XPGX.

100. Lisa Gartner and Barbara Laker, "At the Nation's Leading Behavioral
Health Nonprofit for Youth, Devereux Staff Abused Children in Their Care for
Years—While Red Flags Were Dismissed," *Philadelphia Inquirer*, August 11,
2020, www.inquirer.com/news/inq/devereux-advanced-behavioral-health-abuse
-children-pennsylvania-20200811.html.

101. Barbara Laker and Wendy Ruderman, "Twenty Chester County
Devereux Staffers Allegedly harmed Children—or Kept Quiet about the
Abuse—since 2018," *Philadelphia Inquirer*, January 27, 2021, www.inquirer
.com/news/inq/devereux-behavioral-health-dhs-child-abuse-20210127.html.

102. Barbara Laker and Wendy Ruderman, "Philly to Remove 53 Kids
from Devereux's Live-In Facilities after It Finds Lax Supervision," *Philadelphia
Inquirer*, September 24, 2020, www.inquirer.com/news/philadelphia/devereux
-philadelphia-abuse-council-remove-children-20200924.html.

103. Devereux Advanced Behavior Health, "Senior Leadership Team," https://www.devereux.org/site/SPageServer/?NONCE_TOKEN=91330397 A1DC4D250566477EC463DA7A&pagename=leadership, [https://perma.cc /6LSN-RXT7].

104. US Securities and Exchange Commission, Geo Group Inc. (GEO), Form 10K, FY 2020, www.sec.gov/Archives/edgar/data/923796/000156459021006003/geo-10k_20201231.htm.

105. Geo Group, Inc., "Geo Completes REIT Conversion," www.geogroup.com/userfiles/337e14c1-4d30-4723-a85d-a02f51816e54.pdf, https://perma.cc /H7A9-VGW7.

106. Jeff Shaw, "The SHB Interview: Rick Matros CEO Sabra Health Care REIT," Seniors Housing Business, July 17, 2017, https://seniorshousingbusiness.com/the-shb-interview-rick-matros-ceo-sabra-health-care-reit/, https://perma.cc /8RFB-4PD9 (describing Sabra as "the seventh largest owner of seniors housing in the country with 182 properties totaling 18,756 beds/units as of the first-quarter" of 2017).

107. US SEC, Geo Group Inc. (GEO), Form 10K.

108. US SEC, Geo Group Inc. (GEO), Form 10K.

109. US SEC, Geo Group Inc. (GEO), Form 10K.

110. US SEC, Geo Group Inc. (GEO), Form 10K.

111. US Department of Justice, Civil Rights Division, "Investigation of the Walnut Grove Youth Correctional Facility Walnut Grove, Mississippi," March 20, 2012, https://www.justice.gov/sites/default/files/crt/legacy/2012/04/09/walnutgrovefl.pdf ("GEO assumed operations of the Facility in August 2010, after acquiring and merging with Cornell Companies, Inc. ('Cornell'), which had operated the Facility since September 2003. Following GEO and Cornell's merger, key personnel, policies and training at WGYCF did not change substantially, despite GEO's claim that it made corrective reforms to reflect the GEO philosophy.").

112. C.B. et al. v. Walnut Grove Correctional Authority, et al., No. 3:10-cv-00663-CWR-FKB, https://www.aclu.org/files/assets/order.pdf, https:// perma.cc/LB6J-WQR7.

113. C.B. et al. v. Walnut Grove Correctional Authority, et al.

114. John Burnett, "Mississippi Prison Operator Out; Facility Called a 'Cesspool,'" NPR, April 24, 2012, www.npr.org/2012/04/24/151276620/firm-leaves -miss-after-its-prison-is-called-cesspool.

115. Hartel v. The Geo Group, Inc., Class Action Complaint, July 7, 2020, www.dandodiary.com/wp-content/uploads/sites/893/2020/07/GEO-Group -Complaint.pdf, https://perma.cc/L424-GKNX.

116. Madison Pauly, "A Judge Says Thousands of Detainees May Sue a Prison Company for Using Them as a 'Captive Labor Force,'" Mother Jones, December 5, 2019, www.motherjones.com/crime-justice/2019/12/immigration -detainee-geo-forced-labor-lawsuit/.

117. Norman Merchant, "Private Prison Industry Backs Trump, Prepares If Biden Wins," Washington Post, August 13, 2020www.washingtonpost.com /health/private-prison-industry-backs-trump-prepares-if-biden-wins/2020/08 /13/a51c8f64-dd8a-11ea-b4f1-25b762cdbbf4_story.html.

118. The White House, "Executive Order on Reforming Our Incarceration System to Eliminate the Use of Privately Operated Criminal Detention Facilities," January 26, 2021, www.whitehouse.gov/briefing-room/presidential -actions/2021/01/26/executive-order-reforming-our-incarceration-system-to -eliminate-the-use-of-privately-operated-criminal-detention-facilities/

119. The Geo Group. Inc., "GEO Group's Statement on President Biden's Executive Order Regarding the Department of Justice and Privately Operated Criminal Detention Facilities," January 26, 2021, www.geogroup.com/EO_DOJ _Statement.pdf, https://perma.cc/459L-V3E4.

120. United States Securities and Exchange Commission, Acadia Healthcare Company, Inc., Form 10-Q, September 30, 2020, https://acadiahealthcare.gcs -web.com/static-files/ca663a0d-060d-4975-a5af-d6589364cf7a.

121. Gary Enos, "Addiction Treatment Inc.: Barry Karlin Has the Drive— and the Financing—to make CRC Health a National Addiction Treatment Enterprise; Will He Shake up the Field? Some Hope So," *Behavioral Healthcare Tomorrow* 12, no. 3 (June 2003), https://go.gale.com/ps/i.do?p=AONE&u= googlescholar&id=GALE%7CA102947823&v=2.1&it=r&sid=AONE&asid= 2d91b95b, https://perma.cc/ET5F-R9QM.

122. Enos, "Addiction Treatment Inc."

123. Enos, "Addiction Treatment Inc."

124. Northern Castle Partners, "CRC Health," www.northcastlepartners .com/portfolio/crc-health-group-inc/, https://perma.cc/94WU-YECL.

125. Ken MacFadyen, "Bain Finalises CRC Purchase," Infrastructure Investor, March 20, 2006, www.infrastructureinvestor.com/bain-finalises-crc-purchase/, https://perma.cc/2WQM-6P9G.

126. Duff McDonald, "Private Equity's Rehab Roll-Up," *Fortune,* July 19, 2012, https://archive.fortune.com/2012/04/26/news/companies/bain-crc-rehab .fortune/index.htm, https://perma.cc/BHW7-93S5.

127. "CRC Health Buys Education Assistance Co., Aspen Education," VentureBeat, Oct. 2, 2006, https://venturebeat.com/2006/10/02/crc-health-buys -education-assistance-co-aspen-education/.

128. Duff McDonald, "Private Equity's Rehab Roll-Up," *Fortune,* July 19, 2012.

129. Nate Rau, "Acadia to Buy CRC Health, Owner of New Life Lodge," *Tennessean,* October 29, 2014, www.tennessean.com/story/money/industries/health -care/2014/10/29/acadia-buy-crc-health-owner-new-life-lodge/18146249/.

130. Altamont Capital Partners, "Jerry Rhodes, Operating Partner," www .altamontcapital.com/employee/jerry-rhodes/, https://perma.cc/QEU8-KYVJ.

131. "Altamont Capital Partners Invests in Sequel Youth & Family Services," *Cision PR Newswire,* September 25, 2017, www.prnewswire.com/news-releases /altamont-capital-partners-invests-in-sequel-youth--family-services-300513614 .html.

132. Altamont Capital Partners, "Jerry Rhodes, Operating Partner."

133. Art Levine, "Dark Side of a Bain Success," *Salon,* July 18, 2012, www .salon.com/2012/07/18/dark_side_of_a_bain_success/.

134. Levine, "Dark Side of a Bain Success."

135. Levine, "Dark Side of a Bain Success."

136. Erica Teichert, "CRC Health Pays \$9.25M to Resolve Medicaid Fraud Claims," *Law 360*, April 17, 2014, https://soberlawnews.com/wp-content/uploads/2014/07/CRC-Health-Pays-9.2-Million.pdf, https://perma.cc/7FPP-DAER.

137. U.S. Department of Justice, "United States Attorney Announces \$17 Million Healthcare Fraud Settlement," press release, May 6, 2019, www.justice.gov/usao-sdwv/pr/united-states-attorney-announces-17-million-healthcare-fraud-settlement.

138. Danielle Prokop, "Problems with Child Welfare Services Persist after Closure of Troubled Facility," *Santa Fe New Mexican*, July 18, 2020, www.santafenewmexican.com/news/local_news/problems-with-child-welfare-services-persist-after-closure-of-troubled-facility/article_aeffb546-1aea-11ea-bff0-fb5f346db6d7.html.

139. *Hearing: Cases of Child Neglect and Abuse at Private Residential Treatment Facilities, House Committee on Education and Labor* (October 10, 2007), https://www.govinfo.gov/content/pkg/CHRG-110hhrg38055/pdf/CHRG-110hhrg38055.pdf, https://perma.cc/WYX3-KDEX.

140. *Hearing: Cases of Child Neglect and Abuse.*

CHAPTER 8. RACIALIZED HARM OF THE INJUSTICE ENTERPRISE

1. Randall G. Shelden, "Origins of the Juvenile Court in Memphis, Tennessee: 1900–1910," *Tennessee Historical Quarterly* 52, no. 1 (1993): 40–41, www-jstor-org.proxy-ub.researchport.umd.edu/stable/42627043?seq=1#metadata_info_tab_contents.

2. Shelden, "Origins of the Juvenile Court in Memphis, Tennessee," 41.

3. Shelden, "Origins of the Juvenile Court in Memphis, Tennessee," 39.

4. Shelden, "Origins of the Juvenile Court in Memphis, Tennessee."

5. Edward Nicholas Clopper, *Child Welfare in Tennessee: An Inquiry*, National Child Labor Committee (US), Tennessee Department of Public Instruction, Tennessee Child Welfare Commission, 1920, https://archive.org/details/cu31924002408684/page/n491/mode/2up.

6. Clopper, *Child Welfare in Tennessee*, 448–52.

7. Clopper, *Child Welfare in Tennessee*, 448–52.

8. Clopper, *Child Welfare in Tennessee*, 448–52.

9. Clopper, *Child Welfare in Tennessee*, 448–52.

10. Clopper, *Child Welfare in Tennessee*, 448–52.

11. Clopper, *Child Welfare in Tennessee*, 448–52.

12. Clopper, *Child Welfare in Tennessee*, 448–52.

13. Clopper, *Child Welfare in Tennessee*, 486.

14. Clopper, *Child Welfare in Tennessee*, 486.

15. Clopper, *Child Welfare in Tennessee*, 452.

16. Nina Bernstein, "Misery Funds a Legal Fiefdom," Alicia Patterson Foundation, 1994, https://aliciapatterson.org/stories/misery-funds-legal-fiefdom, https://perma.cc/A3YQ-EHQB.

17. Bernstein, "Misery Funds a Legal Fiefdom."

18. Bernstein, "Misery Funds a Legal Fiefdom."

19. Bernstein, "Misery Funds a Legal Fiefdom."

20. Bernstein, "Misery Funds a Legal Fiefdom."

21. Yolanda Jones, "A Look Inside the Shelby County Juvenile Detention Center Shows the Human Side of Controversy," *Daily Memphian*, January 21, 2019, https://dailymemphian.com/article/2522/A-look-inside-the-Shelby-County-Juvenile-Detention-Center-shows-the-human-side-of-controversy, https://perma.cc/X8CN-7X7W.

22. Juvenile Court of Memphis and Shelby County, *Annual Report*, 2012, 2, 7, www.shelbycountytn.gov/DocumentCenter/View/13735/2012-Anual-Report?bidId=, https://perma.cc/BH4L-WGQL.

23. US Department of Justice, *Investigation of the Shelby County Juvenile Court*, 2012, 1, www.justice.gov/sites/default/files/crt/legacy/2012/04/26/shelbycountyjuv_findingsrpt_4-26-12.pdf.

24. Wendi C. Thomas, "Juvy Court's Discrimination Goes On, but Mayor Wants Federal Oversight to End," *MLK50*, June 18, 2017, https://mlk50.com/juvy-courts-discrimination-goes-on-but-mayor-wants-federal-oversight-to-end-cc8e6af6f4a3, https://perma.cc/P5CR-DRRU.

25. For example, Adam Serwer, "Jeff Session's Blind Eye," *Atlantic*, April 5, 2017, www.theatlantic.com/politics/archive/2017/04/jeff-sessions-blind-eye/521946/.

26. Sandra Simkins, *Final Report on Shelby County Juvenile Court*, Department of Justice, 2018, 1, www.scribd.com/document/395400277/Final-report-from-a-Department-of-Justice-monitor-on-Shelby-County-Juvenile-Court#from_embed, https://perma.cc/6CDV-SDFL; see also Sarah Macaraeg, "Final DOJ Report: 'Blatantly Unfair' Practices Persist at Shelby County Juvenile Court," www.commercialappeal.com/story/news/2018/12/10/shelby-county-juvenile-court-federal-oversight-doj-report/2266028002/ (providing copy of final report).

27. Simkins, *Final Report on Shelby County Juvenile Court*, 3.

28. Simkins, *Final Report on Shelby County Juvenile Court*, 3.

29. Simkins, *Final Report on Shelby County Juvenile Court*, 34–37.

30. Simkins, *Final Report on Shelby County Juvenile Court*, 34–37.

31. Toby Sells, "Juvenile Judge Declares 'Mission Accomplished,'" *Memphis Flyer*, February 22, 2019, www.memphisflyer.com/NewsBlog/archives/2019/02/22/juvenile-judge-declares-mission-accomplished.

32. Toby Sells, "Rate of Juvenile Transfer to Adult Court 'Appalling,'" *Memphis Flyer*, January 7, 2020, www.memphisflyer.com/rate-of-juvenile-transfer-to-adult-court-appalling.

33. Juvenile Court of Memphis and Shelby County, "Juveniles Admitted to Detention Center and Reception and Release: 2013–2020," www.shelbycountytn.gov/DocumentCenter/View/30616/JUVENILES-ADMITTED-TO-DETENTION-CENTER-and-RECEPTION--RELEASE-2013---2019?bidId=, https://perma.cc/7Y3R-R7JE; and Juvenile Court of Memphis and Shelby County, "Top 10 Delinquent Charges Grouped," www.shelbycountytn.gov/DocumentCenter/View/30615/TOP-10-DELINQUENT-CHARGES-GROUPED-BY-RACE-2015---2020-COUNTING-CHARGESINCIDENTS-AMENDED-CHARGES?bidId=, https://perma.cc/9NAW-6JM3.

34. Yolanda Jones, "Records Show Increase, Racial Disparity in Juvenile Transfers to Adult Court," *Daily Memphian*, January 13, 2020, https://dailymemphian.com/section/metrocriminal-justice/article/9914/transfer-of-juveniles-to-adult-court-increases.

35. National Council of Juvenile and Family Court Judges, "Judge Dan H. Michael Elected as Treasurer to NCJFCJ Board of Directors," September 1, 2018, www.ncjfcj.org/news/judge-dan-h-michael-elected-as-treasurer-to-the-ncjfcj-board-of-directors-2/#:~:text=%E2%80%93%20The%20National%20Council%20of%20Juvenile,%2C%E2%80%9D%20said%20Judge%20John%20J, https://perma.cc/DBK5-R3LZ.

36. National Council of Juvenile and Family Court Judges, "Judge Dan H. Michael Elected as 76th President of the NCJFCJ," July 22, 2020, www.ncjfcj.org/news/judge-dan-h-michael-elected-as-76th-president-of-the-ncjfcj/.

37. Shelby County Juvenile Justice Consortium, "A Summary of Final Department of Justice Recommendations, Juvenile Court of Memphis and Shelby County Progress, and Remaining Concerns," June 2021, https://agenda.shelbycountytn.gov/OnBaseAgendaOnline/Documents/ViewDocument/EXHIBIT%20A%20CJJC%20REPORT%20AUGUST%202021.PDF.pdf?meetingId=2870&documentType=Agenda&itemId=66067&publishId=159689&isSection=false, https://perma.cc/4WC8-DYPC.

38. Katherine Burgess, "Shelby County Commission Asks DOJ to Reevaluate Juvenile Court," *Memphis Commercial Appeal*, September 27, 2021, www.commercialappeal.com/story/news/2021/09/27/shelby-county-commission-asks-doj-reevaluate-juvenile-court/5893303001/.

39. Shelden, "Origins of the Juvenile Court in Memphis, Tennessee."

40. Shelden, "Origins of the Juvenile Court in Memphis, Tennessee."

41. Shelden, "Origins of the Juvenile Court in Memphis, Tennessee." ("There was a significant relationship between race and offense, and between race and disposition. Blacks were far more likely to be referred to the court for delinquent offenses. . . . This reflects a prevailing view in Memphis as elsewhere that black youths and their behavior were more often viewed as "criminal" than their white counterparts.").

42. Cedric J. Robinson, *Black Marxism: The Making of the Black Radical Tradition* (Chapel Hill: University of North Carolina Press, 1983).

43. Michele Alexander, *The New Jim Crow: Mass Incarceration in the Age of Colorblindness* (New York: The New Press, 2012).

44. Dorothy Roberts, *Shattered Bonds: The Color of Child Welfare* (New York: Basic Books, 2002); and Dorothy Roberts, *Torn Apart: How the Child Welfare System Destroys Black Families—And How Abolition Can Build a Safer World* (New York: Basic Books, 2022).

45. Cuyahoga County, *2017 Results of Operations*, https://fiscalofficer.cuyahogacounty.us/pdf_fiscalofficer/en-US/obm/2017ResultsOfOperations.pdf, https://web.archive.org/web/20210707173513/https://fiscalofficer.cuyahogacounty.us/pdf_fiscalofficer/en-US/obm/2017ResultsOfOperations.pdf, https://perma.cc/VF98-NN9Q; and Cuyahoga County, "2018-2019 Biennial Budget," 168, https://fiscalofficer.cuyahogacounty.us/pdf_fiscalofficer/en-US/obm/2018-2019Budget Plan.pdf, https://perma.cc/T7XY-KTHG.

46. Cuyahoga County, *2019 Court of Common Pleas Juvenile Division Annual Report*, 30, Table 2, http://juvenile.cuyahogacounty.us/pdf_juvenile/en-US/AnnualReports/2019AnnualReport.pdf, https://perma.cc/J83J-SXTG (listing 1,433 dispositions of delinquency or "unruly" against Black youth, compared to 1,893 total); and US Census Bureau, "QuickFacts: Cuyahoga County, Ohio," 2021, https://www.census.gov/quickfacts/fact/table/cuyahogacountyohio,US/PST045219.

47. Cuyahoga County, *2019 Court of Common Pleas Juvenile Division Annual Report*, tables 1 and 2.

48. Summit County Court of Common Pleas Juvenile Division, *2015 Annual Report*, https://juvenilecourt.summitoh.net/images/AR/annrep15.pdf, https://perma.cc/2M7F-GEVG.

49. Summit County Court of Common Pleas Juvenile Division, *2016 Annual Report*, https://juvenilecourt.summitoh.net/images/AR/annrep16.pdf, https://perma.cc/8NX6-YBA8.

50. US Department of Justice, Office of Juvenile Justice and Delinquency Prevention, State of Ohio 2019 DMC/RED Action Plan, https://ojjdp.ojp.gov/sites/g/files/xyckuh176/files/media/document/OH-FY18-DMC-PLAN-508.pdf.

51. US Department of Justice, Office of Juvenile Justice and Delinquency Prevention, Louisiana DMC Update 2019, https://ojjdp.ojp.gov/sites/g/files/xyckuh176/files/media/document/la-fy18-dmc-plan_508.pdf.

52. Georgia Department of Juvenile Justice, Office of Federal Programs, https://djj.georgia.gov/djj-divisions/division-financial-services/office-federal-programs, https://web.archive.org/web/20210427104822/https://djj.georgia.gov/djj-divisions/division-financial-services/office-federal-programs.

53. Georgia Department of Juvenile Justice, Policy no. 24.1, www.djj.state.ga.us/Policies/DJJPolicies/Chapter24/DJJ24.1MedicaidApplicationIV-EForYouthIn NonSecureResidentialPrograms.pdf, https://web.archive.org/web/202010191 92155/http://www.djj.state.ga.us/Policies/DJJPolicies/Chapter24/DJJ24.1Medicaid ApplicationIV-EForYouthInNonSecureResidentialPrograms.pdf.

54. Georgia Department of Juvenile Justice, Policy no. 24.5, www.djj.state.ga.us/Policies/DJJPolicies/Chapter24/DJJ24.5SocialSecurityandSupplemental SecurityIncomeBenefitsforCommittedYouth.pdf, https://perma.cc/5TGD-AHF8.

55. Georgia Criminal Justice Coordinating Council, *Disproportionate Minority Contact in Georgia's Juvenile Justice System: A Three Prong Approach to Analyzing DMC in Georgia*, 2018, https://cjcc.georgia.gov/document/full-analysis-available-here/download, https://perma.cc/ETE4-CS5F.

56. Vinnie Giordano, "Florida Has Work to Do to Treat African American Youth Fairly," Juvenile Justice Information Exchange, December 4, 2019, https://jjie.org/2019/12/04/florida-has-work-to-do-to-treat-african-american-youth-fairly/#:~:text=From%202013%20to%202014%2C%20the,at%209 %2C315%20by%202017%2D18, https://perma.cc/4TD2-KWKW. Similarly, a 2021 study focused on girls in Florida's juvenile justice system found that "even though just 21 percent of Florida girls are Black, they're arrested and incarcerated at a rate more than double that." Dawn White, "New FL Study Finds Black Girls Receive Unfair Punishment," *First Coast News*, March 12, 2021, www.firstcoastnews.com/article/news/local/new-florida-study-finds-black

-girls-receive-unfair-punishment-in-school-criminal-justice-systems-trouble/77
-516a0820-a441-4da0-9ac2-d635bdc7bff0.

57. US Department of Justice, Office of Juvenile Justice and Delinquency Prevention, *Disproportionate Minority Contact Plan for Texas*, https://ojjdp.ojp .gov/sites/g/files/xyckuh176/files/media/document/tx-fy18-dmc-plan_509.pdf.

58. Hunter Bassler, "Arizona Has Almost 4 Times as Many Black Children Incarcerated Compared to White Kids, Report Shows, *12 News*, February 17, 2021, www.12news.com/article/news/crime/arizona-four-times-as-many-black -kids-incarcerated-in-jail-compared-to-white-sentencing-project-report-shows /75-cc61404f-b6b5-478a-a1ea-6353a7ab71ed; and Juvenile Justice Geography, Policy, Practice & Statistics, "Arizona: Racial/Ethnic Fairness," www.jjgps.org /racial-fairness/arizona, https://perma.cc/2TJH-AASC.

59. Emily Putnam-Hornstein, Eunhye Ahn, John Prindle, Joseph Magruder, Daniel Webster, and Christopher Wildeman, "Cumulative Rates of Child Protection Involvement and Terminations of Parental Rights in a California Birth Cohort, 1999–2017," *American Journal of Public Health* 111 (2021): 1157–63, https://doi.org/10.2105/AJPH.2021.306214.

60. Laura Ridolfi, "California Youth Face Heightened Racial and Ethnic Disparities in Division of Juvenile Justice," W. Haywood Burns Institute, August 2020, https://files.eric.ed.gov/fulltext/ED610669.pdf, https://perma.cc/5D48 -PTYL.

61. US Department of Justice, Office of Juvenile Justice and Delinquency Prevention, Missouri DMC Action Plan - FY2019, https://perma.cc/S5TJ-4TR7. https://ojjdp.ojp.gov/sites/g/files/xyckuh176/files/media/document/mo-fy18-dmc -plan_508.pdf; and City of St. Louis, Missouri, "Juvenile Referrals to Court," www.stlouis-mo.gov/government/departments/mayor/initiatives/resilience/equity /youth/wellbeing/juvenile-referrals-to-court.cfm.

62. Anne Hobbs, Elizabeth Neely, Candace Behrens, and Timbre Wulf-Ludden, "Nebraska State DMC Assessment," University of Nebraska Juvenile Justice Institute, March 21, 2012, https://ncc.nebraska.gov/sites/ncc.nebraska .gov/files/pdf/others/DMCAssessment2012.pdf; see also Juvenile Justice Geography, Policy, Practice & Statistics, "Nebraska: Racial/Ethnic Fairness," www .jjgps.org/racial-fairness/nebraska, https://perma.cc/ED4H-HPVQ.

63. National Juvenile Court Data Archive, "Juvenile Court Statistics 2019," 21, www.ojjdp.gov/ojstatbb/njcda/pdf/jcs2019.pdf.

64. William P. Quigley, "Work or Starve: Colonial American Poor Laws," *University of San Francisco Law Review* 31 (1996): 35.

65. General Assembly, "An Act Concerning Servants and Slaves" (1705), in *Encyclopedia Virginia*, https://encyclopediavirginia.org/entries/an-act-concerning -servants-and-slaves-1705, https://perma.cc/547T-2WDT.

66. *Revised Statutes of the State of Delaware of Eighteen Hundred and Fifty-Two* (Wilmington, DE: printed by James & Webb, 1874), 485, https://books .google.ci/books?id=88xJAQAAIAAJ&printsec=frontcover&hl=fr&source= gbs_ge_summary_r&cad=0#v=onepage&q&f=false. For additional history regarding the development of juvenile courts, including "binding out" children, see Jane C. Murphy and Jana B. Singer, *Divorced from Reality: Rethinking Family Dispute Resolution* (New York: NYU Press, 2015).

67. James W. Ely Jr., "Poor Laws of the Post-Revolutionary South, 1776–1800," *Tulsa Law Journal* 21 (2013): 1.

68. Ely, "Poor Laws of the Post-Revolutionary South."

69. Gabriel Loiacono, "Using Poor Laws to Regulate Race in Providence in the 1820s," Organization of American Historians, January 11, 2018, www.process history.org/loiacono-poor-laws/, https://web.archive.org/web/20200707024012 /http://www.processhistory.org/loiacono-poor-laws/.

70. Loiacono, "Using Poor Laws to Regulate Race."

71. Gabriel Loiacono, "Poor Laws and the Construction of Race in Early Republican Providence, Rhode Island," *Journal of Policy History* 25, no. 2 (2013): 264–87.

72. Loiacono, "Poor Laws and the Construction of Race."

73. Ely, "Poor Laws of the Post-Revolutionary South."

74. Ely, "Poor Laws of the Post-Revolutionary South," 16.

75. Quigley, "Work or Starve," 78.

76. Tim Lockley, "Rural Poor Relief in Colonial South Carolina," *Historical Journal* 48, no. 4 (2005): 955–76, https://warwick.ac.uk/fac/arts/cas/staff /lockley/tlhistj.pdf.

77. Lockley, "Rural Poor Relief in Colonial South Carolina."

78. Lockley, "Rural Poor Relief in Colonial South Carolina." ("In northern colonies, where whites far outnumbered blacks, poor relief was broadly comparable to English levels, but in Charles-Town, where there were roughly equal numbers of whites and blacks, poor relief was considerably more generous. Outside Charles-Town, where whites were heavily outnumbered, relief was more generous still, and it marked a clear boundary between poorer whites and slaves.")

79. Lockley, "Rural Poor Relief in Colonial South Carolina." For another historical account of poor relief used to support White supremacy, see Anne O'Connell, "Building Their Readiness for Economic 'Freedom': The New Poor Law and Emancipation," *Journal of Sociology & Social Welfare* 36, no. 2 (2009): art 6.

80. Dorothy E. Roberts, "Welfare and the Problem of Black Citizenship," *Yale Law Journal* 105 (1996): 1563.

81. Roberts, "Welfare and the Problem of Black Citizenship."

82. Alma Carten, "How Racism Has Shaped Welfare Policy in America since 1935," *Conversation*, August 21, 2106, https://theconversation.com/how -racism-has-shaped-welfare-policy-in-america-since-1935-63574.

83. Roberts, "Welfare and the Problem of Black Citizenship."

84. Roberts, "Welfare and the Problem of Black Citizenship."

85. Tonya L. Brito, "From Madonna to Proletariat: Constructing a New Ideology of Motherhood in Welfare Discourse," *Villanova Law Review* 44 (1999): 415, 416.

86. Ann Cammett, "Deadbeat Dads & Welfare Queens: How Metaphor Shapes Poverty Law," Boston College Journal of Law & Social Justice 34 (2014): 233, 237–38; see also Daniel L. Hatcher, "Don't Forget Dad: Addressing Women's Poverty by Rethinking Forced and Outdated Child Support Policies," *Journal of Gender, Social Policy & the Law* 20 (2012): 775, 793.

87. See generally Daniel L. Hatcher, "Child Support Harming Children: Subordinating the Best Interests of Children to the Fiscal Interests of the State," *Wake Forest Law Review* 42 (2007): 1029.

88. *The Welfare Mess: A Scandal of Illegitimacy and Desertion, US Senate Committee on Finance* (December 14, 1971) (address by Hon. Russel B. Long), www.finance.senate.gov/imo/media/doc/Sprt21.pdf, https://perma.cc/EX6H-LWS7.

89. *Welfare Reform—Or Is It?, US Senate Committee on Finance,* (August 6, 1971) (address by Hon. Russel B. Long), https://www.finance.senate.gov/imo/media/doc/Sprt15.pdf, https://perma.cc/4UP5-2TYZ.

90. *Welfare Reform—Or Is It?*

91. Alison Lefkovitz, "Men in the House: Race, Welfare and the Regulation of Men's Sexuality in the United States, 1961–1972," *Journal of the History of Sexuality* 20, no. 3 (2011): 594–614.

92. Shawn Fremstad, "TANF and Two-Parent Families," Institute for Family Studies, July 25, 2016, https://ifstudies.org/blog/tanf-and-two-parent-families#:~:text=Married%20and%20unmarried%20two%2Dparent,the%20parents%20ohas%20a%20disability, https://web.archive.org/web/20201219152016/https://ifstudies.org/blog/tanf-and-two-parent-families.

93. Bernstein, "Misery Funds a Legal Fiefdom."

94. Bernstein, "Misery Funds a Legal Fiefdom."

95. Bernstein, "Misery Funds a Legal Fiefdom."

96. Shelby County, Tennessee, "Juvenile Court Judge," www.shelbycountytn.gov/382/Juvenile-Court-Judge, https://perma.cc/4APZ-SZ84.

97. Bernstein, "Misery Funds a Legal Fiefdom."

98. Bernstein, "Misery Funds a Legal Fiefdom."

99. Bernstein, "Misery Funds a Legal Fiefdom."

100. Daniel L. Hatcher and Hannah Lieberman, "Breaking the Cycle of Defeat for 'Deadbroke' Noncustodial Parents through Advocacy on Child Support Issues," *Clearinghouse Review*, May–June 2003, https://ssrn.com/abstract=1275918.

101. See US Department of Health & Human Services, Office of Child Support Enforcement, *FY 2019 Preliminary Data Report*, June 23, 2020, www.acf.hhs.gov/css/policy-guidance/fy-2019-preliminary-data-report (over 14.3 million children in the IV-D system in 2019); and US Department of Health & Human Services, Office of Child Support Enforcement, "Characteristics of Families Served by the Child Support (IV-D) Program," November 19, 2018, www.acf.hhs.gov/archive/css/report/characteristics-families-served-child-support-iv-d-program-2016-census-survey. The federal agency data show that 27 percent of custodial parents in the IV-D system are Black parents, while the Census Bureau estimates that Black individuals account for 13.4 percent of the US population. US Census Bureau, "QuickFacts: Population Estimates," July 1, 2021, www.census.gov/quickfacts/fact/table/US/PST045219.

102. US Department of Health & Human Services, Office of Child Support Enforcement, "Who Owes the Child Support Debt?," September 15, 2017, www.acf.hhs.gov/css/ocsedatablog/2017/09/who-owes-the-child-support-debt.

103. Vicki Turetsky, "Reforming Child Support to Improve Outcomes for Children and Families," *Abell Report* 32, no. 5, June 2019, https://abell.org

/sites/default/files/files/Abell%20Reforming%20Child%20Support(1).pdf; see also Tonya L. Brito, David J. Pate Jr., and Jia-Hui Stefanie Wong, "'I Do for My Kids': Negotiating Race and Racial Inequality in Family Court," *Fordham Law Review* 83 (2015): 3027.

104. Turetsky, "Reforming Child Support."

105. Turetsky, "Reforming Child Support."

106. Turetsky, "Reforming Child Support."

107. Maryland General Assembly, House Judiciary Committee, Testimony in Support of HB 580, The University of Baltimore School of Law Legal Data and Design Clinic, February 9, 2021.

108. Michele Alexander, *The New Jim Crow: Mass Incarceration in the Age of Colorblindness* (New York: The New Press 2010).

109. Noah Zatz, "Get to Work or Go to Jail," UCLA Institute for Research on Labor and Employment, March 2016, www.labor.ucla.edu/wp-content /uploads/2018/06/Get-to-Work324.pdf.

110. Zatz, "Get to Work or Go to Jail," 8.

111. National Conference of State Legislators, "Child Support and Incarceration," www.ncsl.org/research/human-services/child-support-and-incarceration .aspx, https://perma.cc/AR47-JNKP.

112. Eli Hager, "For Men in Prison, Child Support Becomes a Crushing Debt," Marshall Project, October 18, 2015, www.themarshallproject.org/2015 /10/18/for-men-in-prison-child-support-becomes-a-crushing-debt.

113. See Wyo. Stat. § 14-2-1003; Neb. Rev. Stat. § 43-1407; Mich. Stat. § 722.712; and Wisconsin Department of Children and Families, "Repaying Birth Costs," https://dcf.wisconsin.gov/cs/benefits-birth-costs, https://perma.cc /2N4T-9MNH.

114. City of Mountain Terrace, "Electronic Home Monitoring Program," www.cityofmlt.com/faq.aspx?TID=18, https://perma.cc/3K2P-62SD.

115. Although "ethicless" may not appear in predominantly recognized dictionaries, I feel the term is more accurate here than "unethical"—because those seeking to hide, dismantle, and distort true history are functioning with the cold demeanor of a narcissistic absence of ethics.

CONCLUSION

1. Since Chief Judge Bell's retirement, the swearing-in ceremony for clinic students has been wonderfully led by another excellent judge, Honorable Shirley M. Watts, the first Black woman appointed to the Maryland Court of Appeals.

2. Dale Wimbrow, "The Guy in the Glass," www.theguyintheglass.com/gig .htm.

3. Morgan State University, "Honorable Robert M. Bell," www2.morgan.edu /centers_and_institutes/robert_m_bell_center_for_civil_rights_in_education /staff/the_honorable_robert_m_bell.html, https://perma.cc/VCN7-42PP.

4. Morgan State University, "Honorable Robert M. Bell." See also Jean Marbella, "Chief Judge of Maryland Court of Appeals Retiring," *Baltimore Sun*,

April 13, 2013, www.baltimoresun.com/maryland/baltimore-city/bs-md-judge-bell-retires-20130413-story.html.

5. Marbella, "Chief Judge of Maryland Court of Appeals Retiring."

6. Martin Luther King Jr., "Letter from Birmingham City Jail," April 16, 1963, https://kinginstitute.stanford.edu/sites/mlk/files/letterfrombirmingham_wwcw_0.pdf.

Selected Bibliography

Alexander, Michele. *The New Jim Crow: Mass Incarceration in the Age of Colorblindness*. New York: The New Press, 2012.

Alexander, Thomas B. "Kukluxism in Tennessee, 1865–1869." *Tennessee Historical Quarterly* 8, no. 3 (1949): 195–219.

Appell, Annette R. "Protecting Children or Punishing Mothers: Gender, Race and Class in the Child Protection System," *South Carolina Law Review* 48 (1997): 577.

Baldwin, James. *No Name in the Street*. New York: Vintage Books, 1972.

Ball, Ankeet. "Ambition & Bondage: An Inquiry on Alexander and Slavery." Columbia University and Slavery, https://columbiaandslavery.columbia.edu/content/ambition-bondage-inquiry-alexander-hamilton-and-slavery.

Bernstein, Nina. "Misery Loves a Legal Fiefdom." Alicia Patterson Foundation, 1994, https://aliciapatterson.org/stories/misery-funds-legal-fiefdom.

Bessler, John D. *Private Prosecution in America: Its Origin, History, and Unconstitutionality in the Twenty-First Century*. Durham, NC: Carolina Academic Press, 2022.

Brett, Sharon, Neda Khoshkhoo, and Mitali Nagrecha, *Paying on Probation: How Financial Sanctions Intersect with Probation to Target, Trap and Punish People Who Cannot Pay* Harvard Law School Criminal Justice Policy Program, June 2020, https://mcusercontent.com/f65678cd73457docbde864do5/files/fo5e951e-60a9-404e-b5cc-13c065b2a630/Paying_on_Probation_report_FINAL.pdf.

Brito, Tonya L. "The Child Support Debt Bubble," *University of California Irvine Law Review* 9 (2019): 953.

———. "From Madonna to Proletariat: Constructing a New Ideology of Motherhood in Welfare Discourse," *Villanova Law Review* 44 (1999): 415, 416.

Brito, Tonya L., David J. Pate Jr., and Jia-Hui Stefanie Wong. "'I Do for My Kids': Negotiating Race and Racial Inequality in Family Court." *Fordham Law Review* 83 (2015): 3027.

Brustin, Stacy L., and Lisa Vollendorf Martin. "Bridging the Justice Gap in Family Law: Repurposing Federal IV-D Funding to Expand Community-Based Legal and Social Services for Parents." Hastings Law Journal 67 (2016): 1265.

Budasoff, Christine A. "Modern Civil Forfeiture Is Unconstitutional." *Texas Review of Law and Politics* 23 (2019): 467.

Cahn, Naomi. "Children's Interests in a Familial Context: Poverty, Foster Care, and Adoption." *Ohio State Law Journal* (1999): 1189.

Cammett, Ann. "Deadbeats, Deadbrokes, and Prisoners." *Georgetown Journal on Poverty Law and Policy* 18 (2011): 127.

Clopper, Edward Nicholas. *Child Welfare in Tennessee: An Inquiry.* National Child Labor Committee (US), Tennessee Department of Public Instruction, Tennessee Child Welfare Commission, 1920.

Condlin, Robert J. "Online Dispute Resolution: Stinky, Repugnant, or Drab." *Cardozo Journal of Conflict Resolution* 18 (2017): 717.

Cooper, Tanya Asim. "Racial Bias in American Foster Care: The National Debate." *Marquette Law Review* 97 (Winter, 2013): 215.

Czapanskiy, Karen Syma. "To Protect and Defend: Assigning Parental Rights When Parents Are Living in Poverty." *William & Mary Bill of Rights Journal* 14 (2006): 943.

Douglas, James W., and Roger E. Hartley. "The Politics of Court Budgeting in the States: Is Judicial Independence Threatened by the Budgetary Process?" *Public Administration Review* 63 (2003): 441.

Dowd, Nancy E. "Fatherhood and Equality: Reconfiguring Masculinities." *Suffolk University Law Review* 45 (2012): 1047, 1048.

Edelman, Peter, Harry J. Holzer, and Paul Offner. *Reconnecting Disadvantaged Young Men* (Washington, DC: Urban Institute Press, 2006).

Ely, James W., Jr. "Poor Laws of the Post-Revolutionary South, 1776–1800." *Tulsa Law Journal* 21 (2013): 1.

Enos, Gary. "Addiction Treatment Inc.: Barry Karlin Has the Drive—and the Financing—to Make CRC Health a National Addiction Treatment Enterprise." *Behavioral Healthcare Tomorrow* 12, no. 3 (June 2003): 12.

Escamilla, Paulina Maqueda. *Unholy Alliance: California Courts Use of Private Debt Collectors.* California Reinvestment Coalition, May 2018, http://ebclc .org/wp-content/uploads/2018/05/Unholy-Alliance-California-Courts-Use -of-Private-Debt-Collectors.pdf.

Ervin, Sam J., Jr. "Separation of Powers: Judicial Independence." *Law & Contemporary Problems* 35 (1970): 108, 121.

Fineman, Martha A. "The Vulnerable Subject and the Responsive State." *Emory Law Journal* (2010): 251, 257.

Fraidin, Matthew I. "Stories Told and Untold: Confidentiality Laws and the Master Narrative of Child Welfare." *Maine Law Review* 63 (2010): 1.

Fremstad, Shawn. *TANF and Two-Parent Families.* Institute for Family Studies, July 25, 2016.

Gilman, Michele Estrin. "Legal Accountability in an Era of Privatized Welfare." *California Law Review* 89 (2001): 569.

Green, Bruce A., and Rebecca Roiphe. "Rethinking Prosecutors' Conflicts of Interest." *Boston College Law Review* 58 (2017): 463.

Guggenheim, Martin. "The Foster Care Dilemma and What to Do About It: Is the Problem That Too Many Children Are Not Being Adopted out of Foster Care or That Too Many Children Are Entering Foster Care?" *University of Pennsylvania Journal of Constitutional Law* 2 (1999): 141.

———. *What's Wrong with Children's Rights* (Cambridge, MA: Harvard University Press, 2005).

Gupta-Kagan, Josh. "Rethinking Family-Court Prosecutors: Elected and Agency Prosecutors and Prosecutorial Discretion in Juvenile Delinquency and Child Protection Cases." *University of Chicago Law Review* 85 (2018): 743.

Hahn, Heather. *Relief from Government-Owed Child Support Debt and Its Effects on Parents and Children*. Urban Institute, August 2019, www.urban .org/sites/default/files/publication/100812/relief_from_government-owed _child_support_debt_and_its_effects_on_parents_and_children_4.pdf.

Harris, Lee A. "From Vermont to Mississippi: Race and Cash Welfare." *Columbia Human Rights Law Review* 38 (2006): 1.

Harvey, Gordon E., Richard D. Starnes, and Glen Feldman. *History and Hope in the Heart of Dixie: Scholarship, Activism and Wayne Flint in the Modern South*. Tuscaloosa: University of Alabama Press, 2006.

Hatcher, Daniel L. "Child Support Harming Children: Subordinating the Best Interests of Children to the Fiscal Interests of the State." *Wake Forest Law Review* 42 (2007): 1029.

———. "Collateral Children: Consequence and Illegality at the Intersection of Foster Care and Child Support." *Brook Law Review* 74 (2009): 1333.

———. "Don't Forget Dad: Addressing Women's Poverty by Rethinking Forced and Outdated Child Support Policies." *Journal of Gender, Social Policy & the Law* 20 (2012): 775.

———. "Foster Children Paying for Foster Care." *Cardozo Law Review* 27 (2006): 1797.

———. "Juvenile Court Interagency Agreements: Subverting Impartial Justice to Maximize Revenue from Children." *NYU Annual Survey of American Law* 76 (2020): 33.

———. *The Poverty Industry: The Exploitation of America's Most Vulnerable Citizens*. New York: NYU Press, 2016.

———. "States Diverting Funds from the Poor." In *Holes in the Safety Net: Federalism and Poverty*, edited by Ezra Rosser, 151–72. New York: Cambridge University Press, 2019.

Hatcher, Daniel L., and Hannah Lieberman, "Breaking the Cycle of Defeat for 'Deadbroke' Noncustodial Parents through Advocacy on Child Support Issues." *Clearinghouse Review* (May–June 2003): 5–22.

Helge, Terri L. "Joint Ventures of Nonprofits and For-Profits." *Texas Tax Law* 41 (2014): 1.

Herrera, Lucero, Tia Koonse, Menanie Sonsteng-Person, and Noah Zatz. *Work, Pay or Go to Jail: Court-Ordered Community Service in Los Angeles.* UCLA Labor Center and UCLA School of Law, October 2019.

Hopkins, Callie. "The Enslaved Household of President Andrew Jackson." The White House Historical Association, n.d., www.whitehousehistory.org /slavery-in-the-andrew-jackson-white-house.

Human Rights Watch. *Profiting from Probation: America's 'Offender-Funded' Probation Industry.* February 5, 2014, www.hrw.org/sites/default/files /reports/us0214_ForUpload_0.pdf.

———. *Rubber Stamp Justice: U.S. Courts, Debt Buying Corporations, and the Poor.* 2016, www.hrw.org/sites/default/files/report_pdf/us0116_web.pdf.

Institute for Justice. "Policing for Profit: The Abuse of Civil Asset Forfeiture." December 2020, https://ij.org/wp-content/uploads/2020/12/policing-for-profit -3-web.pdf.

Jackson, Jeffrey. "Judicial Independence, Adequate Court Funding, and Inherent Judicial Powers." *Maryland Law Review* 52 (1993): 217.

Kay, Marvin L. Michael, and Lorin Lee Cary, "The Planters Suffer Little or Nothing: North Carolina Compensations for Executed Slaves, 1748–1772." *Science & Society* 40, no. 3 (Fall 1976): 288–306.

Klarman, Michael J. "Brown, Racial Change, and the Civil Rights Movement." *Virginia Law Review* 80 (1994): 7.

Lefkovitz, Alison. "Men in the House: Race, Welfare and the Regulation of Men's Sexuality in the United States, 1961–1972." *Journal of the History of Sexuality* 20, no. 3 (2011): 594–614.

Lockley, Tim. "Rural Poor Relief in Colonia South Carolina." *Historical Journal* 48, no. 4 (2005): 955–76.

Loiacono, Gabriel. "Poor Laws and the Construction of Race in Early Republican Providence, Rhode Island." *Journal of Policy History* 25, no. 2 (2013): 264–87.

———. "Using Poor Laws to Regulate Race in Providence in the 1820s." Organization of American Historians, January 11, 2018, www.processhistory.org /loiacono-poor-laws/, https://perma.cc/H65P-VJSV.

Maldonado, Solangel. "Deadbeat or Deadbroke: Redefining Child Support for Poor Fathers." *University of California Davis Law Review* 39 (2006): 991.

Marston, Allison. "Guiding the Profession: The 1887 Code of Ethics of the Alabama State Bar Association." *Alabama Law Review* 49 (1998): 471.

Minow, Martha. "Public and Private Partnerships: Accounting for the New Religion." *Harvard Law Review* 116 (2003): 1229.

Murphy, Jane C. "Legal Images of Fatherhood: Welfare Reform, Child Support Enforcement, and Fatherless Children." *Notre Dame Law Review* 81 (2005): 325.

Murphy, Jane C., and Jana B. Singer. *Divorced from Reality: Rethinking Family Dispute Resolution.* New York: NYU Press, 2015.

O'Connell, Anne. "Building Their Readiness for Economic 'Freedom': The New Poor Law and Emancipation." *Journal of Sociology & Social Welfare* 36, no. 2 (2009): art 6.

Paulsen, Monrad G. "Juvenile Courts, Family Courts, and the Poor Man." *California Law Review* 54 (1966): 694.

Peskin, Allan. "Was There a Compromise of 1877?" *Journal of American History* 60, no. 1 (1973): 63–75.

The Pew Charitable Trusts, "How Debt Collectors Are Transforming the Business of State Courts," May 6, 2020. www.pewtrusts.org/en/research-and-analysis/reports/2020/05/how-debt-collectors-are-transforming-the-business-of-state-courts.

Phelps, Michele S. "Ending Mass Probation: Sentencing, Supervision, and Revocation." *Future of Children* 28, no. 1 (Spring 2018): 125–46.

Quigley, William P. "Backwards into the Future: How Welfare Changes in the Millenium Resemble English Poor Law of the Middle Ages." *Stanford Law & Policy Review* 9 (1998): 101.

———. "Five Hundred Years of English Poor Laws, 1349–1834: Regulating the Working and Nonworking Poor." *Akron Law Review* 30 (1997): 1349.

———. "Work or Starve: Colonial American Poor Laws." *University of San Francisco Law Review* 31 (1996): 35.

Ratcliffe, Donald. "The Right to Vote and the Rise of Democracy, 1787 to 1828." *Journal of the Early Republic* 221 (Summer 2013): 219–54.

Rickard, Erika. "Online Dispute Resolution Moves from E-Commerce to the Courts." The Pew Charitable Trusts, June 4, 2019, www.pewtrusts.org/en/research-and-analysis/articles/2019/06/04/online-dispute-resolution-moves-from-e-commerce-to-the-courts, https://perma.cc/KT9S-S779.

Ridolfi, Laura. "California Youth Face Heightened Racial and Ethnic Disparities in Division of Juvenile Justice." W. Haywood Burns Institute, August 2020, https://files.eric.ed.gov/fulltext/ED610669.pdf, https://perma.cc/96P8-PNZN.

Rhode, Deborah L., and Amanda K. Packel. "Ethics and Nonprofits." *Stanford Social Innovation Review* (Summer 2009): 29–35.

Roberts, Dorothy. *Shattered Bonds: The Color of Child Welfare.* New York: Basic Books, 2002.

———. *Torn Apart: How the Child Welfare System Destroys Black Families—And How Abolition Can Build a Safer World.* New York: Basic Books, 2022.

———. "Welfare and the Problem of Black Citizenship." *Yale Law Journal* 105 (1996): 1563.

Robinson, Cedric J. *Black Marxism: The Making of the Black Radical Tradition.* Chapel Hill: University of North Carolina Press, 1983.

Rodebush, Curtis. "Separation of Powers in Ohio: A Critical Analysis." *Cleveland State Law Review* 51 (2004): 505.

Rosser, Ezra. *Holes in the Safety Net: Federalism and Poverty.* New York: Cambridge University Press, 2019.

Russell, Thomas D. "South Carolina's Largest Slave Auctioneering Firm—Symposium on the Law of Slavery: Criminal and Civil Law of Slavery." *Chicago-Kent Law Review* 68 (1992): 1241.

Serfilippi, Jessie. "'As Odious and Immoral a Thing': Alexander Hamilton's Hidden History as an Enslavor." Schuyler Mansion State Historic Site, 2020, https://parks.ny.gov/documents/historic-sites/SchuylerMansionAlexander HamiltonsHiddenHistoryasanEnslaver.pdf, https://perma.cc/74LV-NLEW.

Shelden, Randall G. "Origins of the Juvenile Court in Memphis, Tennessee: 1900–1910." *Tennessee Historical Quarterly* 52, no. 1 (Spring 1993): 33–43.

Tarr, Alan G. "Interpreting the Separation of Powers in State Constitutions." *NYU Annual Survey of American Law* 59 (2003): 329.

tenBroek, Jacobus. "California's Dual System of Family Law: Its Origin, Development, and Present Status, Part I." *Stanford Law Review* 16 (1964): 257.

Turetsky, Vicki. "Reforming Child Support to Improve Outcomes for Children and Families," *Abell Report* 32, no. 5 (June 2019), https://abell.org /wp-content/uploads/2022/02/Abell2oChild2oSupport2oReform20-20 Full2oReport2o2_20_202o2oedits2oV1_3.pdf.

Verkuil, Paul R. "Separation of Powers, The Rule of Law and the Idea of Independence." *William & Mary Law Review* 30 (1989): 301.

Williams, Lucy A. "The Ideology of Division: Behavior Modification Welfare Reform Proposals." *Yale Law Journal* 102 (1992): 719.

Woodhouse, Barbara Bennett. "Child Abuse, the Constitution, and the Legacy of Pierce v. Society of Sisters." *University of Detroit Mercy Law Review* 78 (2001): 479.

Woodward, C. Vann. *Reunion and Reaction: The Compromise of 1877 and the End of Reconstruction*. Boston: Little, Brown, 1951.

Zatz, Noah. "Get to Work or Go to Jail." UCLA Institute for Research on Labor and Employment, March 2016, www.labor.ucla.edu/wp-content/uploads /2018/06/Get-to-Work324.pdf.

Index

Founded in 1893,
UNIVERSITY OF CALIFORNIA PRESS
publishes bold, progressive books and journals
on topics in the arts, humanities, social sciences,
and natural sciences—with a focus on social
justice issues—that inspire thought and action
among readers worldwide.

The UC PRESS FOUNDATION
raises funds to uphold the press's vital role
as an independent, nonprofit publisher, and
receives philanthropic support from a wide
range of individuals and institutions—and from
committed readers like you. To learn more, visit
ucpress.edu/supportus.